EATING DISORDERS:
A BIBLIOGRAPHY WITH INDEXES

EATING DISORDERS:
A BIBLIOGRAPHY WITH INDEXES

J. STANGO (EDITOR)

Nova Science Publishers, Inc.
Huntington, NY

Senior Editors: Susan Boriotti and Donna Dennis
Coordinating Editor: Tatiana Shohov
Office Manager: Annette Hellinger
Graphics: Wanda Serrano
Book Production: Matthew Kozlowski, Jonathan Rose and Jennifer Vogt
Circulation: Cathy DeGregory, Ave Maria Gonzalez, Ron Hedges and Andre Tillman

Library of Congress Cataloging-in-Publication Data

Stango, J.
Eating disorders: a bibliogrphy with indexes / J. Stango, editor.
p. cm.
Includes bibliographical references and index.
ISBN 1-59033-008-0.
1. Eating disorders—Bibliography. 2. Eating disorders—Indexes. I. Title.

Z6665.7.E28 S73 2001
[RC552.E18]
016.61685'26—dc21

2001045277

227 Main Street, Suite 100
Huntington, New York 11743
Tele. 631-424-6682 Fax 631-425-5933
E Mail: Novascience@earthlink.net

Printed in the United States of America

CONTENTS

PREFACE

Television, movies, and others that pass for cultural activities worship the body thin. This distortion of reality and the abundance of food in the developed countries of the world have spawned an epidemic of disorders connected to the food. Extremes such as intensive concern about one's body image and total disregard for it have resulted in many countries which contain enormous segments of the population who are either obese and proud of it or bordering on anorexia nervosa. Unfortunately, these diseases are not trivial in their consequences, leading sometimes to fatal outcomes and almost always to a state of depression. Recent research has shown a startling correlation between obesity and heart disease, cancer, kidney failure, and numerous other diseases. Anorexia nervosa, bulemia, and binging form a triad of diseases which threaten the well-being of several million mostly young people.

This bibliography consists of carefully selected citations which have been categorized for easy access.

General

(1):1-24
The eating attitudes test: twenty-five years later.
This manuscript reviews the literature involved with the Eating Attitudes Test (EAT), first developed in the late 1970s as a self-report, indicative of the symptoms of eating disorders. It is used to screen eating disturbances in general as the first part of a two-part diagnostic screen, as an ability to compare across groups and to measure change between groups and over time.

Acta Paedopsychiatr 1968 Oct;35(10):317-23
Eating disorders in a child population.
Brandon S.

Acta Psychiatr Scand 1988 Sep;78(3):314-9
Prevalence and incidence of eating disorders in a suburban area.
Cullberg J, Engstrom-Lindberg M.
Research and Development Unit, Nacka-Varmdo Psychiatric Sector, Nacka Hospital, Sweden.
There has been no previous epidemiological study on anorexia nervosa (AN) and bulimia (BU) where non-medical care givers have also been included in the case-finding procedure. In this study, psychiatric, somatic, child psychiatric, social and primary care personnel were systematically asked for information on patients. Fifty-one cases of eating disorder (17 AN, 34 BU) according to slightly modified DSM-III criteria were traced in a suburban catchment area of 78,000 inhabitants during a two-year period. It was found that there seems to be no clear social class grouping. Twenty (56%) of the adult patients had been hospitalized for eating disorder during the last six-year period.

Acta Psychiatr Scand 1999 Jul;100(1):27-32
Temperament, character and suicide attempts in anorexia nervosa, bulimia nervosa and major depression.
Bulik CM, Sullivan PF, Joyce PR.
Medical College of Virginia of Virginia Commonwealth University, Department of Psychiatry, Virginia Institute for Psychiatric and Behavioral Genetics, Richmond 23298-0126, USA.
Examined were the relation between personality traits as measured by the

Temperament and Character Inventory (TCI) and a reported history of suicide attempts in women with anorexia nervosa, bulimia nervosa and major depression. Suicide attempts are equally common in women with eating disorders and women with depression. Whether the observed association between temperament and suicide attempts reflects correlates, causal factors or sequelae of suicide attempts is unknown.

Am J Nurs 1998 Nov;98(11):22-4
Screening for anorexia and bulimia.
Muscari ME.
University of Scranton, PA, USA.

Am J Psychiatry 1991 Jul;148(7):950-1
Natural histories of anorexia nervosa and bulimia nervosa.
Woodside DB, Rockert W, Garfinkel PE.
Publication Types: Letter

Am J Psychiatry 1992 Aug;149(8):1122
Comment on: Am J Psychiatry. 1991 Dec;148(12):1627-37
Twins and eating disorders.
Solomon JG.
Publication Types: Comment Letter

Am J Psychiatry 1999 Jun;156(6):982
Comment on: Am J Psychiatry. 1998 Feb;155(2):244-9
Obsessive-compulsive disorder with eating disorders.
Cumella EJ.
Publication Types: Comment Letter

Am J Psychiatry 2000 Jun;157(6):886-95
Comment in:Am J Psychiatry. 2000 Jun;157(6):851-3
An empirical study of the classification of eating disorders.
Bulik CM, Sullivan PF, Kendler KS.
Department of Psychiatry, Virginia Institute for Psychiatric and Behavioral Genetics, Medical College of Virginia of Virginia Commonwealth University, Richmond 23298-0126, USA.
The nosology for eating disorders, despite having been extensively revised over time, may not capture the natural clustering of eating-related pathology as it occurs in general population samples. Detailed information about anorectic and bulimic behaviors was assessed through personal interviews of 2,163 Caucasian female twins from a population-based registry. The authors found within a community sample, and through an empirical method, classes of eating-related pathology that broadly resembled the current classifications of anorexia nervosa, bulimia nervosa, and binge-eating disorder. Additional classes were marked by either the psychological features of eating disorders or low body weight. Individuals in the three eating-disorder classes had similar personality profiles but displayed differences in symptom expression and co-twin risk for anorexia nervosa, bulimia nervosa, and obesity.
Publication Types: Twin study

Am J Psychiatry 2001 Apr;158(4):515-7
Progress in eating disorders research.
Andersen AE.
Publication Types: Editorial

Am J Psychother 1998 Spring;52(2):147-65
The contributions of self psychology

to the treatment of anorexia and bulimia.
Bachar E.
Department of Psychiatry, Hadassah University Medical Center, Jerusalem, Israel.
This article reviews the contribution of self psychology to the treatment and understanding of anorexia and bulimia. It tries to show that the unique conceptualization of self, selfobject relations, and this theory's conceptualization of resistance and defenses constitutes a therapeutic stance which especially fits the therapeutic needs of eating-disordered patients.

Am Pharm 1978 Dec;18(13):44-5
The mystery of anorexia nervosa.
Lucas AR.

Ann Clin Biochem 1987 Nov;24 (Pt 6):643-4
Biochemical abnormalities in anorexia nervosa and bulimia.
Fonseca V, De Souza V, Agnew J, Mikhailidis DP, Wakeling A, Dandona P.
Publication Types: Letter

Ann Intern Med 1987 Mar;106(3):480-1
Eating disorders.
Eckert ED, Mitchell JE, Pyle RL.
Publication Types: Letter

Ann N Y Acad Sci 1997 May 28;817:120-6
Childhood-onset anorexia nervosa is a serious illness.
Lask B, Waugh R, Gordon I.
Great Ormond Street Hospital for Children, London, United Kingdom.
101530.1275@compuserve.com
Publication Types: Review; Review, tutorial

Annu Rev Med 1987;38:373-80
Anorexia nervosa and bulimia.
Halmi KA.
This article is an update on the research and treatment of anorexia nervosa and bulimia. In the past five years, endocrine research has focused on neurotransmitters in anorexia nervosa and treatment research has centered on bulimia.
Publication Types: Review

Annu Rev Public Health 1986;7:535-43
Anorexia nervosa and bulimia.
Autry JH, Stover ES, Reatig N, Casper R.
Publication Types: Clinical trial

Appetite 1988 Apr;10(2):119-31
Fat aversion in eating disorders.
Drewnowski A, Pierce B, Halmi KA.
University fo Michigan, School of Public Health, Ann Arbor 48109.
Patients with eating disorders are reported to show an irrational dislike of starchy foods, sometimes described as a "carbohydrate phobia". In the present study, food-related attitudes and self-reported food preferences of women patients with anorexia nervosa (N = 13), anorexia with bulimia (N = 16) and bulimia (N = 14) were mapped using multidimensional scaling (MDS) procedures and compared to those of normal-weight controls (N = 49).
MDS (SINDSCAL) and property fitting (PROFIT) procedures revealed that eating disorder patients associated calories with fat content to a greater extent than did controls, and tended to

dislike high-fat foods. In contrast, no differences in perceptions or preferences for carbohydrate foods were observed. The present multivariate techniques of mapping perceptual space may help to distinguish between diagnostic subgroups in studies of eating disorders.

Arch Fam Med 1993 Aug;2(8):813-4
Comment on: Arch Fam Med. 1993 Mar;2(3):309-16
Compulsive eating disorders.
Barnes ME.
Publication Types: Comment Letter

Arch Gen Psychiatry 1982 Apr;39(4):487-9
Anorexia nervosa and bulimia.
Katz JL, Sitnick T.
Publication Types: Letter

Arch Psychiatr Nurs 1993 Dec;7(6):342-6
A focused overview of anorexia nervosa and bulimia: Part I--Etiological issues.
Irwin EG.
Saint Albans Psychiatric Hospital, Radford, VA.
The origin of eating disorders as a major mental illness may be explored by investigating several related concepts. Examination of biological, social, and psychological perspectives facilitates understanding of these disorders; neurobiological origin may be especially enlightening because of its exciting relevancy to new developments in the study and understanding of mental illness in general. This focus on the neurobiology of eating disorders may better explain the relationship between the eating disorders and the mood disorders, particularly major depression. Through the understanding of this relationship, new avenues of treatment possibilities are open, consistent with interventions and pharmacological developments in the treatment of major depression.
Publication Types: Review; Review, tutorial

Arch Psychiatr Nurs 1998 Aug;12(4):181-94
A comparison of inpatient and outpatient women with eating disorders.
White JH, Litovitz G.
School of Nursing, Catholic University of America, Washington, DC 20064, USA.
The purpose of this study was to compare two groups of women with eating disorders, one inpatient and one outpatient, on selected variables. Implications for practice that focus on more comprehensive assessments and early detection of eating disorders are presented.

Aust N Z J Psychiatry 1997 Aug;31(4):525-31
The use of guardianship legislation for anorexia nervosa: a report of 15 cases.
Griffiths RA, Beumont PJ, Russell J, Touyz SW, Moore G.
Lynton Hospital, Chatswood, New South Wales, Australia.
This paper investigates compulsory treatment under guardianship legislation for 15 anorexia nervosa patients admitted to four eating disorders units in New South Wales (NSW), Australia, between 1991 and 1994. A retrospective follow-up was

conducted. This involved an analysis of sociodemographic, clinical, eating and weight history, and Guardianship Order details obtained from medical records. This small sample was compared to a larger sample of anorexia nervosa patients admitted voluntarily to a specialised eating disorder unit in NSW. It was noted that the guardianship sample comprised a more severely Ill group than anorexic patients treated voluntarily. The nature of guardianship legislation compared to mental health law is discussed and advice offered to clinicians contemplating and implementing compulsory treatment.

Aust N Z J Psychiatry 2001 Feb;35(1):99-103
An analysis of consumer perspectives following contact with an eating-disorders service.
Swain-Campbell NR, Surgenor LJ, Snell DL.
Eating Disorders Service, HealthLink South, The Princess Margaret Hospital, Christchurch, New Zealand.
The views of consumers following contact with treatment for eating disorders represent an underresearched aspect of service provision. People with eating disorders form a unique group of mental health consumers to survey for satisfaction. While approval ratings prompted by both structured and open-ended questions were high, and centred around the theme of therapeutic alliance, the most frequent source of negative commentary was activities and structures considered essential by traditional treatment modalities. This provides important insights into the predicaments of people with eating disorders presenting for treatment, and the importance of developing satisfaction surveys to accommodate such predicaments and concerns.

Baillieres Clin Obstet Gynaecol 1989 Dec;3(4):705-27
Eating disorders.
Holden NL.
Publication Types: Review; Review, tutorial

Behav Med 1999 Fall;25(3):125-33
Semistarvation-associated eating behaviors among college binge eaters: a preliminary description and assessment scale.
Hagan MM, Whitworth RH, Moss DE.
Department of Psychiatry, University of Cincinnati Medical Center, Ohio, USA.
haganmm@email.uc.edu
Binge eating is a consequence of semistarvation in victims of war and famine and in volunteers in rare semistarvation experiments. These behaviors include bizarre mixing of ingredients and adulteration of food; eating inappropriate, soiled, or discarded food; secrecy; deception; and defensiveness. A Semistarvation-Associated Behaviors Scale was constructed and administered to 40 college students. Among binge eaters, reports of bizarre semistarvation-like behaviors were common and frequent and were associated with dieting.

Behav Res Ther 1995 Nov;33(8):985-90
Body size estimation in eating

disorder patients: testing the video distortion method on a life-size screen.
Probst M, Vandereycken W, Van Coppenolle H, Pieters G.
University Center St. Joseph, Kortenberg, Belgium.
The video distortion method on a life-size screen is a new method for studying eating disordered patients' estimations of their own body width. Testing this method in female patients (53 with anorexia nervosa, 38 with bulimia nervosa) and 36 normal females, yielded high to very high reliability scores (consistency and test-retest stability). Bulimics differ significantly from anorectics and controls on their optative responses (i.e. what they wanted to look like) and their affective responses (i.e. what they felt they looked like).

Biol Psychiatry 2000 May 1;47(9):777-86
Research on eating disorders: current status and future prospects.
Vitiello B, Lederhendler I.
Child & Adolescent Treatment & Preventive Inteventions Research Branch, National Institute of Mental Health, Bethesda, Maryland 20892-9633, USA.
This report summarizes the main themes addressed at a workshop on research on eating disorders (EDs), which was hosted by the National Institute of Mental Health in December 1998. Both basic behavioral neuroscientists and clinical investigators met in an effort to integrate areas of research and foster collaborations. Closer interface between neuroscientists and clinical researchers is required for advancing our understanding of ED pathogenesis and developing effective treatments. Recent studies are suggestive of a substantial genetic contribution to EDs that deserves further investigation.
Publication Types: Review; Review, tutorial

BMJ 1999 Dec 4;319(7223):1508A Eating disorders
Carnall D.
BMJ dcarnall@ bmj.com.

Br J Clin Psychol 1989 Sep;28 (Pt 3):285-6
Eating disorders and family interaction.
Waller G, Calam R, Slade P.
Sub-Department of Clinical Psychology, University of Liverpool, UK.
The McMaster Model of Family Functioning was used to compare women with eating disorders with a normal comparison group. The anorexia nervosa and bulimia nervosa groups showed similar perceived family pathologies but bulimics with no history of anorexia showed a pattern of family interaction that was more severely 'unhealthy' than that of the other clinical groups. The McMaster Model could be a useful tool in clinical assessment and in planning therapy in this particular area.

Br J Hosp Med 1993 Apr 21-May 4;49(8):531-3
Eating disorders.
Lask B, Bryant-Waugh R.
Publication Types: Editorial

Br J Med Psychol 2000 Mar;73 (Pt 1):35-51
Attachment research in eating disorders.
Ward A, Ramsay R, Treasure J.
Psychotherapy Unit, Maudsley Hospital, London, UK.
In a recent review, disturbances in attachment have been linked with eating disorder symptomatology. However, because of the limitations of study design, few inferences could be drawn about these processes in the aetiology and maintenance of eating disorder. Since that review, there has been further development in the instruments used and the publication of several further studies of attachment processes in eating disorders. The vast majority of studies found that attachment processes, by whatever method measured, are abnormal in eating disordered populations. Attachment style (dismissing versus preoccupied) may be linked with eating disorder diagnostic subgroup. CONCLUSIONS: Insecure attachment is common in eating disordered populations, with implications for therapy. Further work with refined instruments may clarify whether or not there is a specific association between attachment style and eating disorder subgroup.
Publication Types: Review; Review, tutorial

Br J Psychiatry 1993 Jun;162:837-40
Media influences on body size estimation in anorexia and bulimia. An experimental study.
Hamilton K, Waller G.
Department of General Practice, University of Aberdeen.
Anorexic and bulimic women overestimate their body sizes substantially more than comparison women, but little is known about the factors that influence this overestimation. This study examined the influence of media portrayal of idealized female bodies in women's fashion magazines. Comparison women were not affected by the nature of the photographs that they saw, but eating-disordered women were--they overestimated more when they had seen the pictures of women than when they saw photographs of neutral objects.

Br J Sports Med 1999 Dec;33(6):434
Eating disorders among male and female elite athletes.
Sundgot-Borgen J.
The Norwegian University of Sport and Physical Education, Olso, Norway.

Br Med J (Clin Res Ed) 1986 Nov 29;293(6559):1412-4
Eating disorders in general practice.
King MB.
A total of 748 patients who attended four south London group practices were screened using the eating attitudes test; 1% of women had bulimia nervosa and a further 3% a partial syndrome eating disorder. Eating and weight control behaviour and psychiatric indicators for an eating disorder were analysed. Patients with bulimia nervosa and partial syndromes were remarkably similar. They were mainly women, from the middle to upper classes, in the normal weight range but having

had considerable weight fluctuation in the past, more likely to have had a history of menstrual irregularity, often psychologically troubled, and tended to have more family psychopathology.

Can Fam Physician 1998 Jul;44:1448
Interest group for eating disorders.
McSherry J.
Publication Types: Letter

Can J Psychiatry 1989 Jun;34(5):419-24
Anorexia nervosa and bulimia in males: lessons from a low-risk population.
Steiger H.
Eating Disorders Program, Douglas Hospital Centre, Montreal, Quebec.
The literature on anorexia nervosa and bulimia in male patients was reviewed with the intention of (a) identifying differences that may exist between male and female sufferers, and (b) isolating, through a study of etiological factors in the low-risk (male) group, those factors that may be specific in the etiology of these disorders in both sexes. Current knowledge suggests that fundamental male-female differences do not exist as far as the etiology or symptomatology of these disorders is concerned. Given such similarities, the lower incidence among males suggests biological, social and intrapsychic determinants, that can be conceived to be more active in female versus male populations.
Publication Types: Review; Review, tutorial

Can Nurse 1968 Jan;64(1):46-8
"I won't eat, I won't".
Sparks D.

CDA J 1985 Aug;13(8):18-22
Anorexia and bulimia: eating functions gone awry.
Levinson NA.

CDS Rev 1996 May;89(4):10-8
Eating disorders: the untold story.
Hamilton J.

Clin Obstet Gynecol 1985 Sep;28(3):588-97
Anorexia nervosa and related eating disorders.
Warren MP.

Clin Obstet Gynecol 1997 Sep;40(3):601-15
Eating disorders.
Gidwani GP, Rome ES.
Department of Pediatrics and Adolescent Medicine, Cleveland Clinic Foundation, OH 44195, USA.
Publication Types: Review; Review, tutorial

Clin Psychol Rev 1998 Jun;18(4):387-90
Neglected topics in eating disorders: guidelines for clinicians and researchers.
Mizes JS.
Department of Psychology, Philadelphia College of Osteopathic Medicine, PA 19131-1693, USA.
jscott@pcom.edu
The purpose of this special series is to address areas of significant clinical importance that have a very modest research literature, and to briefly summarize the existing research. The authors of the individual papers, all noted experts in eating disorders treatment, then offer practical clinical

management recommendations drawing both on the modest available research and their extensive clinical experience.

Community Nurse 1997 Oct;3(9):27-8
Eating disorders: a growing trend among young people.
Blades M.
Publication Types: Review; Review, tutorial

Compendium 1988 Mar;9(3):244-7
Anorexia nervosa and bulimia: a review.
Knewitz JL, Drisko CL.
Publication Types: Review; Review, tutorial

Cult Med Psychiatry 1999 Jun;23(2):245-68
Fat, loathing and public health: the complicity of science in a culture of disordered eating.
Austin SB.
Department of Health and Social Behavior, Harvard School of Public Health, Boston, MA, USA.
baustin@hsph.harvard.edu

Dent Teamwork 1996 May-Jun;9(3):24-9
A look at anorexia nervosa and bulimia.
Sprouls LS.

Dent Today 1999 May;18(5):132-5
Eating disorders. A multidisciplinary approach.
Silber L, Wynne B.

East Mediterr Health J 1999 Mar;5(2):354-60
Eating disorders: a transcultural perspective.
Shuriquie N.
King Hussein Medical Centre, Amman, Jordon.
Publication Types: Review; Review, tutorial

Epidemiol Psichiatr Soc 1998 Jan-Apr;7(1):32-41
The epidemiology of eating disorders.
King M.
Publication Types: Editorial Review; Review, tutorial

Eur J Prosthodont Restor Dent 1997 Dec;5(4):161-7
Eating disorders and the dental practitioner.
Schmidt U, Treasure J.
Bethlem and Maudsley Hospital Trust, London, UK.
Eating disorders are an increasing problem for society and the medical professions. The dental practitioner has an important role both in identifying the illnesses and in minimising its affects on the dentition. This paper highlights the features of the most common eating disorders and discusses the possible role of the dental profession in the long-term care of patients suffering from the problem.
Publication Types: Review; Review, tutorial

Eur Psychiatry 1999 Dec;14(8):434-41
Gender-related clinical differences in obsessive-compulsive disorder.
Bogetto F, Venturello S, Albert U, Maina G, Ravizza L.
Department of Neurosciences, Psychiatric Unit, University of Turin, Via Cherasco 11, 10126 Turin, Italy.
The purpose of the present study was

to investigate the gender-related differences of clinical features in a sample of obsessive-compulsive (OCD) patients. We found three gender-related features of OCD: males show an earlier age at onset with a lower impact of precipitant events in triggering the disorder; OCD seems to occur in a relative high proportion of males who already have phobias and/or tic disorders; and a surfeit of chronic course of the illness in males in comparison with females.

Fla Nurse 1992 Jan;40(1):9
Eating disorders: a look at the basics.
Rhim L.

Gac Sanit 2001;15(1):18-24
Quality of life in patients with eating disorders
Gonzalez N, Padierna A, Quintana J, Arostegui I, Horcajo M.
Unidad de Investigacion. Hospital de Galdakao. Vizcaya.
Objective: To evaluate the quality of life of ambulatory patients with eating disorders in relation to the severity of their symptomatology and in comparison with other psychiatric disorders and general population values. This study shows the severity of these disorders, which have a special incidence in young active women. This fact isbecoming an important public health problem and raises the need of specialized assistance.

Harv Ment Health Lett 1998 Sep;15(3):6-7
Race and eating disorders.

Harv Ment Health Lett 1999 Feb;15(8):7
Culture and eating disorders.
Publication Types: News

Harv Rev Psychiatry 1996 Sep-Oct;4(3):163-7
Culture, the media, and eating disorders.
Becker AE, Hamburg P.
Department of Social Medicine, Harvard Medical School, Boston, MA 02115, USA.

Helping people with eating disorders. a clinical guide to assessment and treatment.

Hosp Med 1999 Jul;60(7):472
Eating disorders: the brain, bones and exercise.
Bryant-Waugh R, Lask B.
Publication Types: Editorial

Hosp Pract (Off Ed) 1988 Nov 30;23(11A):58-62, 67-9, 73-4 passim
Eating disorders.
Mickley DW.
Wilkins Center for Eating Disorders, Greenwich, Conn.
Publication Types: Review; Review, tutorial

Indian J Pediatr 1998 Jul-Aug;65(4):487-94
Eating disorders.
Patel DR, Phillips EL, Pratt HD.
Department of Pediatrics, Michigan State University College of Human Medicine, Kalamazoo Centre for Medical Studies 49008, USA.
Anorexia nervosa and bulimia nervosa are primarily psychiatric disorders characterized by severe disturbances of eating behaviour. Anorexia nervosa

has been well documented in pre-pubertal children. Eating disorders are most prevalent in the Western cultures where food is in abundance and for females attractiveness is equated with thinness. Eating disorders are rare in countries like India. As Western sociocultural ideals become more widespread one may expect to see an increase in number of cases of eating disorders in non-Western societies. Etiological theories suggest a complex interaction among psychological, sociocultural, and biological factors. Patients with anorexia nervosa manifest weight loss, fear of becoming fat, and disturbances in how they experience their body weight and shape. Patients with bulimia nervosa present with recurrent episodes of binge eating and inappropriate methods of weight control such as self-induced vomiting, and abuse of diuretics and laxatives.
Publication Types: Review; Review, tutorial

Int J Clin Pract 1999 Jul-Aug;53(5):386-8
The stigma of eating disorders.
Gowers SG, Shore A.
Section of child and Adolescent Psychiatry, University of Liverpool, England, UK.
Those who suffer from eating disorders often carry the added burden of stigmatizing attitudes from the lay public and the medical profession. This review explores the truth of these beliefs and suggests ways in which a more positive approach to the management of eating disorders might help to reduce the stigma. This includes empathy with the patient's predicament and an approach to treatment in which the patient's wishes are paramount.

Int J Eat Disord 1993 Dec;14(4):439-43
History of eating disorders in female patients with obsessive-compulsive disorder.
Fahy TA, Osacar A, Marks I.
Institute of Psychiatry, De Crespigny Park, London, UK.
The prevalence of eating disorders was assessed in a casenote study of 105 female patients with obsessive-compulsive disorder (OCD). The comorbidity of the two syndromes among females may point to common vulnerability factors. Patients with early onset OCD may be at increased risk of developing eating disorders. The assessment of OCD in young female patients should include a careful check for evidence of eating disorders.

Int J Eat Disord 1995 May;17(4):413-6
Comparison of eating disorder patients with and without compulsive exercising.
Brewerton TD, Stellefson EJ, Hibbs N, Hodges EL, Cochrane CE.
Eating Disorders Program, Institute of Psychiatry, Medical University of South Carolina, Charleston 29425-0742, USA.
Several studies have examined the occurrence of eating disorders in athletes. However, little has been written about the frequency and phenomenology of compulsive exercising in eating disorder (ED) patients. Given this, we studied a series of 110 patients who presented to the Medical University of South Carolina Eating Disorders Program

and met lifetime DSM-III-R criteria for bulimia nervosa (n = 71), anorexia nervosa (n = 18), or both disorders (n = 21). All patients completed the Diagnostic Survey of the Eating Disorders (DSED), a self-report measure of demographic and clinical characteristics including time spent exercising daily. Found was a trend for a significantly higher frequency of compulsive exercising in the patients with anorexia nervosa (38.5%) than those with bulimia nervosa (22.5%) (p < or = .06, chi 2).

Int J Eat Disord 1995 Nov;18(3):209-19
The spectrum of eating disturbances.
Shisslak CM, Crago M, Estes LS.
Department of Family and Community Medicine, University of Arizona, Tucson 85719, USA.
OBJECTIVE: The purpose of this paper was to review and summarize the research literature on the spectrum of eating disturbances. METHOD: Literature was searched using a computer data base to identify recent articles related to the prevalence and occurrence of disturbed eating patterns as well as full and partial syndrome eating disorders (EDs). The findings suggest the need for careful, scientific evaluation of risk factors for EDs in both children and adults. A longitudinal research program in progress isdescribed which aims to identify the risk factors for EDs.
Publication Types: Review; Review, tutorial

Int J Eat Disord 1996 Sep;20(2):115-27
Attachment disruption in anorexia nervosa and bulimia nervosa: a review of theory and empirical research.
O'Kearney R.
Department of Psychology, University of Queensland, Brisbane, Australia.
To critically review both the theoretical propositions about the connections between attachment disruption and eating disorders and the empirical work directly examining these associations.
Because of the limitation of the single pathway conceptualization adopted by the theoreticians and researchers reviewed, few inferences about the role of attachment processes in the etiology and maintenance of eating disorders can be drawn from the existing literature. The paper argues for the development of multifactorial and process-orientated models of the role of attachment functions in the pathogenesis of eating disorders.
Publication Types: Review; Review, tutorial

Int J Eat Disord 1998 Dec;24(4):449-52
Eating disorder in a transgendered patient: a case report.
Surgenor LJ, Fear JL.
Department of Psychological Medicine, Christchurch School of Medicine, University of Otago, New Zealand.
This paper reports the case of a 25-year-old biological male transgendered patient referred to a specialist eating disorder service, and presenting with persistent purging, subjective binging, and restricting. She articulated a close link between transgender issues and the development of eating disorder symptoms. By virtue of its emphasis on estrangement from body, biological gender, and expected social role,

transgenderism may constitute a risk factor for developing an eating disorder in certain men.

Int J Eat Disord 1999 Dec;26(4):349-58
Twin studies and the etiology of eating disorders.
Fairburn CG, Cowen PJ, Harrison PJ.
Department of Psychiatry, University of Oxford, Oxford, England.
OBJECTIVE: To evaluate the major twin studies of eating disorders in order to consider the empirical standing of the suggestion that these disorders, notably bulimia nervosa, are largely genetically determined.
Publication Types: Twin study

Int J Eat Disord 1999 Jan;25(1):65-70
Perfection as acculturation: psychological correlates of eating problems in Chinese male and female students living in the United States.
Davis C, Katzman MA.
University of California, Los Angeles, USA.
The purpose of this study was to assess the relationship between acculturation, self-esteem, depression, and characteristics associated with eating disorders among Chinese university students in the United States. METHOD: The impact of perfecting onself or one's body as a means of acculturating is discussed along with potential gender differences in perceived efficacy in a new culture.

Int J Eat Disord 2000 Jan;27(1):1-20
Twin studies of eating disorders: a review.
Bulik CM, Sullivan PF, Wade TD, Kendler KS.
Virginia Institute for Psychiatric and Behavioral Genetics, Department of Psychiatry, Medical College of Virginia of Virginia Commonwealth University, Richmond, VA 23298-0126, USA. cbulik@hsc.vcu.edu
Twin methodology has been used to delineate etiological factors in many medical disorders and behavioral traits including eating disorders. Although twin studies are powerful tools, their methodology can be arcane and their implications easily misinterpreted. On the basis of this review, it is not possible to draw firm conclusions regarding the precise contribution of genetic and environmental factors to anorexia nervosa. Twin studies confirm that bulimia nervosa is familial and reveal significant contributions of additive genetic effects and of unique environmental factors in liability to bulimia nervosa.
Publication Types: Review; Review, tutorial

Int J Eat Disord 2001 Apr;29(3):314-8
Sexual orientation and eating psychopathology: The role of masculinity and femininity.
Meyer C, Blissett J, Oldfield C.
Department of Psychology, University Warwick, Coventry, UK.
Previous research suggests that eating disorders are related to homosexuality in men, although links with female sexual orientation are less clear. In relation to homosexual men and women, the results support a model where femininity might be seen as a specific risk factor for eating disorders, whereas masculinity is likely to be a protective factor.

Int J Eat Disord 2001 May;29(4):393-400
Pretreatment motivational enhancement therapy for eating disorders: A pilot study.
Feld R, Woodside DB, Kaplan AS, Olmsted MP, Carter JC.
Department of Psychiatry, Toronto General Hospital and University of Toronto, Toronto, Canada.
Eating disorder patients are notoriously ambivalent about treatment and often lack motivation to change. These characteristics may decrease the number of patients entering treatment and increase the number of patients dropping out of treatment prematurely. The results of this study suggest that MET could be valuable for the treatment of eating disorder patients and provide a rationale to conduct further research in this area.

Int J Fertil Womens Med 1998 May-Jun;43(3):133-8
"A body to die for": eating disorders and body-image distortion in women.
Ressler A.
The Renfrew Center, Coconut Creek, Florida 33073, USA.
This article presents an overview of anorexia nervosa, bulimia, and eating disorders not otherwise specified (including binge eating disorder) and their psychological and medical complications. Also included are strategies that enhance the communication process with patients who may be in denial or reluctant to share fears and concerns.
Publication Types: Review; Review, tutorial

Int J Psychosom 1986;33(3):3-8
Aspects of the family with anorexia nervosa or bulimia.
Gross M.
PMID: 3466880 [PubMed - indexed for MEDLINE]

Int Psychiatry Clin 1970;7(1):335-51
Psychotherapy and eating disorders.
Bruch H.

J Abnorm Psychol 2000 May;109(2):239-51
Age differences in genetic and environmental influences on eating attitudes and behaviors in preadolescent and adolescent female twins.
Klump KL, McGue M, Iacono WG.
Department of Psychology, University of Minnesota, USA.
A sample of 680 11- and 602 17-year-old female twins was used to examine (a) age differences in genetic and environmental influences on disordered eating attitudes and behaviors and (b) associations between body mass index (BMI) and eating attitudes and behaviors. Univariate, biometrical model-fitting analyses indicated that 11-year-old twins exhibited less genetic and greater shared environmental influence on eating attitudes and behaviors than 17-year-old twins. Bivariate model-fitting analyses indicated that the relationship between BMI and eating attitudes was mediated primarily by common shared environmental influences in 11-year-old twins and common genetic influences in 17-year-old twins.
Publication Types: Twin study

J Adolesc Health 1998 Dec;23(6):354-63
Review of options for primary prevention of eating disturbances among adolescents.
Rosen DS, Neumark-Sztainer D.
Department of Pediatrics, University of Michigan Medical School, Ann Arbor 48109-0318, USA.
Publication Types: Review; Review, tutorial

J Adolesc Health Care 1988 Sep;9(5):384-8
A method for the assessment of body image disturbance in patients with eating disorders.
Manley RS, Tonkin R, Hammond C.
British Columbia's Children's Hospital, Vancouver, Canada.
This paper describes a new method for assessing body image disturbances in eating disordered patients. Fifteen bulimic, 25 anorexic, and 24 normal controls served as subjects. All subjects were matched for age and height, and bulimics and controls were matched for weight as well. All subjects completed the Perceived Body Image Scale (PBIS), which required subjects to report on how they see themselves when they look in the mirror, how they think they look, and how they feel themselves to be, reflecting the perceptual, cognitive, and affective aspects of body image, respectively. Results showed that both eating disorder groups demonstrated more apparent body image disturbance than controls, and that the bulimics showed significantly greater body image dissatisfaction than anorexics or controls.

J Am Acad Psychoanal 1994 Summer;22(2):299-317
Eating disorders, female psychology, and the self.
de Groot JM, Rodin G.
University of Toronto.
Publication Types: Review; Review, tutorial

J Am Acad Psychoanal 1998 Spring;26(1):165-77
All about Barbie: distortions of a transitional object.
Turkel AR.
Columbia University College of Physicians & Surgeons, USA.

J Am Diet Assoc 1993 Sep;93(9):1037-9
Predictors of body satisfaction in college women.
Mortenson GM, Hoerr SL, Garner DM.
Birchwood Care Center, Grand Rapids, Mich.

J Am Diet Assoc 1996 Jan;96(1):62-4
Change in eating attitudes: an outcome measure of patients with eating disorders.
Eiger MR, Christie BW, Sucher KP.
Cottage Hospital, Santa Barbara, Calif. 93102, USA.

J Am Osteopath Assoc 1988 May;88(5):685-9
Taking the lid off eating disorders.
Reich M.
Publication Types: Review; Review, tutorial

J Child Adolesc Psychiatr Nurs 1998 Apr-Jun;11(2):51-60
An eating disorders prevention program.

Chally PS.
College of Health, University of North Florida, Jacksonville, USA.
Developing, implementing, and evaluating a school personnel training program on eating disorders. Training school personnel to identify students at risk for eating disorders holds promise as a strategy for dealing with this disease. All at-risk students for eating disorders should be further evaluated and additional treatment initiated as needed.
Publication Types: Clinical trial; Controlled clinical trial

J Consult Clin Psychol 1987 Oct;55(5):628-34
Scope and significance of eating disorders.
Mitchell JE, Eckert ED.
Publication Types: Review; Review, academic

J Consult Clin Psychol 1987 Oct;55(5):660-7
Primary prevention of eating disorders.
Shisslak CM, Crago M, Neal ME, Swain B.
Publication Types: Review; Review, academic

J Gen Intern Med 2001 Feb;16(2):140-1
On Walsh JME, Wheat ME, Freud K. Detection, evaluation and treatment of eating disorders.

J Gend Specif Med 1999 Jan-Feb;2(1):47-54
Gender-related aspects of eating disorders: a guide to practice.
Andersen AE.
Department of Psychiatry, University of Iowa, 200 Hawkins Dr, Iowa City, IA 52242, USA. arnold-andersen@uiowa.edu
Eating disorders have significantly different rates of incidence in males and females. Although there is ample scientific evidence supporting gender-specific diagnostic criteria, common stereotypes prevent accurate diagnosis of eating disorders in males. This article focuses on areas of practical consequence to physicians and other health professionals, emphasizing topics for which evidence-based studies can direct treatment guidelines for both female and male patients.
Publication Types: Review; Review, tutorial

J Hum Nutr Diet 2001 Apr;14(2):i-ii
How can weight control be promoted without encouraging eating disorders?
Publication Types: Editorial

J Midwifery Womens Health 2000 Jul-Aug;45(4):301-7
Critical issues in the care of pregnant women with eating disorders and the impact on their children.
Little L, Lowkes E.
University of New Hampshire, School of Health and Human Services, Department of Nursing, Durham 03824, USA.
Pregnancy and eating disorders is a subject that has received relatively little attention in the literature. Nevertheless, serious complications have been found in both the mother and the baby during both pregnancy and post partum period. This article alerts practitioners to the physical and psychological risks that imperil pregnant women with histories of recent eating disorders, describes the experiences of three women with

eating disorders during pregnancy whose children developed eating difficulties, and suggests some guidelines for the screening and care of women with eating disorders and their babies.

J Nerv Ment Dis 1987 Oct;175(10):620-3
Eating disorder and socioeconomic class. Anorexia nervosa and bulimia in nine communities.
Pope HG Jr, Champoux RF, Hudson JI.
Epidemiology Laboratory, McLean Hospital, Belmont, Massachusetts 02178.
To compare the prevalence of eating disorders in lower income vs. upper income communities, we administered a previously validated questionnaire to 394 women at nine state-regulated bingo tournaments. Surprisingly, eating disorders were more commonly reported by lower income respondents.

J Nerv Ment Dis 1990 Aug;178(8):531-5
Anorexia nervosa in 19th century America.
Vandereycken W, Lowenkopf EL.
University Psychiatric Center, Kortenberg, Belgium.
Compared with late 19th century publications in Great Britain and France, medical writers in the United States of the same era apparently had less interest in anorexia nervosa as a distinct clinical syndrome. A review of the literature of that period shows that American physicians very rarely referred to the "new" syndrome described in 1873 by Gull and Lasegue. Except for some short or oblique references, the first explicit clinical description of a case of anorexia nervosa by an American author (James Hendrie Lloyd) did not appear until 1893. The present article documents and discusses this hitherto little known fragment in the history of medicine and psychiatry.
Publication Types: Historical article

J Pediatr 1981 Nov;99(5):830-1
Family relationships in anorexia nervosa.
Monroe B.
Publication Types: Letter

J Pract Nurs 1993 Sep;43(3):47-55; Quiz 55-7
Eating disorders: anorexia nervosa & bulimia.
Tolstoi LG.

J Psychiatr Res 1985;19(2-3):143-53
The epidemiology of anorexia nervosa and bulimia.
Szmukler GI.

J Psychosoc Nurs Ment Health Serv 1988 Nov;26(11):6-11, 15
Eating disorders. Promoting continuity of care.
Deering CG, Niziolek C.
Psychiatric-Mental Health Nursing Program, Yale University, School of Nursing, New Haven, Connecticut.

J Psychosom Res 1970 Sep;14(3):321-5
On compulsive eating.
Thorner HA.

J Soc Psychol 1996 Apr;136(2):269-71
The relationship between eating disorders and depression.
Willcox M, Sattler DN.
Department of Psychology, College of

Charleston, SC 29424, USA.

J Voice 1998 Mar;12(1):89-90
Reflux and vocal disorders in singers with bulimia.
Rothstein SG.
Department of Otolaryngology, SONY Vocal Health Center, New York University Medical Center, New York 10016, USA.
Dysphonia associated with bulimia has been described in the literature associated with vocal fold edema and polypoid changes. Laryngopharyngeat reflux (LPR) has been documented to cause reflux vocal fold pathology including edema and polypoid changes. We studied eight singers with bulimia and documented vocal fold pathology, including edema, posterior commissure hypertrophy, ventricular obliteration, and telangiectasia. Reflux was demonstrated in all eight. The results of this study showed that LPR may be a contributing factor to vocal disorders in singers with bulimia.

Mayo Clin Proc 1976 May;51(5):266-72
The treatment of eating disorders.
Bruch H.

Med Clin North Am 1993 Jul;77(4):899-909
Obesity, anorexia, and bulimia.
Edwards KI.
Department of Medicine, University of Florida, Gainesville.
Eating disorders are common in our society. They represent a heterogeneous group of disorders with respect to pathophysiology (biological, social-cultural, psychological, familial, and developmental), presentation, and treatment. The patient may have superimposed comorbid psychiatric illnesses and may even exhibit features common to both anorexia and bulimia. Regardless, the health care provider must remain cognizant of these illnesses to be able to offer prompt referral to an appropriate center with expertise in treating these pervasive illnesses.
Publication Types: Review; Review, tutorial

Med J Aust 1998 Sep 21;169(6):342-3
Comment on: Med J Aust. 1998 May 4;168(9):458-63
Eating disorders from a primary care perspective.
Hay PJ.
Publication Types: Comment Letter

Midwife Health Visit Community Nurse 1988 May;24(5):189-92
Impact of eating disorders on pregnancy.
Beary MD.

Mil Med 2001 Mar;166(3):264-8
Abnormal eating behaviors in female reserve officer training corps cadets.
Lauder TD, Campbell CS.
Madigan Army Medical Center, Tacoma, WA, USA.
The objective of this study was to evaluate the prevalence of abnormal eating behaviors in Reserve Officer Training Corps (ROTC) female cadets. A total of 310 female ROTC cadets participated in a prospective, cross-sectional study during summer training at Fort Lewis, Washington. All subjects completed the Eating Disorder Inventory and a

supplemental questionnaire. Because of time constraints, clinical interviews were not administered. Of the 310 ROTC cadets, 20% met the screening criteria for being at risk for an eating disorder. The cadets at risk for eating disorders had significantly higher Drive for Thinness, Bulimia, and Body Dissatisfaction subscale scores and were more dissatisfied with their weight than cadets not at risk. There was no significant difference in reported ideal body weight and exercise intensity between the two groups. In the female ROTC cadet population evaluated, 20% practiced abnormal eating behaviors and were at risk for developing an eating disorder.

N C Med J 1988 Oct;49(10):533-5
Eating disorders: evaluation and treatment.
Rockwell WJ.
Publication Types: Review; Review, tutorial

N Engl J Med 1999 Apr 8;340(14):1092-8
Comment in: N Engl J Med. 1999 Aug 19;341(8):614-5; discussion 615-6
N Engl J Med. 1999 Aug 19;341(8):615-6
Eating disorders.
Becker AE, Grinspoon SK, Klibanski A, Herzog DB.
Department of Psychiatry, Massachusetts General Hospital and Harvard Medical School, Harvard Eating Disorders Center, Boston 02116, USA.
Eating disorders are common among adolescent girls and young women and are associated with potentially serious medical complications, yet they often go undetected and untreated. All patients with eating disorders should be evaluated and treated for medical complications of the disease at the same time that psychotherapy and nutritional counseling are undertaken. Pharmacologic agents are often useful as adjuncts to psychotherapy for bulimia nervosa or binge-eating disorder; in the case of anorexia nervosa, psychotropic medication is generally reserved for patients with a concurrent psychiatric illness or those who have recovered some weight.
Publication Types: Review; Review, tutorial

N Engl J Med 1999 Aug 19;341(8):614-5; discussion 615-6
Comment on: N Engl J Med. 1999 Apr 8;340(14):1092-8
Eating disorders.
Mehler PS.
Publication Types: Comment Letter

N Engl J Med 1999 Aug 19;341(8):615-6
Comment on: N Engl J Med. 1999 Apr 8;340(14):1092-8
Eating disorders.
Bravender T.
Publication Types: Comment Letter

New Dir Ment Health Serv 1986 Fall;(31):1-127
Eating disorders.

New Dir Ment Health Serv 1986 Fall;(31):39-46
Males with eating disorders.
Andersen AE.

Nippon Naika Gakkai Zasshi 1997 Sep 10;86(9):1718-22

[Clinical study on eating behavior disorders].
[Article in Japanese]
Suematsu H.
Publication Types: Lectures

NT Learn Curve 1997 Jul 2;1(5):5-8
Eating disorders--knowledge for practice.
Cremin D, Halek C.
Annex Nursing Development Unit, Pathfinder NHS Trust Springfield Hospital, London.

Nurs Stand 1999 Jan 27-Feb 2;13(19):19
Fit to eat.
Brown L.
Derby City General Hospital.
PMID: 10085913 [PubMed - indexed for MEDLINE]

Nurs Times 1995 Nov 29-Dec 5;91(48):42-3
Weight on their minds.
Halek C, Cremin D, Chandran U, Parnell J.

Nurs Times 1997 Jul 30-Aug 5;93(31):24-5
Unhappy eater.
Green C.

Nurs Times 1997 Jul 30-Aug 5;93(31):25-7
In search of perfection.
Wiseman H.
A&E Department, Royal Liverpool University Hospital.
Publication Types: Review; Review, tutorial

Nutr Health 1987;4(4):217-25
Anorexia nervosa and related conditions in schoolchildren.
Salmons PH.
The clinical features of anorexia nervosa and the prevalence of the eating orders in different societies is described. The role of physiological, cultural and biological factors in the aetiology of eating are reviewed. Finally ways of preventing eating disorders are considered.
Publication Types: Review

Nutrition 2000 Jul-Aug;16(7-8):547-51
Eating disorders: diagnosis, etiology, and prevention.
Hetherington MM.
From the Department of Psychology, University of Dundee, Scotland, UK. m.mhetherington@dundee.ac.uk
Publication Types: Review; Review, tutorial

Occup Health (Lond) 1988 May;40(5):547-50
The control of eating disorders.
Williamson J.

Panminerva Med 1968 Nov;10(11):465-71
Anorexia in the first year of life as an expression of changes in the mother-child relationship. A catamnestic study and psychopathological findings in 30 cases.
Di Cagno L, Ravetto F.

Practitioner 1986 May;230(1415):445-50
The eating disorders.
Birtchnell SA, Lacey JH.

Practitioner 1989 Nov 22;233(1479):1525-7
Bulimia nervosa and anorexia nervosa.
Treasure J.
Anorexia and bulimia nervosa are

aetiologically distinct diseases with different treatments. Though it was described more recently, bulimia nervosa occurs more commonly. Accurate diagnosis and early treatment should reduce the mortality of both conditions.

Practitioner 2000 Feb;244(1607):129-32, 134-6
Eating disorders: a strategic approach.
Launer M.
Burnley Healthcare NHS Trust.
Publication Types: Review; Review, tutorial

Prev Med 2001 Mar;32(3):268-83
Population-based prevention of eating disorders: an application of the rose prevention model.
Austin SB.
Division of Adolescent Medicine, Children's Hospital Several decades of concerted research on eating disorders have generated a broad range of proposed causal influences, but much of this etiologic research does not elucidate practical avenues for preventive interventions. Theoretical and empirical evidence suggests that a population-wide reduction in dieting may be a justifiable and effective strategy for prevention of eating pathology. Copyright 2001 American Health Foundation and Academic Press.

Prim Care 1987 Dec;14(4):737-44
Anorexia and bulimia.
Yates WR, Sieleni B.
Department of Psychiatry, University of Iowa College of Medicine, Iowa City.
Eating disorders are receiving increasing attention in the lay press and in psychiatric research. Young women are most often affected by eating disorders, frequently with additional psychiatric syndromes. This article focuses on accurate diagnosis, medical and psychiatric complications, and current management techniques.

Probe 1987 Dec;21(4):173-6
Anorexia and bulimia. Where will they end?
Yochim JR.

Proc Annu Meet Am Psychopathol Assoc 1970;59:181-202
Eating disorders in adolescence.
Bruch H.

Prog Behav Modif 1985;19:255-92
The assessment of anorexia nervosa and bulimia.
Chiodo J.

Psychiatr Dev 1983 Autumn;1(3):247-62
The state of research in anorexia nervosa and bulimia.
Halmi KA.
Recent studies suggest that some of the DSM III criteria for anorexia nervosa require revision. In particular exclusion for onset beyond 25, and a requirement for 25 per cent weight loss appear inappropriate, whereas amenorrhoea correlates better with anorectic psychology than weight. Although an increased incidence of affective disturbance among the relatives of anorectics and bulimics has been shown, the precise relationship with affective disorder remains unclear. Of the behavioral therapies, operant positive

reinforcement that restores weight in a hospital setting has had the best results. Successful pharmacological approaches have included cyproheptadine (a serotonin antagonist), chlorpromazine and metoclopramide.
Publication Types: Review

Psychiatr Med 1989;7(3):75-87
Laxative abuse in eating disorders.
Willard SG, Winstead DK, Anding R, Dudley P.
Department of Psychiatry and Neurology, Tulane University School of Medicine, New Orleans, Louisiana.

Psychiatr Med 1992;10(4):105-18
The use of hypnosis with eating disorders.
Torem MS.
Department of Psychiatry, Northeastern Ohio Universities College of Medicine, Akron.
This paper reviews the literature on the use of hypnosis in the assessment and treatment of eating disorders. A number of hypnotherapeutic techniques are explained and discussed, such as: general relaxation and calmness, guided imagery, teaching self-hypnosis, ego-strengthening, direct and indirect suggestions for healing and recovery, cognitive restructuring and reframing, symbolic guided imagery, age progression ("back from the future" technique), metaphorical prescriptions, age regression and abreactions, and ego state therapy. Verbatim examples of these techniques are given as illustrations of how to use them.

Psychiatry Res 1995 Apr 28;56(3):205-12
Anger attacks in eating disorders.
Fava M, Rappe SM, West J, Herzog DB.
Department of Psychiatry, Massachusetts General Hospital, Boston 02114, USA.
As central nervous system serotonergic dysregulation has been postulated to exist in both eating and aggression disorders, we hypothesized that anger attacks would be more common among patients with eating disorders than among control subjects. In addition, we wanted to examine possible relationships between the presence of anger attacks and the type or severity of the eating disorder. Subjects were 39 normal female volunteers and 132 female outpatients with anorexia nervosa, bulimia nervosa, or both. The higher prevalence of anger attacks among patients than among control subjects may reflect central hyposerotonergic function, found in previous studies to be present in both eating disorders and pathologic aggression.

Psychiatry Res 1996 Apr 16;62(1):3-9
Epidemiology of anorexia nervosa.
Wakeling A.
University Department of Psychiatry, Royal Free Hospital, London, UK.
Findings of epidemiological studies of the rates, incidence, and prevalence of eating disorder over time and in different populations are reviewed. Risk factors for anorexia nervosa and bulimia nervosa are also addressed. Methodological recommendations for future directions in epidemiological studies of eating disorders are presented.

Publication Types: Review; Review, tutorial

Psychol Assess 2000 Jun;12(2):123-31
Development and validation of the Eating Disorder Diagnostic Scale: a brief self-report measure of anorexia, bulimia, and binge-eating disorder.
Stice E, Telch CF, Rizvi SL.
Department of Psychology, University of Texas at Austin 78712, USA. stice@psy.utexas.edu
This article describes the development and validation of a brief self-report scale for diagnosing anorexia nervosa, bulimia nervosa, and binge-eating disorder. Results implied that this scale was reliable and valid in this investigation and that it may be useful for clinical and research applications.

Psychol Med 1977 Aug;7(3):363-7
The present status of anorexia nervosa.
Russell G.

Psychol Med 2000 Nov;30(6):1249-62
Prevention research in eating disorders: theory and new directions.
Austin SB.
Division of Adolescent Medicine, Children's Hospital and Harvard School of Public Health, Boston, MA, USA.
BACKGROUND: Over the past two decades, scores of articles and several books have been published calling for more attention to the prevention of eating disorders, but less than two dozen prevention intervention studies have been conducted to date. This paper concludes with a recommendation for new attention to a model of proactive primary prevention targeted at environmental change and cross-disciplinary collaboration to achieve a reduction in the incidence of eating disorders.
Publication Types: Meta-analysis

Psychol Med 2001 Feb;31(2):361-5
A preliminary population-based twin study of self-reported eating disorder.
Kortegaard LS, Hoerder K, Joergensen J, Gillberg C, Kyvik KO.
Department of Child Psychiatry, Institute of Clinical Research, Faculty of Medical Sciences, University of Southern Denmark, Odense University.
Twin studies have concluded that there is a substantial genetic contribution to the aetiology of eating disorders. The aim of the present study was to estimate the genetic contribution to the aetiology of self-reported eating disorders in a sample of representative twins. There is a genetic contribution to the aetiology of self-reported eating disorders in the general population. The relationship between self-reported and clinical eating disorder remains to be examined.

Psychol Rep 1998 Dec;83(3 Pt 2):1197-8
Fear of fat and the dream process: a correlational investigation.
Kroth J, Yoneda D, Hammond A.
Graduate Division of Counseling Psychology and Education, Santa Clara University, CA 95053, USA.
Dream characteristics of 27 women from a graduate counseling program were correlated with the Goldfarb Fear of Fat Scale. Significant positive correlations were obtained for scores with recurrent nightmares (.38) and dreaming one is dreaming (.40). An

inverse relationship was noted between sexual content of dreams and scores for fear of fat (-.41). Results were discussed in terms of associations among dissociation, body image, and the dream process.

Psychosomatics 1998 Jul-Aug;39(4):371-8
The evaluation of eating and weight symptoms. A comparison of medically ill and eating disorder patients.
Carney CP, Yates WR.
Department of Psychiatry, University of Iowa College of Medicine, Iowa City 52242, USA.
The purpose of this study was to determine the utility of hospitalization in a medical-psychiatry unit for eating disorder patients. A retrospective chart review of 48 patients given an International Classification of Disease-9 diagnosis of an eating disorder was conducted. Presenting symptoms, functional status using the Karnofsky Index, medical and psychiatric evaluation, diagnosis, treatment, and outcome were evaluated. Initial evaluation of patients presenting with eating or weight symptoms may be difficult given similarities between the patients with primary eating disorders and those with other underlying medical causes. The medical-psychiatry unit provides comprehensive initial evaluation and treatment of patients with eating and weight symptoms.

Qual Life Res 2000;9(6):667-74
The health-related quality of life in eating disorders.
Padierna A, Quintana JM, Arostegui I, Gonzalez N, Horcajo MJ.
Psychiatric Service, Galdakao Hospital, Bizkaia, Spain.
This study investigated the perception of health-related quality of life (HRQoL) in ambulatory patients with eating disorders in relation to the severity of eating symptomatology and psychological comorbidity. The evaluation of HRQoL in these patients confirms the impact of these disorders on daily life in areas not directly related to eating disorders. The SF-36 isuseful for discriminating among different levels of severity of eating disorders and other psychological comorbidities of these patients.

Science 1998 May 29;280(5368):1387-90
Eating disorders: progress and problems.
Walsh BT, Devlin MJ.
New York State Psychiatric Institute and the College of Physicians & Surgeons, Columbia University, 722 West 168th Street, New York, NY 10032, USA.
btw1@columbia.edu
Recent research on Anorexia Nervosa and Bulimia Nervosa has yielded an increasingly detailed understanding of the range of biological and psychological abnormalities associated with these eating disorders. This article reviews current thinking on the etiology and treatment of the two major eating disorders and a related syndrome, Binge Eating Disorder.
Publication Types: Review; Review, tutorial

Semin Gastrointest Dis 1998 Oct;9(4):183-8
Nutritional management of anorexia.
Jeejeebhoy KN.

Nutrition and Digestive Disease Program, St. Michael's Hospital, and the University of Toronto, Ontario, Canada.

The prevalence of eating disorders, such as anorexia nervosa, is increasing in young adults, particularly young adult women. Sometimes, gastrointestinal complaints in patients with anorexia nervosa may lead to an erroneous diagnosis of gastrointestinal disease and unnecessary diagnostic studies and therapies. A careful history and physical examination and laboratory tests are needed to make the correct diagnosis and begin appropriate treatment.

Publication Types: Review; Review, tutorial

Singapore Med J 1994 Apr;35(2):201-3

Anorexia and bulimia nervosa.

Chan S.

Child Psychiatric Clinic, Institute of Health, Singapore.

Anorexia and bulimia nervosa are eating disorders characterised by abnormal eating behaviour, a morbid concern over body weight and a distorted perception of body size. It commonly occurs in young postpubertal girls in developed societies. Aetiological factors are a complex interplay of biological, psychological and social factors. Bizarre eating patterns can lead to life-threatening medical situations which require urgent in-hospital care. Comprehensive management should be effected by a multi-disciplinary team with contributions from the internist, the psychiatrist, the nurse, the psychologist, the social worker and the teacher. There is significant psychiatric morbidity and mortality in the outcome of these eating disorders.

Publication Types: Review; Review, tutorial

Singapore Med J 1994 Dec;35(6):631-4

Eating disorders.

Low BL.

Institute of Mental Health/Woodbridge Hospital, Singapore.

The main forms of eating disorders are anorexia and bulimia nervosa and obesity. The clinical features, aetiology, treatment and prognosis of anorexia and bulimia nervosa are described to highlight the similarities and differences between these two conditions. Both conditions affect predominantly the young female population with body image disturbance as one of the core symptoms.

Publication Types: Review; Review, tutorial

Soc Work Health Care 1998;28(1):61-73

Eating disorders and the cultural forces behind the drive for thinness: are African American women really protected?

Williamson L.

African American females have been largely excluded from studies, due to the assumption that the Black community's acceptance of women with fuller shapes protects its women from eating problems. However, recent studies are beginning to show that race, class, and exposure to a dominant culture which denigrates Black features and physiques impact body image among Black women and may play a role in the development of

eating problems.
Publication Types: Review; Review, tutorial

Tex Med 1988 Sep;84(9):51-4
Erratum in: Tex Med 1988 Oct;84(10):7
Eating disorders: role of the primary care physician.
Waller DA.

Trends Mol Med 2001 Mar;7(3):102
Insights into eating disorders.
Weitzman J.

WMJ 1998 Oct;97(9):14-5, 18-9, 37
Eating disorders: a weighty issue for clinicians and their patients.
Kennedy M.

CAUSES

Acta Psychiatr Scand 1995 Jan;91(1):5-9
Life events and severe anorexia nervosa in adolescence.
Horesh N, Apter A, Lepkifker E, Ratzoni G, Weizmann R, Tyano S.
Department of Psychology, Bar Ilan University, Ramat Gan, Israel.
The purpose of this study was to study the influence of life events on adolescent patients suffering from anorexia nervosa. Twenty one hospitalized adolescent inpatients with severe anorexia nervosa were compared with 79 adolescent nonanorectic psychiatric inpatients and 40 healthy adolescents for stressful life events throughout their lives. The anorectic patients showed significantly higher negative life event scores than healthy controls in all the areas of life events examined. In addition, they showed significantly more negative life events concerning parents than patients in the other psychiatric diagnostic categories. These findings have relevance for the growing literature on the association between eating disorders and certain forms of child abuse.

Acta Psychiatr Scand 1997 Aug;96(2):101-7
Eating disorders and antecedent anxiety disorders: a controlled study.
Bulik CM, Sullivan PF, Fear JL, Joyce PR.
Department of Psychiatry, Medical College of Virginia/Virginia Commonwealth University, Richmond 23298, USA.
We compared the prevalence and age of onset of adult and childhood anxiety disorders relative to the primary diagnosis in 68 women with anorexia nervosa (AN), 116 women with bulimia nervosa (BN), 56 women with major depression with no eating disorder (MD) and 98 randomly selected controls (RC) in order to determine whether antecedent anxiety disorders are plausible risk factors for AN and BN. These data suggest that certain anxiety disorders are non-specific risk factors for later affective and eating disorders, and others may represent more specific antecedent risk factors.

Acta Psychiatr Scand Suppl 1990;361:7-13
Anorexia/bulimia nervosa: the

development of anorexia nervosa and of mental symptoms. Treatment and the outcome of the disease.
Bassoe HH.
Medical Department, School of Medicine, University of Bergen, Norway.
Since 1958 we have conducted a prospective study of anorexia/bulimia nervosa (A/BN) covering a total of 550 patients. This paper presents a new idea of the development of A/BN. For a variety of reasons, a predisposition for developing A/BN is triggered by a minor and non-specific loss of weight. The development of mental symptoms with pathological thoughts and behaviour, and disturbances in the satiety and hunger centres suggest a cerebral dysfunction. Educating patients in pathophysiology enables them to use their intelligence, logical thinking and strong will to evaluate the importance of an adequate supply of nutrients.

Addict Behav 1998 Jul-Aug;23(4):463-75
The eating disorders as addiction: a psychobiological perspective.
Davis C, Claridge G.
Graduate Programme in Exercise and Health Science, York University, Toronto, Canada.
A number of theories have been proposed to explain the substantial comorbidity between the eating disorders and the substance-related disorders. The present study was designed to determine the degree to which anorexic and bulimic patients display addictive personality characteristics, and whether these traits are useful in predicting the severity of the patient's weight preoccupation and their degree of excessive exercising. Results confirmed that both anorexic and bulimic patients had high scores on the Addiction Scale of the Eysenck Personality Questionnaire, and that addictiveness and obsessive-compulsiveness were related simultaneously to weight preoccupation and excessive exercising in both patient groups.

Adolescence 1999 Winter;34(136):671-9
Onset of disordered eating attitudes and behaviors in early adolescence: interplay of pubertal status, gender, weight, and age.
O'Dea JA, Abraham S.
Faculty of Education, School of Professional Studies, University of Sydney, New South Wales, Australia.
The interplay of puberty, gender, weight, and age in regard to body image and disordered eating behaviors and attitudes was investigated in a sample of early adolescents. It was found that, after menarche, females had increased personal expectations and were dissatisfied with weight/shape changes. They wanted to reduce their weight and between-meal eating (which was associated with increased feelings of inadequacy, loss of control, and decreased self-esteem). Young males at puberty desired to build up their bodies, believing that appearance was important to their sexual appeal. They were also more willing to form close relationships. Postpubertal males felt most in control of their lives, had the highest self-esteem, and were more trusting of their body cues. Overall, high achieving, more anxious

postmenarcheal females were at greatest risk for eating disturbances. These results indicate that the interaction of pubertal status and gender must be considered when developing intervention programs.

Alcohol Clin Exp Res 1996 Aug;20(5):878-81
Bulimia nervosa and substance dependence: association and family transmission.
Kaye WH, Lilenfeld LR, Plotnicov K, Merikangas KR, Nagy L, Strober M, Bulik CM, Moss H, Greeno CG.
Department of Psychiatry, Western Psychiatric Institute and Clinic, University of Pittsburgh School of Medicine, Pennsylvania 15213, USA.
Alcohol and drug use disorders are common among women with bulimia nervosa (BN) and their family members. However, it is not known whether there is a familial relationship between BN and substance use disorders. Compared were 47 women with BN and 44 non-eating-disordered community control women, and their first-degree relatives (177 and 190, respectively). BN probands were stratified by the presence (43%) or absence (57%) of lifetime alcohol and/or drug dependence. The first-degree relatives of substance-dependent BN probands had significantly higher lifetime rates of alcohol/drug dependence (38%), compared with relatives of nonsubstance-dependent BN probands (10%) or relatives of community controls (18%). These data suggest that BN and substance dependence are transmitted independently in families.

Am J Psychiatry 1991 Dec;148(12):1627-37
Comment in: Am J Psychiatry. 1992 Aug;149(8):1122
The genetic epidemiology of bulimia nervosa.
Kendler KS, MacLean C, Neale M, Kessler R, Heath A, Eaves L.
Department of Psychiatry, Medical College of Virginia, Richmond.
The authors seek to clarify, from both an epidemiologic and genetic perspective, the major risk factors for bulimia nervosa and to understand the relationship between narrowly defined bulimia and bulimia-like syndromes. METHOD: Personal structured psychiatric interviews were conducted with 2,163 female twins from a population-based register. It was shown that the liability to fully syndromal bulimia nervosa, which affects around one in 25 women at some point in their lives, is substantially influenced by both epidemiologic and genetic risk factors. The same factors that influence the risk for narrowly defined bulimia also influence the risk for less severe bulimia-like syndromes.

Am J Psychiatry 1995 Jan;152(1):64-71
Anorexia nervosa and anorexic-like syndromes in a population-based female twin sample.
Walters EE, Kendler KS.
Department of Psychiatry, Medical College of Virginia/Virginia Commonwealth University, Richmond.
The authors explored the epidemiologic characteristics and risk factors of anorexia nervosa and examined the relationship between

narrowly defined anorexia nervosa and anorexia-like syndromes. The authors' analyses support the hypothesis of a spectrum of anorexic-like syndromes in women. These syndromes are familial and share familial etiologic factors with major depression and bulimia nervosa.

Am J Psychiatry 1998 Feb;155(2):244-9
Comment in: Am J Psychiatry. 1999 Jun;156(6):982
Thirty-month outcome in patients with anorexia or bulimia nervosa and concomitant obsessive-compulsive disorder.
Thiel A, Zuger M, Jacoby GE, Schussler G.
Department of Psychological Medicine and Psychotherapy, University of Innsbruck, Austria.
This study examines whether concomitant obsessive-compulsive disorder (OCD) indicates a poorer prognosis for patients with anorexia or bulimia nervosa. Analysis of variance for repeated measures revealed significant improvement over time on six of the eight Eating Disorder Inventory subscales for all patients regardless of OCD presence. The results suggest that concomitant OCD does not indicate a significantly poorer prognosis for patients with anorexia or bulimia nervosa.

Am J Psychoanal 1980 Summer;40(2):169-72
Preconditions for the development of anorexia nervosa.
Bruch H.

Appetite 1994 Dec;23(3):287
Beauty is in the eye of the beholder: media influences on the psychopathology of eating problems.
Waller G, Shaw J, Hamilton K, Baldwin G, Harding T, Summer A.
School of Phychology, University of Birmingham, U.K.

Arch Gen Psychiatry 1999 May;56(5):468-76
Risk factors for anorexia nervosa: three integrated case-control comparisons.
Fairburn CG, Cooper Z, Doll HA, Welch SL.
Department of Psychiatry, Oxford University, Warneford Hospital, England.
Many risk factors have been implicated in the development of anorexia nervosa. A case-control design was used involving the comparison of 67 female subjects with a history of anorexia nervosa with 204 healthy control subjects, 102 subjects with other psychiatric disorders, and 102 subjects with bulimia nervosa. The subjects with anorexia nervosa and the healthy controls differed in their exposure to most of the putative risk factors. There appears to be a broad range of risk factors for anorexia nervosa and bulimia nervosa, some of which are shared with other psychiatric disorders. Factors that increase the likelihood of dieting seem to have more important influence as risk factors for bulimia nervosa than anorexia nervosa. Perfectionism and negative self-evaluation appear to be particularly common and characteristic antecedents of both eating disorders.

Arch Pediatr Adolesc Med 1999 Nov;153(11):1184-9
Relation of peer and media influences to the development of purging behaviors among preadolescent and adolescent girls.
Field AE, Camargo CA Jr, Taylor CB, Berkey CS, Colditz GA.
Channing Laboratory, Department of Medicine, Brigham and Women's Hospital and Harvard Medical School, Boston, Mass 02115, USA.
Alison.Field@channing.harvard.edu
OBJECTIVE: To assess prospectively the relation of peer and media influences on the risk of development of purging behaviors. Both peers and popular culture, independent of each other, exert influence on girls' weight control beliefs and behaviors. Therefore, to make eating disorder prevention programs more effective, efforts should be made to persuade the television, movie, and magazine industries to employ more models and actresses whose weight could be described as healthy, not underweight.

Aust Fam Physician 2000 Apr;29(4):328-33
The recognition and management of eating disorders.
Buist A.
Austin Repatriation Medical Centre, Heidelberg, Victoria.
a.buist@medicine.unimelb.edu.au
Eating disorders--anorexia nervosa and bulimia nervosa--are increasingly recognised in our community, and appear to be increasing in frequency and affecting girls at a younger age, though the disorder is not restricted to females. This article provides a current overview of eating disorders and their management. There continues to be controversy over the reason for the increase in eating disorders. Changes in societal ideas and pressures, as well as the massive increase this century in the role of the mass media, have been highlighted as having a likely role. Early engagement and a multifaceted approach are recommended.

Aust N Z J Psychiatry 1978 Sep;12(3):145-9
The onset of anorexia nervosa.
Beumont PJ, Abraham SF, Argall WJ, George CW, Glaun DE.
In a retrospective study of case notes a number of experiential and psychological factors were discerned of possible importance to the psychogenesis of anorexia nervosa. These factors included issues of dependence and independence, sexual challenge, concern about obesity, and a variety of other, less specific stresses. Attempts to confirm the findings by means of a prospective study were impeded by difficulties in defining the onset of the illness.

BMJ 1999 Jun 26;318(7200):1761-2
Onset of adolescent eating disorders. Dieting may be an early sign, rather than a cause, of eating disorder.
Stettler N, Tershakovec AM, Leonard MB.
Publication Types: Letter

BMJ 1999 Mar 20;318(7186):765-8
Onset of adolescent eating disorders: population based cohort study over 3 years.
Patton GC, Selzer R, Coffey C, Carlin JB, Wolfe R.

Centre for Adolescent Health, Department of Paediatrics, University of Melbourne, Parkville Victoria 3052, Australia.
patton@cryptic.rch.unimelb.edu.au
To study the predictors of new eating disorders in an adolescent cohort. In a cohort study over 3 years with six waves. Dieting was found to be the most important predictor of new eating disorders. Differences in the incidence of eating disorders between sexes were largely accounted for by the high rates of earlier dieting and psychiatric morbidity in the female subjects. In adolescents, controlling weight by exercise rather than diet restriction seems to carry less risk of development of eating disorders.

Br J Med Psychol 1998 Dec;71 (Pt 4):525-47
The sexual competition hypothesis for eating disorders.
Abed RT.
Department of Psychiatry, Rotherham District General Hospital, UK.
A hypothesis is presented for eating disorders, based on Darwinian theory, that contends that these syndromes together with the phenomenon of the pursuit of thinness are manifestations of female intra-sexual competition. The present hypothesis deals with the ultimate level of causation and is therefore compatible with a range of theories of proximate causation. Although the present hypothesis is not directly testable, it makes predictions that are testable and refutable.

Br J Psychiatry 1979 Jan;134:71-8
Pretreatment predictors of outcome in anorexia nervosa.
Halmi KA, Goldberg SC, Casper RC, Eckert ED, Davis JM.
The relationship of selected pretreatment characteristics to weight gain during treatment was examined in 81 anorexia nervosa patients. Good prognostic indicators correlating positively with weight gain were: no previous hospitalizations for anorexia nervosa, a great amount of overactivity before treatment, less denial of illness, less psychosexual immaturity and the admission to feeling hunger. A perinatal history of delivery complications was associated with the poor outcome predictor of prior hospitalizations.

Br J Psychiatry 1991 Dec;159:846-9
The prediction of treatment response in bulimia nervosa. A study of patient variables.
Maddocks SE, Kaplan AS.
Department of Psychology, Women's College Hospital, Toronto, Ontario, Canada.
To investigate the predictive value of a wide range of variables fordistinguishing subjects who demonstrate a favourable treatment response from those who do not, 86 women with a DSM-III-R diagnosis of bulimia nervosa who completed a group treatment programme for eating disorders were studied.

Br J Psychiatry 1999 Jan;174:63-6
Comment in: Br J Psychiatry. 1999 Jul;175:89-90
Difficulties in family functioning and adolescent anorexia nervosa.
Gowers S, North C.
Academic Unit, Young People's Centre, Chester.

BACKGROUND: Difficulties in family functioning are often evident when an adolescent has anorexia nervosa, and the possible causative or contributory role of such difficulties in the illness is unclear. Thirty-five adolescents with anorexia nervosa and their mothers completed the Family Assessment Device (FAD) while clinicians administered the McMaster's Structured Interview of Family Functioning (McSIFF). Severity of anorexia nervosa was rated at baseline and at one year follow-up using the Morgan-Russell Schedule. Concluded were the difficulties in family functioning do not appear to be directly associated with severity of anorexia nervosa nor do these difficulties reduce with clinical improvement, in the short term.

Compr Psychiatry 1989 Mar-Apr;30(2):179-88

A family study of anorexia nervosa and bulimia.

Logue CM, Crowe RR, Bean JA.

Department of Preventive Medicine and Environmental Health, University of Iowa, Iowa City.

A family study is presented that examines the association between eating disorders and affective illness. 307 relatives of 30 eating disorder patients, of 16 patients with major depression, and of 20 normal controls, were interviewed to determine lifetime histories of psychiatric illness. Using logistic regression analyses, the results supported previous findings of a familial association between eating disorders and major depression. However, there was no evidence that clinical features of eating disorder patients (presence of bulimia or major depression) can be used to predict morbid risk. In addition, the results failed to reveal a familial aggregation of either alcoholism or drug abuse in eating disorder families.

Compr Psychiatry 1996 Sep-Oct;37(5):368-74

Lifetime anxiety disorders in women with bulimia nervosa.

Bulik CM, Sullivan PF, Carter FA, Joyce PR.

Department of Psychology, University of Canterbury, Christchurch, New Zealand.

We examined the prevalence and ages at onset of additional childhood and adult psychiatric disorders in women with bulimia nervosa and evaluated the differential impact of a mood or anxiety disorder on the presentation of bulimia nervosa. One hundred fourteen women participating in a clinical trial of cognitive-behavioral therapy for bulimia nervosa were assessed at pretreatment with structured diagnostic methodology. The presence of a mood disorder was associated with greater body dissatisfaction, lower Global Assessment of Functioning Scales (GAFS) score, more externalizing disorders of childhood, and, as expected, higher Hamilton Depression Rating Scale (HDRS) scores. The presence of an anxiety disorder was related to a history of anorexia nervosa and earlier age at onset of drug or alcohol dependence. Early-onset anxiety disorders are prevalent and may represent one potential pathway to bulimia nervosa.

Compr Psychiatry 1998 Nov-Dec;39(6):392-9
Familial factors in anorexia nervosa: a community-based study.
Nilsson EW, Gillberg C, Rastam M.
Child Neuropsychiatry Clinic, Goteborg University, Sweden.
A group of 51 cases with teenage anorexia nervosa (AN; including a total population of cases from one birth cohort) were compared with a sex-, age-, and school-matched group of 51 cases on familial factors. Found were PDD symptoms, major depression, and death in first-degree relatives pervasive developmental disorders in the AN group.

Curr Opin Pediatr 1993 Aug;5(4):415-8
Erratum in: Curr Opin Pediatr 1993 Dec;5(6):750
Anorexia nervosa and bulimia nervosa in children and adolescents.
Woodside DB.
Eating Disorders Inpatient Unit, Toronto Hospital, Ontario, Canada.
There are significant advances in many areas in the field of the eating disorders anorexia nervosa and bulimia nervosa. The publication of treatment guidelines by the American Psychiatric Association provides clear direction forclinicians involved in the care of these patients. Research continues to elucidate those factors in family therapies that are associated with significant change, suggesting that the psychoeducational component of these treatments iscritical. There is increased interest in the heritable genetic components of these conditions, with some evidence available to support a heritable component. There is also a growing body of literature examining the occurrence of eating disorders in members of nonwestern cultural groups.
Publication Types: Review; Review, tutorial

Dev Med Child Neurol 1979 Jun;21(3):393-5
Early recognition and prevention of anorexia nervosa.
Crisp AH.

Eat Weight Disord 1998 Jun;3(2):95-9
Analyzing the relation between self-esteem and eating disorders: differential effects of self-liking and self-competence.
Silvera DH, Bergersen TD, Bjorgum L, Perry JA, Rosenvinge JH, Holte A.
University of Tromso, Norway.
Research in the past has demonstrated an association between low self-esteem and eating disorders. Recent research on self-esteem has shown, however, that self-esteem is composed of two distinct factors--self-liking and self-competence. The present study examined the relation between these two self-esteem factors and both eating disorders and eating disturbed cognitions. A strong relationship was found between self-liking and eating disorders, but no relationship was found between self-competence and eating disorders.

Health Psychol 2000 Mar;19(2):115-23
The relation between risk factors for binge eating and bulimia nervosa: a population-based female twin study.
Wade TD, Bulik CM, Sullivan PF, Neale MC, Kendler KS.
Department of Psychology, Flinders

University of South Australia, Adelaide, Australia.
This study investigated the differential risk factors for the initiation of binge eating and the transition from binge eating to bulimia nervosa. Genetic risk factors for binge eating and bulimia nervosa may be largely similar, whereas nonshared environment may be important in influencing the risk for bulimia nervosa once binge eating is initiated.
Publication Types: Twin study

Hum Genet 1995 Jan;95(1):1-11
Anorexia nervosa viewed as an extreme weight condition: genetic implications.
Hebebrand J, Remschmidt H.
Department of Child and Adolescent Psychiatry, Philipp's University Marburg, Germany.
In anorexia nervosa, psychopathological features and reduced body weight are inseparable, suggesting a prominent role of behavioral factors in achievement and maintenance of extreme underweight. By reviewing the relevant literature we examined whether genetic research in anorexia nervosa can profit from considering this disorder as an extreme weight condition.

Int J Eat Disord 1995 Apr;17(3):291-7
Premorbid onset of psychopathology in long-term recovered anorexia nervosa.
Deep AL, Nagy LM, Weltzin TE, Rao R, Kaye WH.
Center for Overcoming Problem Eating, Western Psychiatric Institute and Clinic, Pittsburgh, PA 15213, USA.
It is recognized that patients with anorexia nervosa commonly have other psychiatric illnesses. We obtained a retrospective history from 24 subjects who were long term (more than 1 year) recovered from anorexia nervosa. We found that 58% reported that they had the onset of one or more childhood anxiety disorder diagnoses at the age of 10 +/- 5 years old. This was 5 years before the mean age of onset of anorexia nervosa. The onset of depression was about 1 year before the onset of anorexia nervosa in about one half the subjects. The early and common onset of childhood anxiety disorders in a substantial percentage of anorexics raises the possibility that childhood anxiety disorders herald the first behavioral expression of a biologic vulnerability in some subjects who develop anorexia nervosa.

Int J Eat Disord 1995 Mar;17(2):147-52
Perfectionism in anorexia nervosa.
Bastiani AM, Rao R, Weltzin T, Kaye WH.
University of Pittsburgh, School of Medicine, PA, USA.
Although it is well accepted that most patients with anorexia nervosa are perfectionistic, little work has been done in characterizing this behavior. Anorexics were assessed by two new multidimensional instruments that were designed to measure multiple aspects of perfectionism. Both scales confirm that underweight, malnourished patients with anorexia nervosa are perfectionistic.
Importantly, elevated perfectionism scores, persisted after weight restoration.
These scales may be of value in

assessing response to treatment.

Int J Eat Disord 1996 Jan;19(1):13-22
Food preferences and desire to eat in anorexia and bulimia nervosa.
Stoner SA, Fedoroff IC, Andersen AE, Rolls BJ.
Nutrition Department, Pennsylvania State University, University Park 16802-2311, USA.
An examination to determine whether eating disordered patients and controls differ in visual analog scale (VAS) ratings of liking and desire to eat various foods and whether ratings differ according to caloric or macronutrient content of the foods. METHOD: Fifty-five female inpatients with eating disorders and 15 controls rated their liking of and desire to eat 50 common foods at admission and discharge using 100-mm VAS. RESULTS: All patient groups rated their desire to eat high-calorie foods significantly lower than their desire to eat low-calorie foods whereas controls rated their desire to eat high- and low-calorie foods equally. Patients also differed from controls more in ratings of desire to eat than in liking when foods were classified according to macronutrient content.

Int J Eat Disord 1996 May;19(4):335-45
Course and outcome in adolescent anorexia nervosa.
Herpertz-Dahlmann BM, Wewetzer C, Schulz E, Remschmidt H.
Department of Child and Adolescent Psychiatry, Philipps University, Marburg, Germany.
Investigated were course, outcome, and psychiatric comorbidity in adolescent anorexia nervosa by repeated follow-up assessment. After 7 years, 1 patient (3%) had anorexia nervosa, 4 patients (12%) bulimia nervosa, and 10 patients (29%) eating disorder not otherwise specified (EDNOS). Anxiety disorders (41%) and affective disorders (18%) were the most prevalent comorbid psychiatric disorders. Concomitant general psychopathology was significantly related to the outcome of the eating disorder.

Int J Eat Disord 1997 Dec;22(4):403-9
Food cravings in women with a history of anorexia nervosa.
Gendall KA, Sullivan PF, Joyce PR, Bulik CM.
Department of Psychological Medicine, Christchurch School of Medicine, New Zealand.
The objective of the present study was to determine the prevalence and characteristics of food cravings in women with a history of anorexia nervosa. A similar prevalence of food craving in cases as in controls suggests that successful control of food intake and/or denial of hunger overrides dietary restriction as a precondition for craving in anorexia nervosa. A dysfunction in the serotonergic system, the provision of intermittent reinforcement by binge episodes, and/or frustration due to unsuccessful attempts at dietary restraint may mediate the association of cravings with the presence of lifetime bulimia.

Int J Eat Disord 1998 Sep;24(2):167-74
The significance of body size estimation in eating disorders: its

relationship with clinical and psychological variables.
Probst M, Vandereycken W, Vanderlinden J, Van Coppenolle H.
Eating Disorders Unit, University Center St. Joseph, Kortenberg, Belgium.
Studying assess the relationship between body size estimation on the one hand and clinical and psychological variables on the other. No significant relationship was found between the body size estimations and the clinical variables. The cognitive and affective responses showed a moderate relationship with self-reported body attitude. Body dissatisfaction was negatively correlated with the optative response (desired body size).

Int J Eat Disord 2000 Jan;27(1):90-5
Body dissatisfaction, bulimia, and depression among women: the ediating role of drive for thinness.
Wiederman MW, Pryor TL.
Department of Psychological Science, Ball State University, Muncie, IN 47306-0520, USA.
Past research has called into question the apparent relationship between body dissatisfaction and bulimia among women once effects of depression are statistically controlled. Investigated were interrelations among body dissatisfaction, depression, and bulimia, as well as considered individual differences in drive for thinness, within two samples of young adult women. In multiple regression analyses using depression and bulimia as predictors of body dissatisfaction, both were uniquely related to body dissatisfaction. These findings were similar to the results of previous research. However, when drive for thinness was added to the regression equations, drive for thinness was a unique predictor of body dissatisfaction whereas bulimia was not (neither was depression among college women).

Int J Fertil Womens Med 1999 May-Jun;44(3):125-30
Managing adolescents with eating disorders.
Slupik RI.
Northwestern University Medical School, Children's Memorial Hospital and Northwestern Memorial Hospital, Chicago, Illinois, USA.
Anorexia nervosa is a complex psychiatric disorder with endocrinologic manifestations primarily affecting adolescent females. The menstrual irregularities may cause the patient or family to seek gynecologic consultation before the diagnosis of primary psychiatric disorder has been made. Bulimia is a separate disease entity characterized by compulsive overeating binges followed by compensatory purging behavior to maintain a desired weight. Depending on the degree of psychiatric disturbance, purging, and ultimate body weight, such patients may or may not present with menstrual abnormalities. Hypoestrogenic hypothalamic amenorrhea in both types of patients may result in osteoporosis, stress fractures, and infertility.
Publication Types: Review; Review, tutorial

Int J Obes Relat Metab Disord 1998 Jul;22(7):641-7
Explaining the effect of ethnic group on weight concern: finding a role forfamily values.
Ogden J, Chanana A.
Department of General Practice, UMDS, London University, UK.
Examining the impact of ethnic group on aspects of weight concern and to assess the role of family values in explaining this association. 20 Asian and 20 white daughters gave a questionnaire to their mother, father and sibling closest in age, concerning their profile characteristics (age, education) values and beliefs and completed a matched questionnaire containing additional measures of aspects of their weight concern.

J Abnorm Psychol 1993 Aug;102(3):438-44
Personality and behavioral vulnerabilities associated with risk status foreating disorders in adolescent girls.
Leon GR, Fulkerson JA, Perry CL, Cudeck R.
Department of Psychology, University of Minnesota 55455.
This article presents first-year cross-sectional findings from a study of the development of eating disorders. Adolescent female (N = 937) 7th through 10th graders completed measures that included information on personality, self-concept, eating patterns, and attitudes. A risk status score was calculated on the basis of comprehensive information regarding DSM-III-R eating disorders criteria and other weight and attitudinal data. All personality measures showed significant differences according to risk, based on subject classification into high, moderate, and mild risk status and comparison groups. The strongest predictor variables for risk were body dissatisfaction, negative emotionality, and lack of interoceptive awareness. The possible diathesis of personality including temperamental factors in the later development of an eating disorder is discussed.

J Abnorm Psychol 1993 Feb;102(1):177-80
Equivalence of body image disturbances in anorexia and bulimia nervosa.
Williamson DA, Cubic BA, Gleaves DH.
Department of Psychology, Louisiana State University, Baton Rouge 70803.
A silhouette method, the Body Image Assessment, was used to measure self-evaluation of current and ideal body size in three groups: Ss with with anorexia nervosa (n = 37), Ss with bulimia nervosa (n = 59), and normal control Ss (n = 95). Current and ideal body size measures were contrasted across the three groups using body mass index as a covariate to control for the Ss actual body size. Both eating disorder groups judged current body size to be larger and ideal body size to be thinner relative to control Ss. When actual body size was not statistically controlled, Ss with anorexia nervosa judged current body size to be thinner than did control Ss and Ss with bulimia nervosa. These data illustrate the importance of controlling for actual body size when investigating the self-evaluation of

body size.

J Abnorm Psychol 1994 Feb;103(1):137-47
Personality variables and disorders in anorexia nervosa and bulimia nervosa.
Vitousek K, Manke F.
Department of Psychology, University of Hawaii, Honolulu 96822.
All dominant models of eating disorders implicate personality variables in the emergence of weight concerns and the development of specific symptoms such as bingeing and purging. Standardized measures of personality traits and disorders generally confirm clinical descriptions of restricting anorexics as constricted, conforming, and obsessional individuals. A less consistent picture suggesting affective instability and impulsivity has emerged from the assessment of subjects with bulimia nervosa. Considerable heterogeneity exists within eating disorder subtypes, however, and a number of special problems complicate the interpretation of personality data in this population.
Publication Types: Review; Review, tutorial

J Abnorm Psychol 1999 May;108(2):255-66
Friendship clique and peer influences on body image concerns, dietary restraint, extreme weight-loss behaviors, and binge eating in adolescent girls.
Paxton SJ, Schutz HK, Wertheim EH, Muir SL.
Psychology Department, University of Melbourne, Parkville, Victoria, Australia.
s.paxton@psych.unimelb.edu.au
This study explored friendship variables in relation to body image, dietary restraint, extreme weight-loss behaviors (EWLBs), and binge eating in adolescent girls. Friendship attitudes contributed significantly to the prediction of individual body image concern and eating behaviors. Use of EWLBs by friends predicted an individual's own level of use.

J Am Med Womens Assoc 1985 Nov-Dec;40(6):169-74
Bulimia: contributing factors and effects.
Andries NG.

J Clin Psychol 1988 Nov;44(6):964-71
Bulimia: a comparison of psychological adjustment and familial characteristics in a nonclinical sample.
Kent JS, Clopton JR.
Department of Psychology, Texas Tech University, Lubbock 79409.
This study examined the relation of eating attitudes and behaviors to family dynamics and psychological adjustment in a nonclinical group of female university freshmen. Family dynamics variables, which were measured by the Family Environment Scale (FES), included Control, Cohesion, Conflict, Organization, Expressiveness, Independence, Achievement-Orientation, Intellectual-Cultural Orientation, Active-Recreational Orientation, and Moral Religious Emphasis. Psychological adjustment was measured by the Hopkins Symptom Checklist (HSC). Variables on this scale included Anxiety, Depression, Somatization, Obsessive-Compulsive, and Interpersonal Sensitivity. Eating

attitudes and behaviors were measured by the Bulimia Test (BULIT), a 32-item self-report inventory. The results suggest that conclusions about the causal relationships between maladaptive family patterns and bulimia presented in previous research should be viewed with caution.

J Consult Clin Psychol 1987 Oct;55(5):654-9

Familial contributions to the etiology and course of anorexia nervosa and bulimia.

Strober M, Humphrey LL.

Publication Types: Review; Review, academic

J Pers Assess 1999 Aug;73(1):133-47

Personality and affectivity characteristics associated with eating disorders: a comparison of eating disordered, weight-preoccupied, and normal samples.

Podar I, Hannus A, Allik J.

Clinic of Psychiatry, University of Tartu.

The purpose of this study was to assess the relative contribution of personality and emotional experience to self-reported eating attitudes in a group of patients with clinically diagnosed eating disorders, a weight-reduction training group (Weight Watchers), and a control group without body weight problems. It was argued that personality dispositions have a larger relevancy in etiology of eating disorders than emotional state.

J Psychiatr Ment Health Nurs 1997 Jun;4(3):179-83

Making our own meanings: a critical review of media effects research in relation to the causation of aggression and social skills difficulties in children and anorexia nervosa in young women.

Barrett RT.

School of Community Health and Social Studies, Anglia Polytechnic University, Colchester, Essex, UK.

This study examines concerns regarding the effects of video and television on certain types of behaviour. Evidence from cultural studies, within an interpretivist tradition, will be cited as a challenge to the 'moral panic of the media', highlighting the incommensurability of diverse research disciplines. Mental health professionals have long been confronted with the failure of science to provide any unitary truth regarding the aetiology of mental health problems. Frustrating as that is, it is proposed that diverse empirical methods in the social sciences enrich debate and serve to expose the quest for a monocasual aetiology as fundamentally flawed. Media effects are thus only part of a myriad possible causes of anorexia nervosa, and yet are seen as central to current alarm regarding the way children learn (or don't learn) to cooperate with, and show concern for, other people.

J Psychiatr Res 1997 Jul-Aug;31(4):467-80

Personality factors and weight preoccupation: a continuum approach to the association between eating disorders and personality disorders.

Davis C, Claridge G, Cerullo D.

Graduate Programme in Exercise and Health Science, York University, Toronto, Canada.

OBJECTIVE: Evidence shows a high

comorbidity of eating disorders and some forms of personality disorder. Adopting a dimensional approach to both, this study explored their connection among a non-clinical sample. Patterns of association between eating pathology and personality disorder, especially borderline and narcissism, can be clearly mapped across to personality traits in the currently non-clinical population. This finding has important implications for understanding dynamics of, and identifying individuals at risk for, eating disorders.

J Psychiatr Res 1999 Mar-Apr;33(2):129-38
Neuropsychological assessments before and after treatment in patients with anorexia nervosa and bulimia nervosa.
Lauer CJ, Gorzewski B, Gerlinghoff M, Backmund H, Zihl J.
Max Planck Institute of Psychiatry, Munich, Germany.
In psychiatric patients the identification of cognitive deficits which predict a poor clinical outcome is important for the development of specific treatment strategies aimed at the amelioration of these impaired cognitive functions to increase the likelihood of full clinical remission. Findings indicate that the cognitive functions in the acute AN and BU are similarly impaired, but also ameliorate in a similar manner with clinical remission.
Publication Types: Clinical trial

J Psychosom Res 1967 Jun;11(1):141-9
The nutritional disorder in anorexia nervosa.
Russell GF.

J Psychosom Res 1984;28(5):397-402
Moderation of bulimia.
Lacey JH.
This paper examines those factors which appear to influence the response of bulimia to treatment. Poorer prognosis is associated with a previous history of weight disorder (in either direction); also, with a personality disorder, particularly one marked by alcohol abuse. The paper indicates the aetiological and clinical structure of what is a heterogeneous disorder and describes the mechanisms of a successful treatment programme.
Publication Types: Review

Lancet 1978 Sep 23;2(8091):674
Sociocultural factors in anorexia nervosa.
Garner DM, Garfinkel PE.
Publication Types: Letter

Lancet 1993 Jun 26;341(8861):1631-5
Pathogenesis of anorexia nervosa.
Garner DM.
Department of Psychiatry, Michigan State University, East Lansing 48824.
Publication Types: Review; Review, tutorial

Life Sci 1976 Jun 15;18(12):1341-8
Biological aspects of anorexia nervosa.
Lupton M, Simon L, Barry V, Klawans HL.
Publication Types: Review

N Z Med J 1979 Mar 14;89(631):171-3
Anorexia nervosa in a male: comment

and illustration.
Galletly C, James B.
Attention is drawn to the possible diagnosis of anorexia nervosa in young males with weight loss. The symptoms and signs are described, along with the setting in which the condition may develop. These points are illustrated by reference to a recently treated case. The poor prognosis of anorexia nervosa in males isemphasised.

Nat Med 1996 Jan;2(1):21-2
Anorexia nervosa, self-starvation and the reward of stress.
Bergh C, Sodersten P.
Karolinska Institute, Department of Clinical Neuroscience, Huddinge, Sweden.
Publication Types: Review; Review, tutorial

Nature 1984 Nov 8-14;312(5990):104
Complexities of cause and effect in anorexia nervosa.
Mrosovsky N.
Publication Types: News

Neurol Clin 1988 Feb;6(1):195-212
The endocrinology of anorexia nervosa and bulimia nervosa.
Newman MM, Halmi KA.
Cornell University Medical College, New York.
Considerable evidence exists of hypothalamic dysfunction in patients with anorexia nervosa and bulimia nervosa. This dysfunction is reflected in disturbances of endocrine function including abnormalities of gonadotropin, growth hormone, and corticotropin-releasing hormone secretion. Endocrine disturbances may be a final common pathway in which disturbances of diet, weight, activity, stress, and mood as well as hypothalamic dysfunction are expressed.
Publication Types: Review; Review, academic

Nursing (Lond) 1991 May 23-Jun 12;4(35):15-7
Causes of anorexia nervosa.
Fretwell A.

Obes Res 1997 Sep;5(5):489-91
Comment on: Obes Res. 1997 Sep;5(5):492-7;
Obes Res. 1997 Sep;5(5):498-502
Obes Res. 1997 Sep;5(5):503-8
Anorexia nervosa and socio-economic status.
Bray GA.
Pennington Biomedical Research Center, Baton Rouge, LA, USA.
Publication Types: Comment; Historical article

Patient Educ Couns 1997 Jun;31(2):103-12
Personalities and alimentary behaviors in obese patients.
Golay A, Hagon I, Painot D, Rouget P, Allaz AF, Morel Y, Nicolet J, Archinard M.
Department of Medicine, University Hospital, Geneva, Switzerland.
The actual tendency in the care of obese patients is the association of dietetic information with an eating behavior therapy. Studies attempting to attribute the origin of obesity to psychiatric pathologies are contradictory. The diversity, even the absence, of eating disorders brought to evidence by tests based upon different personality types should allow better

understanding of the psychological and behavioral causes of weight gain and the means for improving compliance in the following of an obese patient.

Physiol Behav 1996 Jul;60(1):1-5
Biological and psychological correlates of intermittent dieting behavior in young women. A model for bulimia nervosa.
Laessle RG, Platte P, Schweiger U, Pirke KM.
Center for Psychobiological and Psychosomatic Research, University of Trier, Germany. The eating disorder bulimia nervosa is characterized by alternating periods of strict dieting and overeating. Patients also report mood fluctuations, frequent eating related thoughts, fear of loss of control over eating, impairment of cognitive abilities such as concentration, and somatic complaints. The present study attempted to clarify to what extent these symptoms are consequences of the dieting behavior. These results found here suggest that a substantial part of symptoms of bulimic patients might be associated with the frequent periods of an extremely restrained eating behavior.

Practitioner 1996 May;240(1562):306, 309, 312-7
Getting to the cause of eating disorders.
Wrate R.
Young Peoples Unit, Royal Edinburgh Hospital.
Publication Types: Review; Review, tutorial

Psychiatr Clin North Am 1998 Jun;21(2):381-96
The role of the central nervous system in the psychoneuroendocrine disturbances of anorexia and bulimia nervosa.
Kaye WH, Gendall K, Kye C.
Department of Psychiatry, University of Pittsburgh School of Medicine, Pennsylvania, USA.
It has been well-recognized that starvation in anorexia and bulimia nervosa causes endocrine disturbances. Such disturbances may help understand why many people with eating disorders cannot easily reverse their illness since people with eating disorders often enter a downward spiraling circle with malnutrition sustaining and perpetuating the desire for more weight loss and dieting. This suggests that therapy should be sustained for months after nutritional normalization.
Publication Types: Review; Review, tutorial

Psychiatry Res 1989 Jan;27(1):39-48
Structural brain abnormalities in patients with bulimia nervosa.
Krieg JC, Lauer C, Pirke KM.
Department of Psychiatry, Max Planck Institute of Psychiatry, Munich, F.R.G.
In this analysis, computed tomographic (CT) brain scans were performed in 50 inpatients with bulimia nervosa, 50 anorectic inpatients, and 50 age-matched control subjects. A number of patients with bulimia nervosa had enlarged ventricles and/or sulcal widening, but the degree and frequency of ventricular dilatation and sulcal

widening were not so pronounced as in patients with anorexia nervosa.

Psychol Med 1997 May;27(3):509-13
Can dieting cause an eating disorder?
Hsu LK.
Publication Types: Editorial Review; Review literature

Psychol Med 2000 Jan;30(1):61-7
Quality of rearing practices as predictor of short-term outcome in adolescent anorexia nervosa.
Castro J, Toro J, Cruz M.
Section of Child and Adolescent Psychiatry, Institute of Psychiatry and Psychology, Hospital Clinic Universitari of Barcelona, Spain.
Studies of family relationships in anorexia nervosa have produced conflicting results. Some authors claim that family factors are related to short-term outcomes. Overall, small differences were observed in the perceptions of rearing practices as expressed by the controls and the anorexic patients. Patients with bad short-term outcome perceived more rejection and control-overprotection from both parents than those with good outcome. In the logistic regression analysis only Rejection from father and the EAT (Eating Attitudes Test) total score gave independent prediction of treatment response. Taken as a whole, these results do not support the idea of altered rearing practices in anorexic patients, at least in young patients with a short evolution of the disease. Perceived rearing practices, especially 'rejection', appear to have an appreciable effect on the short-term outcome.

Psychopathology 1996;29(1):64-70
Perceived parental bonding in anorectic and bulimic patients.
Sordelli A, Fossati A, Devoti RM, La Viola S.
Medical Psychology and Psychotherapy Unit, Scientific Institute H San Raffaele, Milan, Italy.
Psychodynamic clinical studies as well as empirical research have pointed out the importance and the specificity of object relations in eating disorders.
Given this, the aim of this work was to identify the presence of significant differences in the object relations patterns, as described by the Parental Bonding Instrument (PBI), between anorectic and bulimic subjects. PBI was administered to 42 anorectic female and 26 bulimic female subjects, consecutively admitted to the Eating Disorders Outpatient Unit of H San Raffaele of Milan. Profile analysis revealed the presence of significant ($T2 = 11.3453$, d.f. 3,64, $p = 0.017$) qualitative differences in PBI profiles between anorectic and bulimic subjects. The most striking difference was represented by the bulimics' view of their parents as both caring and overwhelming, which contrasted with the anorectics' perception of their parents as absolutely caring.

Psychosom Med 1988 Nov-Dec;50(6):591-9
Psychologic and physiologic reactivity to stressors in eating disordered individuals.
Cattanach L, Malley R, Rodin J.

Psychology Department, Yale University, New Haven, CT 06520.
The present study explored a potential mechanism for the relationship between stressors and binge eating: specifically, whether subjects with behaviors and attitudes reflecting disordered eating show distinctive psychologic or physiologic reactivity to stressors. The results suggest that the increased desire to binge in response to stressors reported by subjects higher in disordered eating cannot be accounted for by differences in cardiovascular reactivity or negative hedonic state, relative to what subjects low in disordered eating showed in response to the same stressors.

Women Health 1999;30(1):71-83
Symptoms of eating disorders among female distance runners: can the inconsistencies be unraveled?
Ryujin DH, Breaux C, Marks AD.
California Polytechnic State University, San Luis Obispo, USA.
Research on eating disorders among female distance runners has produced a modest, but inconsistent body of findings. Operational definitions to further test the model are discussed.

[B]Eat Weight Disord 1998 Jun;3(2):53-63
Earliest recollections in anorexia and bulimia.
Fassino S, Abbate Daga G, Garzaro L, Rovera GG.
Psychiatric Clinic, University of Torino, Italy.
Earliest Recollections (ER) are very useful as they reveal information about a person's main aims and lifestyle, according to the Individual Psychology assumption of the inner coherence of the personality. This paper looks at the utility of analyzing ER in psychopathological research, diagnosis and therapy.

TEENAGERS/YOUNG ADULTS

Acta Psychiatr Scand 1992 Dec;86(6):432-6
Anorexia nervosa and bulimia: a prevalence study.
de Azevedo MH, Ferreira CP.
Department of Medical Psychology, Faculty of Medicine, Coimbra, Portugal.
This study determined the prevalence of anorexia nervosa and bulimia in a large sample of students attending a secondary school on the island of Sao Miguel (Azores) using the Diagnostic Interview for Children and Adolescents, which enabled us to collect the information necessary to make DSM-III diagnoses. Although the prevalence of anorectic and bulimic behaviour was rather high, the partial syndrome of anorexia nervosa was found in only 0.48% of the students (0.76% for girls and 0.17% for boys) and the syndrome of bulimia in only 0.16% (0.30% of the girls; there were no boys with bulimia). The overall prevalence of eating disorders, including partial syndromes, was rather low (0.64%). These results stand in sharp contrast to reports that eating disorders are common and probably getting more common. The low prevalence found in the present survey is probably due to the absence of sociocultural pressures to control eating and weight.

Addict Behav 1986;11(4):415-24
Bulimia and binge eating in adolescent females: a comparison.
Crowther JH, Chernyk B.
The present study compared the following four groups on characteristics commonly associated with eating disorders: bulimics (n = 17) who met the DSM-III criteria for bulimia; severe bingers (n = 16) who binged frequently and experienced negative emotions associated with the binging but did not meet the DSM-III criteria for bulimia; mild bingers (n = 16), who only reported engaging in binge eating; and normals (n = 17), who neither binged, fasted, or purged. Theoretical and diagnostic implications of these findings are discussed.

Adolesc Med 1991 Jun;2(2):369-374
Management of Adolescents with Eating Disorders: Role of the Primary Physician and Family.
Shenker IR, Frank S.

It has been demonstrated that family dynamics and relationships are important in the development, promulgation, and potential resolution of eating disorders in adolescents. This text emphasizes the role of the health care provider in working with the adolescent patient with eating disorders and his or her family.

Adolesc Med 1993 Oct;4(3):543-550
Television, Obesity, and Eating Disorders.
Dietz WH.
Division of Pediatric Gastroenterology and Nutrition, Boston Floating Hospital, Box 213, 750 Washington Street, Boston, MA 02111, USA.
Two national survey from the early 1960s indicate that the prevalence of obesity is directly related to the amount of time spent in viewing television in young people aged 6 to 17 years. The author discusses the mechanisms by which television affects obesity and other eating disorders.

Adolesc Psychiatry 1995;20:267-85
A review of eating disorders in adolescents.
Ponton LE.
Langley Porter Psychiatric Institute, University of California, San Francisco, USA.
Many review articles address the diverse and rapidly developing field of eating disorders, but there are far fewer articles addressing the specific population of adolescents. Increased public awareness regarding the need for treatment of these illnesses is a high priority. If untreated, chronicity appears inevitable. Examination and study of the most cost effective methods of treatment are very important.
Publication Types: Review; Review, tutorial

Adolescence 1985 Fall;20(79):525-36
Adolescent eating disorder: anorexia nervosa.
Muuss RE.
Anorexia nervosa is an eating disorder observed with increasing frequency, especially among adolescent females. No consensus exists concerning the causes of the disorder. Social, psychosexual, family system, biological theories, and the regression hypothesis have been advanced to explain the phenomenon. Anorexic adolescents resist treatment and may die if not cured. The following therapeutic modalities have been effective: hospitalization, and cognitive, behavioral, and family therapy. Some of the typical family patterns, early characteristics, social adjustment problems, and society's contribution to the disorder are presented.

Adolescence 1986 Summer;21(82):257-67
Adolescent eating disorder: bulimia.
Muuss RE.
Bulimia, an eating disorder, recently has emerged as a major mental health problem, especially among adolescent females. The physical side effects include dental problems, inflamed esophagus, EEG abnormalities, abdominal or urinary disturbances, and changes in blood sugar level. Cognitive disturbances related to binging and purging are perfectionistic, egocentric, and

distorted thinking, misconceptions about nutritional requirements, unreasonable goals and expectations, and disturbed affect. Bulimics resist treatment; however, such methods as cognitive, group, family, behavior, and drug therapy, and hospitalization appear promising.

Adolescence 1987 Fall;22(87):617-23
Anorexia nervosa: a misdiagnosis of the adolescent male.
Svec H.
School Psychology Program, Michigan State University, East Lansing 48824.
The rarity of anorexia nervosa among the male population is discussed with primary reference to differences from female symptomology. A case is presented which implies that anorexia nervosa in the male may be a marker for other more severe pathology. These findings suggest a diagnostic strategy based on familial, behavioral, environmental, educational, and psychological factors.

Adolescence 1988 Summer;23(90):303-12
Eating disorders in a nonclinical adolescent population: implications fortreatment.
Lachenmeyer JR, Muni-Brander P.
Department of Psychology, Fairleigh Dickinson University, Teaneck, New Jersey 07666.
The present study investigates the prevalence of adolescent eating disorders across gender, cultural groupings, and socioeconomic status. The Eating Attitudes Test, the Binge-Eating Questionnaire, and a demographic questionnaire were administered to students at two high schools. The results indicate a high rate of eating disorders in a nonclinical adolescent population. Given such high rates of eating problems in a nonclinical population, the issue of prevention and early detection must be addressed. Additionally, more specific information on male eating disorders is needed.

Adolescence 1994 Fall;29(115):643-7
Adolescent boys and anorexia nervosa.
Romeo F.
College of Education, Florida Atlantic University, Boca Raton 33431.
Anorexia nervosa is an eating disorder that primarily affects adolescent girls and young adult females, and is considered to be rare among males. It isestimated that one in 200 adolescents between the ages of 12 and 18 years, the high risk group, develop anorexia nervosa with 90% of those affected being females. However, there has been a steady increase in the reported incidence of male anorectics. Since educators and counselors can serve a vital role in the early identification of this disorder, the young anorectic male has a better prognosis for recovery if they receive treatment during the early stages.

Adolescence 1994 Winter;29(116):821-34
The relationship of gender and family environment to eating disorder risk in adolescents.
Felker KR, Stivers C.
Department of Health Promotion, University of New Mexico, Albuquerque.
Incidence and prevalence rates of both

anorexia nervosa and bulimia among adolescents have steadily increased during the past decade. The purpose of this study was to examine the relationship of gender and family environment to the risk of developing anorexia nervosa or bulimia in adolescents. The Family Environment Scale (FES; Moos & Moos, 1981) and the Setting Conditions for Anorexia Nervosa Scale (SCANS; Slade, Phil, & Dewey, 1986) were used to measure select components of family environment and risk of developing anorexia nervosa or bulimia, respectively. Multiple regression using a unique approach revealed a significant relationship between family environment and the risk of developing anorexia nervosa or bulimia in adolescents. Simple correlation of the FES subscales was conducted by means of Pearson product moment and results indicated that lower cohesion, expressiveness, and organization were significantly associated with greater eating disorder risk ($p < .01$). Lower independence was significantly associated with increased eating disorder risk, but to a lesser degree ($p < .05$). Greater conflict ($p < .01$) and control ($p < .05$) were significantly associated with greater eating disorder risk.

Adolescence 1998 Summer;33(130):291-300
Personality features and expressed concerns of adolescents with eating disorders.
Pryor T, Wiederman MW.
Department of Psychiatry and Behavioral Sciences, University of Kansas School of Medicine-Wichita, Kansas 67214, USA.
Differences between adolescent females diagnosed with either anorexia nervosa ($n = 26$) or bulimia nervosa ($n = 30$) were investigated using the Millon Adolescent Personality Inventory (MAPI; Millon, Green, & Meagher, 1982). Results are compared with clinical observations of adolescents with eating disorders and findings for adult eating-disordered samples.

Adolescence 1999 Fall;34(135):621-33
Anorexic eating attitudes and behaviors of male and female college students.
Nelson WL, Hughes HM, Katz B, Searight HR.
Division of AIDS, National Institute of Allergy and Infectious Diseases/National Institutes of Health, Bethesda, Maryland 20892, USA.
This study examined gender differences in eating attitudes and behaviors in a sample of 471 undergraduate college students. The prevalence of symptomatology indicative of anorexia was determined using the Eating Attitudes Test (EAT-26).. In general, students without symptomatic attitudes and behaviors had a more positive self-concept and reported less psychological distress than did those with eating disturbances. The findings suggest that eating problems may be more prevalent among males than previously estimated.

Alcohol abuse and dysfunctional eating in adolescent girls: The influence of individual differences in sensitivity to reward and punishment.

Loxton NJ, Dawe S.
OBJECTIVE: An unusually high comorbidity of eating disorders and alcohol abuse has been found in clinical and community samples of young women. This paper proposes that individual differences in sensitivity to reward and punishment may influence the propensity of young women to engage in dysfunctional eating and drinking behaviour. These findings suggest that girls who abuse alcohol and have dysfunctional eating may share a vulnerability to heightened sensitivity to reward, yet be differentiated by sensitivity to punishment. Copyright 2001 by John Wiley & Sons, Inc.

Am J Dis Child 1982 Nov;136(11):985-9
Bulimia in the adolescent.
Herzog DB.
We report clinical and demographic data from the first eight bulimic adolescents seen at an outpatient eating disorders unit. The frequently chronic course and associated physical consequences make diagnosis and early intervention necessary. A relationship between bulimia and depressive illness may exist.

Am J Dis Child 1988 Oct;142(10):1114-8
Body image and eating behavior in adolescent girls.
Moore DC.
Department of Pediatrics, Madigan Army Medical Center, Tacoma, Wash. 98431-5000.
To determine attitudes toward body weight and shape and eating and weight control practices among adolescent girls, an anonymous questionnaire was administered to 854 adolescent girls and young women aged 12 through 23 years who were seen in a military adolescent outpatient clinic. Overall, 67% were dissatisfied with their weight, and 54% were dissatisfied with their body shape.
These who desired an excessive loss, exhibited an increased prevalence of weight control behaviors and were less likely to believe that they had an eating problem. Dissatisfaction with body weight and shape, and eating behaviors, such as dieting, binge eating, fasting, and vomiting, are common in adolescent girls, many of whom are attempting weight control without an accurate perception of what is normal.

Am J Nurs 1967 Nov;67(11):2356-9
Care of adolescents with anorexia nervosa.
Miesem ML, Wann F.

Am J Nurs 1974 Sep;74(9):1649-51
A boy with anorexia nervosa.
Melton JH.

Am J Psychiatry 1988 Jun;145(6):753-5
Bulimia in college women: incidence and recovery rates.
Drewnowski A, Yee DK, Krahn DD.
Department of Community Health Programs, University of Michigan School of Public Health, Ann Arbor 48109-2029.
In a longitudinal survey of college freshmen, the incidence of bulimia nervosa was 4.2 cases per 100 women per year. Prevalence remained stable (2.9%-3.3%) as new cases were offset by partial remissions. Some women continued bulimic behaviors without

meeting the DSM-III-R criteria.

Am J Psychiatry 1995 Nov;152(11):1623-9
Body weight, dieting, and eating disorder symptoms among college students, 1982 to 1992.
Heatherton TF, Nichols P, Mahamedi F, Keel P.
Department of Psychology, Dartmouth College, Hanover, NH 03755, USA.
The authors sought to examine changes in prevalence of dieting behavior and eating disorder symptoms from 1982 to 1992. RESULTS: On almost all measures there were significant reductions of problematic eating behaviors and disordered attitudes about body, weight, and shape from 1982 to 1992. The prevalence of problematic eating behaviors and eating disorder symptoms appears to be abating. However, they remain a significant problem that affects a substantial segment of this population.

Am J Public Health 1986 Sep;76(9):1135-7
The prevalence of bulimia among college students.
Zuckerman DM, Colby A, Ware NC, Lazerson JS.
A survey was conducted to determine the prevalence of bulimia and bulimic symptoms in a nonclinical sample of 907 college freshmen and seniors. Using criteria based on the Diagnostic and Statistical Manual of Mental Disorders, 4 per cent of the women and 0.4 per cent of the men were classified as bulimic. Symptoms of bulimia, such as binge eating, purging behaviors, and extreme fear of gaining weight, were much more prevalent.

Am J Public Health 1988 Oct;78(10):1322-5
The prevalence of bulimia nervosa in the US college student population.
Drewnowski A, Hopkins SA, Kessler RC.
Department of Community Health Programs, School of Public Health, University of Michigan, Ann Arbor 48109-2029.
A phone survey to determine the prevalence of bulimia nervosa was conducted with a national probability sample of 1,007 male and female students from a stratified sample of 53 universities and colleges in the continental United States. Using the revised (DSM IIIR) diagnostic criteria, 1 per cent of the women and 0.2 per cent of the men were classified as bulimic. Bulimia was most prevalent (2.2 per cent prevalence rate) among undergraduate women living in group housing on campus.

Ann N Y Acad Sci 1997 May 28;817:359-60
Racial differences in bulimic behaviors among high school females.
Field AE, Colditz GA, Peterson KE.
Brigham and Women's Hospital, Harvard Medical School, Channing Laboratory, Boston, Massachusetts 02115, USA.
alison.field@channing.harvard.edu

Ann Paediatr Fenn 1965;11(2):98-100
Anorexia nervosa. A study on a boy.
Frisk M, Backstrom-Jarvinen L.

Arch Pediatr Adolesc Med 1998 Sep;152(9):884-8
Problem dieting behaviors among young adolescents.
Krowchuk DP, Kreiter SR, Woods CR, Sinal SH, DuRant RH.
Department of Pediatrics, Wake Forest University School of Medicine and Brenner Children's Hospital of Wake Forest University Baptist Medical Center, Winston-Salem, NC 27157, USA. krowchuk@wfubmc.edu
Examining dieting, eating and exercise behaviors, use of diet pills, and vomiting or use of laxatives to lose weight among younger adolescents. DESIGN: Analysis of data from a modified version of the Youth Risk Behavior Survey administered to middle school students in North Carolina in 1995. It was found that younger adolescents trying to lose weight engage in a variety of problem dieting and weight loss behaviors that can compromise health and may be associated with eating disorders.

Aust Fam Physician 1988 May;17(5):334-6
Eating disorders in the adolescent.
Young D.
Publication Types: Review; Review, tutorial

Br J Hosp Med 1988 Nov;40(5):362-4, 368-9
Anorexia nervosa in childhood.
Treasure J, Thompson P.
Institute of Psychiatry, London.
Anorexia nervosa in childhood can be difficult to diagnose and without adequate treatment can lead to a severe developmental disturbance. These problems and the aetiology and treatment are discussed in this article.
Publication Types: Review; Review, tutorial

Br J Med Psychol 1985 Jun;58 (Pt 2):193-5
Anorexia nervosa in adolescents.
Margo JL.
This paper is a retrospective study of 40 carefully defined cases of anorexia nervosa in adolescents. The illness in adolescence appears similar to that in older patients with regard to most clinical features, an increased referral rate since the 1960s, an upper social class predominance, and the importance of antecedent events. Bingeing and vomiting appear to be relatively rare features of anorexia nervosa in adolescents.

Br J Psychiatry 1976 Jun;128:549-54
How common is anorexia nervosa? A prevalence study.
Crisp AH, Palmer RL, Kalucy RS.
During 1972-74 nine populations of schoolgirls were surveyed in respect of the occurrence of anorexia nervosa. The condition in severe form was found to be relatively common in the independent sector of education, probably implying a social class factor. In all such schools, the prevalence was one severe case in approximately every 200 girls. In those aged 16 and over it amounted to one severe case in about every 100 girls.
The condition is likely to be even more common than this study allows because of the stringent limits set here on inclusion of cases and the age-bands studied.

It is concluded that severe anorexia nervosa is a common condition and isprobably getting more common.

Br J Psychiatry 1991 Sep;159:383-9
Long-term outcome in early-onset anorexia nervosa.
Walford G, McCune N.
Forster Green Hospital, Belfast.
Fifteen children who developed anorexia nervosa aged 13 years or less were followed up at least three years later (mean 5.3 years). Outcome measures included the Morgan & Russell Outcome Schedule and the PSE. The general outcome was good in seven, intermediate in four, and poor in four, one of whom had died. A high incidence of psychiatric symptoms at follow-up, which has been suggested in other studies, was not confirmed in the 11 subjects who completed the PSE.
Where onset was very early (11 years and under) and where hospital stay was prolonged, outcome tended to be poor.

Br J Psychiatry 1995 Nov;167(5):673-8
Family functioning in adolescent anorexia nervosa.
North C, Gowers S, Byram V.
Department of Child and Adolescent Psychiatry, University of Manchester, Prestwich.
Difficulties in family functioning have been noted since early descriptions of anorexia nervosa and may be of importance aetiologically.
A diagnostic interview and a questionnaire, the Family Assessment Device (FAD) were administered to control subjects and their mothers. Anorexic families only received the McMaster Structured Interview of Family Functioning.
RESULTS. Multivariate analyses of FAD scores showed pathological ratings forpsychiatric control but not anorexic families, compared with community controls. By contrast objective ratings revealed marked dysfunction in anorexic families (greater in the purging subgroup).

Br J Psychiatry 1999 Jul;175:89-90
Comment on: Br J Psychiatry. 1999 Jan;174:63-6
Family functioning and adolescent anorexia nervosa.
Dare C, Key A.
Publication Types: Comment Letter

Can J Psychiatry 1999 May;44(4):374-8
A comparison of male and female adolescents referred to an eating disorder program.
Geist R, Heinmaa M, Katzman D, Stephens D.
Department of Psychiatry, Hospital for Sick Children, Toronto, Ontario.
rose.geist@sickkids.on.ca Comparing gender-related psychopathology and psychiatric diagnoses in male and female adolescents referred to an adolescent eating disorder program.
The results suggest that male and female adolescents with EDs are clinically similar to each other and therefore resemble adults for lack of gender-specific effects on self-reported psychopathology, family functioning, and comorbid psychiatric disorders.

Can Psychiatr Assoc J 1978 Apr;23(3):159-62
Anorexia nervosa in boys.

Sreenivasan U.
The literature on primary anorexia nervosa in the male is reviewed and the case histories of 3 new patients are reported. All the mothers and fathers were overweight, but obesity was marked only in the fathers, who also showed moderate to severe degrees of alcoholism. The mothers were oversensitive, insecure individuals, and the marriages suffered in proportion to the severity of the husband's alcoholism. Preoccupation with food was observed on home visits. There was overt mutual hostility between each father and anorexic son; the boys showed pronounced obsessional traits in their personalities.
Speculative reasons for this are discussed.

Child Psychiatry Hum Dev 1990 Winter;21(2):79-94
Anorexia nervosa in adolescent males: a review and case study.
Hamlett KW, Curry JF.
Case Western Reserve University School of Medicine, Cleveland, OH 44106.
The clinical presentation of anorexia nervosa among males is quite rare. This paper examines the personality and developmental issues of anorexia nervosa in adolescent males through a comprehensive review of the literature and a case presentation.
Publication Types: Review; Review, tutorial

Child Psychiatry Hum Dev 1991 Spring;21(3):179-84
Bulimia and body image dissatisfaction in adolescence.
Dacey CM, Nelson WM, Clark VF, Aikman KG.
Department of Psychology, Xavier University, Cincinnati, OH 45207.
This study examined body image dissatisfaction in bulimic adolescent girls.
Subjects were screened with the Bulimia Test and the Eating Disorder Inventory, followed by clinical interviews using Russell's diagnostic criteria. Results indicated that bulimic subjects were significantly more dissatisfied with their bodies as measured by the Color-A-Person Test than matched controls.

Child Psychiatry Hum Dev 2001 Spring;31(3):249-65
Associated health risks of adolescents with disordered eating: how different are they from their peers? Results from a high school survey.
Lock J, Reisel B, Steiner H.
Department of Psychiatry and Behavioral Sciences, Stanford University School of Medicine, 401 Quarry Road, Palo Alto, CA 94301, USA.
In this study, we compare health risks of adolescents with disordered eating to those of their peers without disordered eating. A self-report health survey from a community sample of 1769 high school students was used to compare emotional, medical, and social behaviors of these two groups.

Child Today 1984 Nov-Dec;13(6):7-11
Eating out of control: anorexia and bulimia in adolescents.
Bayer AE.

Clin J Sport Med 2001 Jan;11(1):32-7
Prevalence of eating disordered behavior in collegiate lightweight women rowers and distance runners.
Karlson KA, Becker CB, Merkur A.
Department of Community and Family Medicine, Dartmouth Medical School, Hanover, New Hampshire, USA.
Kristine.Karlson@Hitchcock.org
OBJECTIVE: This study examined eating behavior in collegiate women lightweight rowers, runners, and controls. Lightweight rowing and distance running were not associated with increased prevalence of eating disorders in this sample, although rowing was associated with increased restraint and diuretic misuse. This use of pathologic weight-making behaviors is of significant clinical concern. These results support ongoing monitoring of disturbed eating and weight-making practices in weight-dependent sports, but do not support discouraging the growth of lightweight women's rowing at the collegiate level.

Curr Opin Pediatr 1998 Aug;10(4):369-77
Childhood eating disorders.
Sokol MS, Steinberg D, Zerbe KJ.
Menninger Clinic, Topeka, KS 66601, USA.
This paper reviews the recent research literature on childhood eating disorders from a developmental perspective. The best-studied areas include epidemiological studies, short-term treatment for bulimia nervosa, and outcome in anorexia nervosa.
Publication Types: Review; Review, academic

Del Med J 1980 Sep;52(9):481-4
A treatment approach to adolescents with anorexia nervosa.
Kramer JP.

Eat Weight Disord 1999 Jun;4(2):63-75
Multidimensionality in adolescent eating problems. A two-phase measurement study.
Engelsen BK.
Department of Psychosocial Sciences, University of Bergen, Christiesgate 12, N-5015 Bergen, Norway.
The aims of this study were, firstly, to examine the factor structure of single items from several self-report methods used to measure eating disorder symptoms, and secondly, in search for a short assessment instrument to reduce the number of items within each factor. The findings are discussed in relation to restraint theory and the continuum hypothesis.

Eat Weight Disord 2000 Jun;5(2):87-91
Prevalence and dimensionality in adolescent eating problems.
Engelsen BK.
Department of Psychosocial Sciences, University of Bergen, Norway.
Prevalence of three eating problem dimensions (body concerns, dieting, and loss of control over eating) was studied in a Norwegian sample consisting of 4129 normal adolescents aged 12-16. It is concluded that the study gives support to the view of the relationship between the three dimensions as cumulative and developmental, and that longitudinal research should be conducted to examine how these eating problems are related to later eating disorders.

Eating disorders and altered eating behaviors in adolescents of normal weight in a spanish city.
Purpose: To study the prevalence of altered eating behaviors or eating disorder-related behaviors among adolescents of normal weight that do not fulfill criteria for anorexia nervosa and bulimia nervosa. A high proportion of adolescents with abnormal eating behaviors and an altered perception of body fat may currently be diagnosed as having atypical eating disorder" (Diagnostic and Statistical Manual of Mental Disorders, Fourth Revision) considering that their body mass index was within normal range.

Eur Child Adolesc Psychiatry 1998 Jun;7(2):79-84
Personality characteristics predict outcome of eating disorders in adolescents: a 4-year prospective study.
van der Ham T, van Strien DC, van Engeland H.
Academisch Ziekenhuis Utrecht, Afd. Kinder- en Jeugdpsychiatrie, The Netherlands.
Results of studies on predictive factors in eating disorders have not been very clear until now. Attention has focused primarily on the predictive value of eating behaviour, duration of illness, comorbidity, and population characteristics for groups with mixed eating disorders, but lately several studies have concentrated on the influence of psychological and personality characteristics. In this 4-year prospective follow-up study of 49 eating-disordered adolescent patients, the predictive value of psychological factors and personality characteristics for the course of eating disorders is determined and discussed.

Eur Child Adolesc Psychiatry 2000;9 Suppl 1:I108-16
Eating disorders in children and adolescents: pharmacological therapies.
Kotler LA, Walsh BT.
Division of Child Psychiatry, College of Physicians and Surgeons, Columbia University, New York, NY 10032, USA.
Anorexia nervosa and bulimia nervosa do exist in childhood, frequently have their onset in adolescence, and can result in serious medical and psychiatric sequelae that impede physical, emotional, and behavioral development. This review article summarizes the current literature on the role of medication in the treatment of anorexia nervosa and bulimia nervosa, with particular emphasis on studies conducted in child and adolescent populations.
Publication Types: Review; Review, tutorial

Gastroenterology 1980 Jun;78(6):1650-1
Anorexia and the adolescent.
Gryboski J.
Publication Types: Letter

Horm Res 1995;43(4):168-70
Treatment and outcome of adolescent anorexia nervosa.
Steinhausen HC.
Department of Child and Adolescent Psychiatry, University of Zurich, Switzerland. Treatment of adolescent anorectic patients includes a comprehensive assessment of the

patient's condition, measures leading to effective weight restoration and the choice of the optimal treatment setting. The main psychotherapeutic approaches include supportive individual psychotherapy, behavioural, and family therapy. There is no evidence that pharmacotherapy, besides treating depressive symptoms, has any beneficial effect in anorectic patients. The outcome and prognosis of an individual patient is unpredictable.
Publication Types: Review; Review, tutorial

Int J Eat Disord 1993 Dec;14(4):487-96
Outcome in adolescent eating disorders.
Steinhausen HC, Seidel R.
Department of Child and Adolescent Psychiatry, University of Zurich, Switzerland.
A consecutive series of 60 adolescent patients in this article with eating disorders was followed up after a mean period of 58 months. Questionnaire findings indicated that the improvements that occurred during inpatient treatment were intact at follow-up. No significant findings were revealed by the analysis of a large scale of potential prognostic factors.

Int J Eat Disord 1993 Mar;13(2):221-7
The self-image of adolescent patients with eating disorders.
Steinhausen HC, Vollrath M.
Department of Child and Adolescent Psychiatry, University of Zurich, Switzerland.
Forty German adolescent anorectic patients were assessed with regard to self-image components as measured by the Offer Self-Image Questionnaire (OSIQ).
The profile of this group deviated negatively from the German standardization group of healthy subjects on measures of impulse control, emotional tone, body image, social relationships, sexual attitudes, and psychopathology. In addition, the OSIQ profile of this German sample was remarkably similar to the profiles of samples reported in two American studies. Finally, it was found that inpatient treatment served to improve the psychological condition of the patients with regard to certain but not all self-image components. Despite a trend of improvement, some of the scores did not fully normalize in this sample.

Int J Eat Disord 1995 Nov;18(3):221-36
Development of body image, eating disturbance, and general psychological functioning in female adolescents: covariance structure modeling and longitudinal investigations.
Thompson JK, Coovert MD, Richards KJ, Johnson S, Cattarin J.
Department of Psychology, University of South Florida, Tampa 33620-8200, USA.
Covariance structure modeling (CSM) and longitudinal analyses were used to identify a possible causal sequence for factors that might lead to the development of body image and eating disturbance in adolescent females. The findings offer important insights into possible causal sequences for the development of body image

and eating disturbance.

Int J Eat Disord 1997 Jul;22(1):15-23
The relationship between socioeconomic status and eating-disordered behaviors in a community sample of adolescent girls.
Rogers L, Resnick MD, Mitchell JE, Blum RW.
Department of Psychiatry, University of Minnesota Hospital and Clinic, Minneapolis, USA.
Although previous research has demonstrated a relationship between socioeconomic status (SES) and weight, the research has not been consistent regarding the relationship between SES and eating disorders. This analysis was designed to examine this relationship in a large community sample of adolescent girls (Grades 7 to 12). This study suggests that while there may be a significant relationship between SES and dieting or other behaviors associated with eating disorders, this relationship does not apply to diagnostically significant behaviors.

Int J Eat Disord 1998 Sep;24(2):223-6
Pregnancy and early 1: factors in the development of anorexia nervosa?
Benton-Hardy LR, Lock J.
Department of Psychiatry and Behavioral Sciences, Stanford University Medical Center, California, USA.
Most psychologic and social theories of anorexia focus on the developmental pressures that challenge adolescent girls. Pregnancy, which causes profound physical, emotional, and cognitive changes, could represent an amplification of these developmental pressures. In this case study, pregnancy is suggested as a possible contributor to the development of anorexia in a 17-year-old female.

Int J Eat Disord 1999 Nov;26(3):245-60
Binge eating and substance use among male and female adolescents.
Ross HE, Ivis F.
Addiction Research Foundation Division, Centre for Addiction and Mental Health, Toronto, Ontario, Canada.
OBJECTIVE: This study examines the relationship between binge eating and substance use behaviors and attitudes in adolescents and explores gender differences and mental health correlates. Adolescent binge eaters who engage in compensatory behaviors may be an appropriate target group for preventive programs in high schools. Copyright 1999 by John Wiley & Sons, Inc.

Int J Eat Disord 1999 Nov;26(3):301-14
Measuring binge eating in adolescents: adolescent and parent versions of the questionnaire of eating and weight patterns.
Johnson WG, Grieve FG, Adams CD, Sandy J.
Department of Psychiatry and Human Behavior, University of Mississippi Medical Center, Jackson, Mississippi 39216-4505, USA.
This study investigated the psychometric properties of an adolescent version of the Questionnaire of Eating and Weight Patterns (QEWP-A). The data suggest that parental perceptions of eating problems approximate those of their

children when no problem is present. However, parents are not as likely to be aware of eating difficulties when they actually exist.

Int J Eat Disord 2000 Jul;28(1):43-57
Improving the body image, eating attitudes, and behaviors of young male and female adolescents: a new educational approach that focuses on self-esteem.
O'Dea JA, Abraham S.
Faculty of Education, University of Sydney, Sydney, Australia.
odeaj@edfac.usyd.edu.au
This study examines the effect of an interactive, school-based, self-esteem education program on the body image and eating attitudes and behaviors of young male and female adolescents following the program and after 12 months. This is the first controlled educational intervention to successfully improve body image and to produce long-term changes in the attitudes and self-image of young adolescents.
This new approach to prevent the development of eating disorders by improving self-esteem may be effective, particularly if reinforced by teachers and family.

Publication Types: Clinical trial; Multicenter study; Randomized controlled trial

Int J Eat Disord 2000 Nov;28(3):317-24
Children into DSM don't go: a comparison of classification systems for eating disorders in childhood and early adolescence.
Nicholls D, Chater R, Lask B.
Behavioural Sciences Unit, Institute of Child Health and Great Ormond Street Hospital, London, United Kingdom.
OBJECTIVE: To evaluate the reliability of diagnostic classification systems for eating disorders when applied to children and young adolescents. DSM-IV and ICD 10 criteria are of little value in the classification of the eating difficulties of children. The GOS criteria, which were developed for this age range, are more reliable. The classification of eating disorders in childhood needs reevaluation.

Int J Eat Disord 2000 Sep;28(2):221-5
The emergence of dieting among female adolescents: age, body mass index, and seasonal effects.
Huon G, Lim J.
School of Psychology, University of New South Wales, Sydney, Australia.
OBJECTIVE: The purpose of this brief report is to document the emergence of dieting in adolescent girls across a 2-year period, and to establish whether the changes in dieting status were related to the girls' age, body mass index, or to seasonal effects. The emergence of dieting occurs in early adolescence and might be triggered by concerns about changes in body shape.

Int J Eat Disord 2000 Sep;28(2):226-30
Initiation of dieting among adolescent females.
Huon GF, Walton CJ.
School of Psychology, University of New South Wales, Sydney, Australia.
OBJECTIVE: This brief report identifies the factors that distinguish girls who have begun dieting recently

from those who have never dieted, using Huon and Strong's (International Journal of Eating Disorders 23:361-369, 1998) model of dieting. Girls who are just beginning to diet differ from those who have never dieted, predominantly in terms of their perceived social influence. The forms of parental influence that distinguish the two groups differ in nature from the type of influence exerted by peers. Copyright 2000 by John Wiley & Sons, Inc.

Int J Soc Psychiatry 2001 Spring;47(1):24-35
A cross-cultural study of parental conflict and eating disorders in a non-clinical sample.
Mujtaba T, Furnham A.
Previous British studies have found that EAT scores of second generation British Asian schoolgirls are higher than those of White schoolgirls, and that these scores are positively associated with parental over-protection (Furnham & Hussain, 1999).
This study looked at the relationship between parental conflict and parental overprotection and EAT scores in three cultures.

Issues Compr Pediatr Nurs 1986;9(5):289-98
The plight of a female adolescent--anorexia or bulimia: an overview.
Twiss JJ.

J Adolesc 1990 Mar;13(1):79-83
Bulimia nervosa in an adolescent boy boxer.
Lovett JW.
Department of Psychological Medicine, Royal Liverpool Children's Hospital, Alder Hey, U.K.

J Adolesc 1999 Jun;22(3):379-88
Eating disorder behaviors of ethnically diverse urban female adolescent athletes and non-athletes.
Rhea DJ.
Texas Christian University, Kinesiology Department, Ft. Worth 76125, USA.
This study compared Caucasian, Hispanic, and African-American urban adolescent athlete and non-athlete females for relative frequency of behavioral and psychological indices of eating disorders, while controlling for physical size. This study suggests that Hispanic and Caucasian urban adolescent females are comparably more at-risk for eating disorders than African-American urban adolescent females. In addition, athletes were no more at-risk than non-athletes for eating disordered behaviors.
Publication Types: Multicenter study
J Adolesc 1999 Jun;22(3):389-96
Subclinical eating disorders in adolescent women: a test of the continuity hypothesis and its psychological correlates.
Franko DL, Omori M.
Department of Psychology, University of Massachusetts Dartmouth, North Dartmouth 02747-2300, USA.
dfranko@umassd.edu
Subclinical eating disorders are common in adolescent women. In this study the severity of disturbed eating and its psychological correlates were examined in 207 college freshmen. Depression, dysfunctional thinking, and disturbed eating attitudes were

found to correlate with the severity of eating pathology. Support was found for the continuity hypothesis of eating disorders.

J Adolesc Health 1995 Jun;16(6):420-37
Comment in: J Adolesc Health. 1995 Jun;16(6):416-7
Eating disorders in adolescents: a background paper.
Fisher M, Golden NH, Katzman DK, Kreipe RE, Rees J, Schebendach J, Sigman G, Ammerman S, Hoberman HM.
Division of Adolescent Medicine, North Shore University Hospital, Cornell University Medical College, Manhasset, New York 11030, USA.
Publication Types: Review; Review, tutorial

J Adolesc Health 1995 Jun;16(6):448-53
Medical complications in male adolescents with anorexia nervosa.
Siegel JH, Hardoff D, Golden NH, Shenker IR.
Division of Adolescent Medicine, Schneider Children's Hospital of Long Island Jewish Medical Center, New Hyde Park, New York 11042, USA.
Medical information on male anorectics is scant. Presented were data on 10 males with anorexia nervosa, who were treated at our Eating Disorders Center during a twelve-year period. Despite the small number of patients, the proportion of male adolescent anorectics with medical abnormalities seems high, and may be due to difficulties in establishing the diagnosis and delay in seeking medical attention. Patients who had heart rates of 80 or greater were perhaps sicker and further along in their development of congestive heart failure, thus explaining their initial relative tachycardia. We suggest a higher index of suspicion forcongestive heart failure and closer medical monitoring when a malnourished adolescent with anorexia nervosa presents with relatively elevated heart rates.
PMID: 7669794 [PubMed - indexed for MEDLINE] individuals of the two genders.

J Adolesc Health 1999 Mar;24(3):206-11
Comment in: J Adolesc Health. 1999 Mar;24(3):157
Self-assessment of sexual maturation in adolescent females with anorexia nervosa.
Hick KM, Katzman DK.
Department of Paediatrics, The Hospital for Sick Children, and the Faculty of Medicine, University of Toronto, Ontario, Canada.
Evaluating the accuracy of self-assessment of pubertal maturation and to determine the desired stage of pubertal maturity in adolescent females with anorexia nervosa. Standardized figure drawings depicting Tanner's sexual maturation stages were given to a consecutive sample of 40 adolescent females with anorexia nervosa who were instructed to assess current and desired pubertal development. Pubertal development was assessed independently by two investigators. The percent agreement between physician and subject ratings was determined. RESULTS: Percent agreement between physician and subject ratings was 30% for

developmental stage for breasts and 50% for pubic hair. Subjects underestimated breast development 3.4 times as often as they overestimated it and overestimated pubic hair development 1.5 times as often as they underestimated it. Multivariate probit analysis showed that inaccuracy in breast self-assessment was inversely related to a desire for sexual maturity ($p < 0.05$). Ninety percent of subjects stated that their desired stage of breast development was equal to or more mature than their present stage. Eighty percent stated that their desired stage of pubic hair development was equal to or more. It was found self-assessment of sexual maturity by adolescents with anorexia nervosa using standardized figure drawings depicting Tanner's stages is not accurate. Patients desiring a sexually immature body were most likely to be inaccurate in their self-assessment of their pubertal stage.

J Adolesc Health 2000 May;26(5):361-7
Eating behavior, depression, and self-esteem in high school students.
Tomori M, Rus-Makovec M.
Department Psychiatry, Medical School University of Ljubljana, Ljubljana, Slovenia.
OBJECTIVE: In a representative sample of 4700 Slovene high school students, we examined their eating behavior and its correlations with some psychosocial and psychological characteristics with the aim of identifying the main risk factors for disordered eating. METHOD: Using a questionnaire which also included Zung's Self-rating Depression Scale and Rosenberg's Self-Esteem Scale, we compared girls (n = 2507) and boys (n = 2193) with regard to their satisfaction with their body weight, weight-reducing activities, and frequency of binge eating.

J Adolesc Health 2001 Mar;28(3):222-7
Differences between adolescents and young adults at presentation to an eating disorders program.
Fisher M, Schneider M, Burns J, Symons H, Mandel FS.
Division of Adolescent Medicine, North Shore University Hospital, Manhasset, New York 11030, USA.
fisher@nshs.edu
OBJECTIVE: To describe differences between adolescents and adults in clinical presentation of eating disorders. The findings in this study document and confirm that there are important differences between adolescents and adults that must be taken into account in the evaluation and treatment of patients with eating disorders.

J Adolesc Health Care 1985 Jan;6(1):21-4
Adolescents with bulimic and nonbulimic eating disorders.
Arroyo D, Tonkin R.
Twenty-eight adolescents with eating disorders were analyzed in a study that included a retrospective examination of their hospital records and a letter to their family doctor and the patient. These 28 patients were dieting to lose weight, with nine reporting episodes of overeating and vomiting. The clinical characteristics of the bulimic patients versus the nonbulimic are contrasted.
Poor outcome was positively

associated with bulimia, longer duration of illness, and older age of presentation, but not with a lower weight during the illness. However, with the exception of the presence of vomiting and being less likely to feel fat, these differences in clinical characteristics between bulimic and nonbulimic groups did not approach the level of statistical significance.

J Am Acad Child Adolesc Psychiatry 1999 Jun;38(6):754-60
Overweight, weight concerns, and bulimic behaviors among girls and boys.
Field AE, Camargo CA Jr, Taylor CB, Berkey CS, Frazier AL, Gillman MW, Colditz
GA.
Channing Laboratory, Department of Medicine, Harvard Medical School, Boston, USA.
Alison.Field@channing.harvard.edu
Assessing the prevalence rates and correlates of overweight, concern with weight, and bulimic behaviors. Misperception of being overweight and concern with weight were common. Purging was a very rare behavior, but increased with pubertal development. Among the girls, the prevalence increased sharply around the onset of adolescence.

J Am Acad Child Adolesc Psychiatry 2001 Mar;40(3):364-72
To examine differential parental influences on eating attitudes and behaviors of 8-year-old children with a specific focus on gender effects and to assess the specificity of this relationship. The impact of maternal eating disorders and disturbances is much stronger than that of fathers and is specifically directed at their daughters. The clinical importance of these disturbances in terms of precursors of adolescent eating disorders has to be determined by monitoring the sample through puberty.

J Am Acad Child Psychiatry 1986 Nov;25(6):826-35
Self-concept in adolescent anorexics.
Swift WJ, Bushnell NJ, Hanson P, Logemann T.

J Am Coll Health 1998 Mar;46(5):199-207
Eating disorders among college women: prevention, education, and treatment responses.
Schwitzer AM, Bergholz K, Dore T, Salimi L.
Department of Educational Leadership and Counseling, Old Dominion University, Richmond, Virginia, USA.
Eating-related problems, particularly among college women, represent a significant health concern on university campuses. A multiple-level model of intervention that includes preventive, intermediate, and remedial responses to varied forms of eating-related concerns is described. The intervention model is illustrated with examples, and limitations of the method are discussed.
Publication Types: Review; Review, tutorial

J Am Coll Health 2001 Jan;49(4):157-66
The eating disorders NOS diagnostic profile among college women.
Schwitzer AM, Rodriguez LE, Thomas C, Salimi L.

Department of Educational Leadership and Counseling, Old Dominion University in Norfolk, Virginia, USA. aschwitz@odu.edu
The authors examined a proposed profile of eating-related behaviors, associated features, developmental issues, and help-seeking behavior among college women, using an eating disorder response program. Implications for practice, including the need to develop a framework for eating disorder responses on campus that includes preventive programs and developmental interventions to target emerging and moderate concerns are discussed; limitations and the preliminary nature of the findings are explicated.

J Am Coll Nutr 1993 Oct;12(5):505-10
Body image and eating behavior in adolescents.
Moore DC.
Department of Clinical Investigation, Madigan Army Medical Center, Tacoma, Washington 98431-5000.
Approximately two-thirds of adolescent girls at any age are dissatisfied with their weight, the proportion increasing with actual weight. Slightly more than half of all girls are dissatisfied with the shape of their bodies, an attitude which also is positively correlated with body weight. Boys who are underweight are most likely to be dissatisfied with their weight and many with normal weight wish to weigh more. Approximately one-third of boys are dissatisfied with their body shape, desiring larger upper arms, chest and shoulders. Body consciousness and altered body image are widespread among adolescents, and may be associated with potentially harmful eating practices in both sexes, but more so in girls.
Publication Types: Review; Review, tutorial

J Ark Med Soc 1997 Oct;94(5):211-4
Diagnosis and treatment of adolescents with eating disorders.
Portilla MG, Smith PD.
Arkansas Adolescent Eating Disorder Program, University of Arkansas for Medical Sciences/Arkansas Children's Hospital, Little Rock, USA.
Publication Types: Review; Review, tutorial

J Child Adolesc Psychiatr Nurs 1998 Oct-Dec;11(4):146-56
Eating disorders and adolescents: an overview of a maladaptive behavior.
Grothaus KL.
Medical College of Ohio, USA.
TOPIC: Eating disorders among the adolescent population are a serious health problem. The author provides an overview of anorexia nervosa and bulimia nervosa. Advanced practice nurses are particularly suited for working with adolescents because of their holistic approach to client care. Inconsistencies and gaps in the knowledge base of eating disorders regarding incidence, etiology, treatment approaches, pharmacology, and outcome are areas for future nursing research.
Publication Types: Review; Review, tutorial

J Child Fam Nurs 1999 Nov-Dec;2(6):447-52
To be thin is in. Or is it? Recognizing

and measuring adolescent eating disorders.
Marsh CL.
Racine Correctional Institution, Wisconsin, USA.

J Child Psychol Psychiatry 1968 Oct;9(1):27-40
A study of anorexia nervosa in young girls.
Warren W.

J Child Psychol Psychiatry 1986 Mar;27(2):261-73
Anorexia nervosa in a pre-adolescent girl: a multimodal behaviour therapy approach.
Fundudis T.
A multimodal method of behavioural therapy was used in the case of a pre-adolescent girl with anorexia nervosa. A focused approach relevant to each of a number of important different, but overlapping, areas is likely to facilitate better potential for treatment effectiveness than a general ('non-specific') management approach.

J Child Psychol Psychiatry 1995 Feb;36(2):191-202
Eating disorders in children.
Bryant-Waugh R, Lask B.
Department of Psychological Medicine, Great Ormond Street Hospital for Children NHS Trust, London, U.K.
Publication Types: Review; Review, tutorial

J Child Psychol Psychiatry 1997 Mar;38(3):299-306
Adolescent dieting: healthy weight control or borderline eating disorder?
Patton GC, Carlin JB, Shao Q, Hibbert ME, Rosier M, Selzer R, Bowes G.
Department of Psychiatry, University of Melbourne, Australia.
Dieting in adolescent girls is ubiquitous but its health significance isuncertain. On the one hand it might be seen as promoting healthy weight control and on the other it might be considered as a risk factor for eating disorders. Dieting levels were systematically assessed in a representative group of 2525 Australian teenagers and classified using item response theory. Body mass carried a strong positive association with intermediate dieting. Most female dieters, nevertheless, fell within a normal weight range. Psychiatric morbidity was the clearest factor associated with extreme dieting and 62% of extreme dieters reported high levels of depression and anxiety.

J Clin Child Psychol 1997 Dec;26(4):358-65
Fear of fat, disregulated-restrained eating, and body-esteem: prevalence and gender differences among eight- to ten-year-old children.
Shapiro S, Newcomb M, Loeb TB.
Division of Counseling Psychology, University of Southern California, Los Angeles, USA.
Examined whether: (a) societal directives to be thin are perceived among children, (b) discontent with body and attitudes and behaviors associated with eating disorders begin before adolescence, and (c) these differ by sex. These issues were assessed in 239 Grade 3 students. The 8- to 10-year-old children expressed weight, dieting, and physique concerns that reflect Western

sociocultural values and preoccupation with body weight and dieting. These findings appear to be consistent with research on adolescents. The components that may lead to the development of an eating disorder or disregulated-restrained eating in a vulnerable adolescent may be both internalized and expressed at a very early age.

J Clin Psychol 1984 Mar;40(2):440-5
The assessment of bulimic symptoms and personality correlates in female college students.
Nagelberg DB, Hale SL, Ware SL.
A screening questionnaire for bulimic symptoms was completed by 244 college women. A subsample of 31 students were interviewed and administered the Restraint Scale, Compulsive Eating Scale, Beck Depression Inventory, Sixteen Personality Factor Questionnaire, and The Tennessee Self Concept Scale. Results showed a number of significant differences among students who binged only (" bingers "), self-induced vomiting (" purgers "), or did not binge or purge ("controls"). Bingers and purgers showed greater restrained eating tendencies and compulsive eating behaviors. On the 16PF, purgers scored lower on Factor Q3, which suggests lowered will control and less regard for social demands. Purgers also showed lower self-esteem, particularly in the areas of identity and family self-concept.

J Consult Clin Psychol 1996 Apr;64(2):282-90
Attachment processes in eating disorder and depression.
Cole-Detke H, Kobak R.
Department of Psychology, University of Delaware, Newark 19716, USA.
This study examines the relationship between attachment strategies and symptom reporting among college women. Sixty-one college women were selected who reported high or low levels of depressive and eating disorder symptoms. The Adult Attachment Interview (AAI) was administered, and interview transcripts were rated with the Attachment Interview Q-Sort. The results indicated that women with hyperactivating AAI strategies were prone to reporting elevated levels of depressive symptoms, whereas women with deactivating strategies were prone to reporting elevated levels of eating-disorder symptoms, when depression was statistically controlled. These findings support the hypothesis that secondary or defensive attachment strategies predispose individuals toward different forms of symptom expression.
Publication Types: Clinical trial; Randomized controlled trial

J Dev Behav Pediatr 1991 Jun;12(3):191-5
Bulimia nervosa in adolescence.
Herzog DB, Keller MB, Lavori PW, Bradburn IS.
Eating Disorders Unit, Massachusetts General Hospital, Boston 02114.
Investigations of bulimia nervosa have focused primarily on adult samples, although bulimia nervosa commonly has its onset in adolescence. Pediatricians are often questioned about its etiology, course, and treatment. In an attempt to provide pediatricians with answers, integrated

were findings from recent epidemiological and treatment studies with a clinical report of 18 women who developed bulimia nervosa during their teens and sought treatment at a eating disorders clinic.

J Hum Nutr Diet 2001 Apr;14(2):111-20
An ethnic comparison of eating attitudes and associated body image concerns in adolescent South African schoolgirls.
The purpose of this study was to investigate whether differences exist in eating attitudes and body shape concerns amongst adolescent schoolgirls representing South Africa's ethnically and culturally diverse population currently undergoing epidemiological transition. These findings reinforce the notion that eating disorders are culture-reactive rather than culture-bound phenomena and provide insight into the extent of eating-related problems and body image issues in developing societies.

J Pediatr 2001 Feb;138(2):158-60
Comment on:J Pediatr. 2001 Feb;138(2):181-7
Body image concerns among children.
Striegel-Moore RH.
Publication Types: Comment; Editorial

J Psychiatr Nurs Ment Health Serv 1972 Nov-Dec;10(6):18-23
Adolescent anorexia nervosa: the patient; an approach.
Hext M, Murchland A.

J Psychiatr Res 1985;19(2-3):509-14
The treatment and outcome of anorexia nervosa in adolescents: a prospective study and five year follow-up.
Martin FE
This study reports the treatment and five year follow-up of 25 adolescent (mean age 14.9 yr) anorexics seen early in their illness (mean duration 8.08 months) and fulfilling Feighner's criteria. Results are reported along four parameters at treatment termination and at follow-up; weight, menstrual function, eating patterns and social life. It is concluded that anorexia nervosa in adolescence can have a good outcome for the majority but it is undemonstrated which are the crucial variables regarding treatment modalities and patient selection nor did any clear prognostic factors emerge. A hypothesis regarding the therapeutic effect of the follow-up is suggested.

J Psychosom Res 1987;31(1):73-8
Bulimia: prevalence and component factors in college women.
Thelen MH, Mann LM, Pruitt J, Smith M.
Using a measure of bulimia (BULIT) that has demonstrated validity and reliability, the prevalence of bulimia among three samples of college females was found to range from 2.0 to 3.8%. These percentages are substantially lower than most previous reports would suggest. The intercorrelations among factors were examined and the implications of these data for the proposed revised DSM-III criteria forbulimia are discussed.

J Sch Health 1985 Apr;55(4):135-7
The assessment of bulimia in high

school students.
Maceyko SJ, Nagelberg DB.
This study attempted to: estimate the prevalence of bulimia among a sample of high school students; identify demographic variables associated with the disorder; and identify possible personality variables associated with bulimia. Gender was the only demographic variable significantly associated with group, and all 12 of the bulimic students were female (7.1% of the female students). Personality differences were assessed with the California Psychological Inventory (CPI). On two of the scales, female students identified as bulimic and binge eaters scored significantly lower than students identified as normal eaters, indicating poorer adjustment. In males, none of the scales discriminated between the binge eater and normal eater groups. Results are discussed in the context of mental health needs among adolescents and high school students.

JAMA 1987 Sep 4;258(9):1213-5
Bulimia vs bulimic behaviors on a college campus.
Schotte DE, Stunkard AJ.
A self-report survey of bulimic behaviors was conducted with 1965 students who were selected to provide a cross section of a large, eastern university. Follow-up interviews of a subsample of respondents were conducted to validate the survey. After correcting for false-positive responses, only 1.3% of the female and 0.1% of the male respondents met diagnostic criteria for bulimia according to either the third edition or the proposed revision of the Diagnostic and Statistical Manual of Mental Disorders.

Lamp 1997 Aug;54(7):6-7
Anorexia nervosa. Complex illness, complex adolescent nursing.
Anderson G.
Westmead Hospital.
Adolescents requiring inpatient care for anorexia nervosa present an exciting challenge for nurses because of the complex biopsychosocial nature of the illness. Nurses currently play a major role in caring, not only for the physical health of these patients, but for many of their psychological, social and family needs as well. With the strong foundation in holistic care which underpins nursing, scientific research and innovative nursing interventions may well hold the key to improving the current less-than-ideal long-term outcome for young people with anorexia nervosa.

Med Clin North Am 2000 Jul;84(4):1027-49, viii-ix
Eating disorders in adolescents and young adults.
Kreipe RE, Birndorf SA.
Department of Pediatrics, University of Rochester, Rochester, New York, USA.
Richard_Kreipe@urmc.rochester.edu
Eating disorders are relatively common and frequently result in medical signs and symptoms. Armed with an appreciation of the protean manifestations of these complex health problems as well as an appreciation of the biopsychosocialapproach needed to help the adolescent or young adult woman recover, the primary care

physician is in an excellent position to have a therapeutic role in the recovery from these chronic conditions. By recognizing the medical aspects of eating disorders, the oversimplified viewpoint of considering them as purely psychiatric disorders can be avoided. Open and consistent communication with patients, with a focus on health rather than dysfunction and mental illness, facilitates the acceptance of a comprehensive approach in which the internist, dietitian, and mental health provider all have a role.
Publication Types: Review; Review, tutorial

Med Health R I 1999 Nov;82(11):391-5
Eating disorders in adolescents: role of the primary care physician.
Riggs S.
Division of Adolescent Medicine, Rhode Island Hospital, Providence 02903, USA.
sriggs@lifespan.org

Newsweek 2000 Jul 3;136(1):44-7
What families should do. Helping children lose weight means walking an emotional tightrope. How, and when, to step in.
Begley S.
Publication Types: News

Nurs Clin North Am 1983 Jun;18(2):343-52
Disorders of eating in adolescence: anorexia nervosa and bulimia.
Carino CM, Chmelko P.
While the clinical syndrome of anorexia nervosa is currently receiving a great deal of scientific and clinical interest, few research findings predict successful outcomes. The most effective approach to date gleans intervention strategies from the behavioral model. The work of the Task Force of the National Group for Classification of Nursing Diagnoses gives guidance for the development of adequate assessment tools and standardized care plans. Ultimately, outcome criteria should be available for prediction and testing.

Obes Res 1997 Sep;5(5):447-54
Racial/ethnic and gender differences in concern with weight and in bulimic behaviors among adolescents.
Field AE, Colditz GA, Peterson KE.
Channing Laboratory, Department of Medicine, Brigham and Women's Hospital, Boston, MA 02115, USA.
This study examined cross-sectional gender and racial/ ethnic differences in bulimic behaviors among adolescents. The results suggest that bulimic behaviors affect male and female adolescents from a variety of racial/ethnic backgrounds. In addition, in contrast to the large gender differences in the prevalence of dieting and binge eating, more modest differences were documented in the prevalence of using vomiting and laxatives to control weight.

Obstet Gynecol Clin North Am 2000 Mar;27(1):101-24
Eating disorders in adolescents and young adults.
Kreipe RE, Mou SM.
Department of Pediatrics, University of Rochester, New York, USA.
Richard_Kreipe@urmc.rochester.edu
Eating disorders are relatively common and frequently result in

gynecologic abnormalities. The gynecologist must appreciate the various manifestations of these complex health problems as well as the biopsychosocial approach needed to help the adolescent or young adult woman recover from these chronic conditions. By recognizing both the medical and gynecologic aspects of eating disorders, the oversimplified viewpoint of considering these conditions as purely psychiatric disorders can be avoided. Open and consistent communication with patients, with a focus on health rather than dysfunction and mental illness, facilitates the acceptance of a comprehensive approach involving the gynecologist, dietitian, and mental health provider.
Publication Types: Review; Review, tutorial

Paediatr Drugs 2001;3(2):91-9
Eating disorders in children and adolescents: epidemiology, diagnosis and treatment.
Kohn M, Golden NH.
Department of Adolescent Medicine, The New Children's Hospital, Westmead, New South Wales, Australia. michaek2@nch.edu.au
Eating disorders such as anorexia nervosa (AN) and bulimia nervosa (BN) are increasingly prevalent among children and adolescents. For children and adolescents, the morbidity from malnutrition is increased because of the biological changes that are interrupted.

Pediatr Ann 1984 Dec;13(12):901-4, 907
Anorexia nervosa and bulimia in adolescent males.
Andersen AE.
Anorexia nervosa or bulimia in adolescent males occurs ten times less frequently than in adolescent females. When they occur, however, they can be clearly identified and differentiated from disorders also associated with weight loss such as swallowing phobias. Treatment seeks to improve quickly the starvation-related aspects of the illness while attempting to find more appropriate methods of dealing with the life crises prompting the illness. The real goal of treatment is to make the anorectic or bulimic illness unnecessary by encouraging the patient to continue the work of individuation and separation so that challenges in development and problems in living are resolved in a direct rather than an indirect way through an eating disorder.

Pediatr Ann 1992 Nov;21(11):769-74
The adolescent male with an eating disorder.
Farrow JA.
Division of Adolescent Medicine, University of Washington, Seattle 98195.
While it is clear that males and females with eating disorders share more features in common than dissimilarities, males are distinctive in their past histories of obesity, sexual identity concerns, defensive dieting, and dieting in relationship to sports participation. All adolescents with an eating disorder are likely to be guarded in terms of disclosing items affecting their psychological state. Young men may be more so. In light of this fact, diagnosisof these disorders in adolescent male patients

still depends on ruling out possible organic etiologies, thoroughly assessing the adolescent's mental status, and looking for underlying psychiatric symptoms. Assessment of developmental and nutritional status is key to the diagnosis and is helpful in monitoring recovery.
Publication Types: Review; Review, tutorial

Pediatr Int 2000 Feb;42(1):1-7
Eating disorders in adolescent girls.
Emans SJ.
Division of Adolescent/Young Adult Medicine, Children's Hospital, Boston, MA, USA.
emansj@al.tch.harvard.edu
New information is emerging on the pathogenesis of anorexia nervosa and bulimia nervosa and includes psychologic, biologic, family, environmental, genetic and social factors. The physician providing care to adolescents is challenged to carry out a careful evaluation and monitor the patient for complications, especially loss of bone mass. Treatment requires a multidisciplinary team.
Publication Types: Review; Review, tutorial

Pediatr Rev 1988 Aug;10(2):37-47
Eating disorders in adolescents.
Comerci GD.

Pediatr Rev 1994 Feb;15(2):72-7; quiz 77
Eating disorders in adolescence.
Harper G.
Children's Hospital, Harvard Medical School, Boston, MA.

Pediatr Rev 1995 Oct;16(10):370-9
Eating disorders among children and adolescents.
Kreipe RE.
Division of Adolescent Medicine, University of Rochester School of Medicine and Dentistry, NY, USA.
Anorexia nervosa and bulimia nervosa represent extreme manifestations of weight control patterns in adolescents. When they occur in children, they often are associated with more severe psychiatric or family dysfunction. By being familiar with the larger issues associated with weight loss, rather than the more narrow topic of eating disorders, the pediatrician will be able to help all patients remain healthy in a culture of thinness, regardless of their diagnosis.

Pediatr Rev 1999 Dec;20(12):410-21
Eating disorders in adolescents and older children.
Kreipe RE, Dukarm CP.
Professor of Pediatrics and Chief, Division of Adolescent Medicine. Senior Instructor in Pediatrics, Division of Adolescent Medicine, The University of Rochester School of Medicine, Rochester, NY.

Pediatrics 1985 Oct;76(4 Pt 2):685-90
Bulimia in adolescents: a review.
Lustick MJ.
This report reviews the occurrence of bulimia in female adolescents, a relatively common disorder. Features contributing to its occurrence in adolescents and treatment modalities are highlighted. A high degree of suspicion is needed to make the diagnosis and further work is required to clarify the unique aspects of this

disorder in adolescents.

Pediatrics 1988 May;81(5):613-23
Medical complications of eating disorders in adolescents.
Palla B, Litt IF.
Department of Pediatrics, Stanford University School of Medicine, Children's Hospital at Stanford, Palo Alto, California 94304.
Anorexia nervosa and bulimia are occurring with increased frequency among adolescents and preadolescents. To determine the range and severity of medical complications encountered in younger anorectic and bulimic patients, we reviewed the medical records of 65 adolescents and preadolescents, aged 10 to 20 years, who were observed in the Eating Disorders Clinic of the Children's Hospital at Stanford. Significant medical instability was present in the majority of our patients. A total of 55% of anorectic patients and 22% of bulimic patients required hospitalization for medical reasons during the study period.
The majority of our pediatric patients with eating disorders had evidence of physiologic derangement requiring medical intervention. The need foradolescents and preadolescents with eating disorders to receive ongoing medical monitoring in concert with psychiatric treatment and the need for therapists and medical practitioners to become familiar with the potential medical sequelae of eating disorders are underscored by our data.

Percept Mot Skills 1994 Feb;78(1):147-54
Body-image perception in pre- and postadolescent females.
Brodie DA, Bagley K, Slade PD.
University of Liverpool, England.
The purpose of this study was to examine both perceived and ideal body-image to establish if the process of adolescence was a contributory factor. A distorting mirror and silhouette pictures were used to examine the image in two groups of 59 pre- and 41 postadolescent girls. The girls' perception of themselves was reasonably accurate yet both groups had a significantly slimmer mean ideal image, irrespective of adolescent status. Scores from the mirror and the pictures question the assumption that body-image dissatisfaction is a postadolescent phenomenon. The comparability between scores for the pictures and the distorting mirror opens the possibility of home-based therapy in the treatment of perceptual and eating disorders.

Postgrad Med J 1998 Nov;74(877):691-2
The young woman who could not stop vomiting.
de Silva AP, Molagoda A, Fernando PL, de Silva HJ.
Department of Medicine, Faculty of Medicine, University of Kelaniya, Ragama, Sri Lanka.

Practitioner 1977 Mar;218(1305):424-7
Anorexia nervosa--a difficult diagnosis in boys. Illustrated by three cases.
Swann I.

Psychiatr Med 1989;7(3):47-58
Eating disorders in college students.
Provost JA.

Health and Counseling Services, Rollins College, Winter Park, Florida.
Certainly eating disorders are a major threat to the physical and mental health of female college students today. The college years, especially for traditional age students, present pressures to complete certain developmental tasks. Some students arrive ill-equipped to complete these tasks and with family pathology as a backdrop.
Eating disorders are one of the prevailing ways these young people try to cope; these disorders may be exacerbated by the college experience.

Psychiatry Res 1988 Nov;26(2):163-9
Prevalence of binge-eating and bulimia among adolescent women in Japan.
Kiriike N, Nagata T, Tanaka M, Nishiwaki S, Takeuchi N, Kawakita Y.
Department of Neuropsychiatry, Osaka City University Medical School, Japan.
This study examined by questionnaire the prevalence of binge-eating and bulimia among 220 women at a school of nursing and 236 women at a junior college, all from 18 to 21 years old, in two different areas of Japan. The difference between these two groups was not significant. These women appeared to meet both DSM-III criteria for bulimia and Russell's criteria for bulimia nervosa.

Psychol Med 1995 Sep;25(5):1019-25
The relationship of partial syndrome eating disorders to anorexia nervosa and bulimia nervosa.
Dancyger IF, Garfinkel PE.
Department of Applied Psychology, Ontario Institute of Studies in Education, University of Toronto, Canada.
A variety of sociocultural, familial and individual features associated with the eating disorders were examined in subjects with full syndrome (FS) and partial syndrome (PS) eating disorders and in normal high school students. The data support a continuum model of the eating disorders, but a continuum of multiple associated features rather than of dieting.
Publication Types: Clinical trial; Randomized controlled trial

Psychosomatics 1972 Jul-Aug;13(4):236-40
Anorexia nervosa in boys.
Taipale V, Larkio-Miettinen K, Valanne EH, Moren R, Aukee M.

Psychother Psychosom 1976-77;27(1):47-53
Anorexia nervosa: a case study.
Steele RL.
D.R., a single 19-year-old female experiencing anorexia nervosa, was admitted to a mental health center inpatient unit weighing 64 lb, approximately 54 lb underweight, with liver, kidney, and pancreas damage. D.R. was hospitalized for59 days. Treatment consisted of utilizing a hierarchy of reinforcements in the form of privileges mutually agreed upon between patient and therapist, psychodynamic and supportive psychotherapy, and involvement in the ward milieu therapeutic program. Five months later D.R.'s weight stabilized between 102 and 104 lb. Two years

later, D.R.'s weight remains at that level. The study cautions against using solely a behavior modification approach in the treatment of anorexia nervosa.

South Med J 1979 Apr;72(4):501-2
Primary anorexia nervosa in an adolescent male.
LaGrone DM.

The spectrum of eating disorder in adolescence. Patton CG
Department of Psychiatry, Royal Free Hospital, London, U.K.
The concept of a spectrum of eating disorder in adolescence ranging from the feeling of being too fat to the syndrome of anorexia nervosa has gained considerable acceptance in epidemiological research into eating disorders. New findings from a prospective study of London schoolgirls support a view that dieting in adolescence, although for the most part unproblematic, is in some instances a precursor to more extreme methods of weight control and concerns about weight. Being of a higher weight and the presence of neurotic and depressive symptoms were found to be the factors, other than concerns about food and weight, which best distinguished the elements of the eating disorder spectrum.

West J Med 2000 Jun;172(6):365
Comment on:West J Med. 2000 Mar;172(3):189-93
Better clinical management of anorexia nervosa in teens.
Vale S.
Publication Types: Comment Letter

Women Health 1998;27(3):73-88
Dating people with anorexia nervosa and bulimia nervosa: attitudes and beliefs of university students.
Sobal J, Bursztyn M.
Division of Nutritional Sciences, Cornell University, Ithaca, NY 14853, USA.
Attitudes and beliefs about dating people with eating disorders were investigated in men and women using a questionnaire administered to 752 university students. Most students believed dating people with anorexia nervosa and bulimia nervosa would not be a positive experience, and men stigmatized people with eating disorders differently than did women.

ADULTS

Addict Behav 1995 Jul-Aug;20(4):491-500
Parental variables associated with bulimia nervosa.
Kanakis DM, Thelen MH.
University of Missouri, Columbia, USA.
The present study examined daughter and parent variables associated with bulimia nervosa, including attitudes about body image, eating and dieting histories, and self-esteem.

Am Fam Physician 1989 Jan;39(1):173-8
Anorexia nervosa in adulthood.
McGlynn TJ, Tinker DE.
Pennsylvania State University College of Medicine, Hershey.
Discussion on how family physicians and other primary care physicians can work with psychotherapists to provide effective treatment for adult women with anorexia nervosa. The major contributions of family physicians include evaluation and treatment of medical complications and supportive reinforcement of long-term psychotherapy. Family physicians can reassure patients that permanent physical disability can be avoided with successful treatment.

Am J Clin Nutr 1997 Oct;66(4):760-73
Comment in: Am J Clin Nutr. 1998 Sep;68(3):758
Anorexia of aging: physiologic and pathologic.
Morley JE.
Division of Geriatrics, St Louis University Medical School, MO 63104, USA.
Morley@SLU.EDU
Despite the increase in body fat and obesity that occurs with aging, there is a linear decrease in food intake over the life span. This conundrum is explained by decreased physical activity and altered metabolism with aging. Approaches to the management of anorexia and weight loss in older persons are reviewed. Although many drugs exist that can enhance appetite, none of these are ideal for use in older persons currently.
Publication Types: Review; Review, tutorial

Am J Orthopsychiatry 1984 Jan;54(1):156-61
Group therapy for bulimic adults.
Stevens EV, Salisbury JD.

Eating disorders are increasingly coming to the attention of mental health practitioners, and effective treatment approaches are a matter of growing concern. This paper describes the structure, process, and outcome of a group therapy project involving eight bulimic women.

Am J Psychiatry 1991 Jul;148(7):831-43
Review of bulimia nervosa in males.
Carlat DJ, Camargo CA Jr.
Langley Porter Psychiatric Institute, San Francisco, CA 94143-0984.
The authors describe the distribution of bulimia nervosa among males and identify characteristics that distinguish male bulimics from their female counterparts. Compared to their female counterparts, male bulimics appear to have a later age of onset; higher prevalences of premorbid obesity, homosexuality, and asexuality; and less concern with strict weight control.
These findings are discussed from biological, psychological, and cultural perspectives to develop a fuller understanding of the pathogenesis of bulimia in males. Bulimia in males has received relatively little attention in the literature. Future research should focus on more rigorous analytic studies that include matched comparison groups of female bulimic and male nonbulimic subjects. Such studies would not only benefit male bulimics but might provide insight into the nature of bulimia in both sexes.
Publication Types: Review; Review, tutorial

Am J Psychiatry 1995 Sep;152(9):1279-85
Eating disorders in college men.
Olivardia R, Pope HG Jr, Mangweth B, Hudson JI.
Department of Psychology, Tufts University, Medford, Mass., USA.
This study was designed to assess the characteristics of men with eating disorders in the community. The authors recruited 25 men meeting DSM-IV criteria for eating disorders and 25 comparison men through advertisements in college newspapers. A second comparison group comprised 33 women with bulimia nervosa who were recruited and interviewed with virtually identical methods. The men with eating disorders closely resembled the women with eating disorders but differed sharply from the comparison men in phenomenology of illness, rates of comorbid psychiatric disorders, and dissatisfaction with body image.

Am J Psychiatry 2001 Apr;158(4):570-4
Comparisons of men with full or partial eating disorders, men without eating disorders, and women with eating disorders in the community.
Woodside DB, Garfinkel PE, Lin E, Goering P, Kaplan AS, Goldbloom DS, Kennedy SH.
Department of Psychiatry, The Toronto Hospital, 200 Elizabeth Street, Toronto, Ontario, Canada M5G 2C4. b.woodside@utoronto.ca The authors compared 62 men who met all or most of the DSM-III-Rcriteria for eating disorders with 212 women who had similar eating disorders and 3,769 men who had no eating disorders on a wide variety of clinical and historical

variables. These results confirm the clinical similarities between men with eating disorders and women with eating disorders. They also reveal that both groups suffer similar psychosocial morbidity. Men with eating disorders show a wide range of differences from men without eating disorders; the extent to which these differences are effects of the illness or possible risk factors for the occurrence of these illnesses in men is not clear.

Ann N Y Acad Sci 1989;575:50-8; discussion 58-9
The anorexia of the elderly.
Morley JE, Silver AJ, Miller DK, Rubenstein LZ.
Geriatric Research, Education and Clinical Center, Sepulveda VA Medical Center, California 91343.
Publication Types: Review; Review, tutorial

Arch Gen Psychiatry 1998 Jul;55(7):603-10
A controlled family study of anorexia nervosa and bulimia nervosa: psychiatric disorders in first-degree relatives and effects of proband comorbidity.
Lilenfeld LR, Kaye WH, Greeno CG, Merikangas KR, Plotnicov K, Pollice C, Rao R, Strober M, Bulik CM, Nagy L.
Department of Psychiatry, Western Psychiatric Institute and Clinic, University of Pittsburgh School of Medicine, PA, USA.
Contemporary family-epidemiological methods were used to examine patterns of comorbidity and familial aggregation of psychiatric disorders for anorexia and bulimia nervosa. It was found that there may be a common familial vulnerability for anorexia nervosa and bulimia nervosa. Major depressive disorder, obsessive-compulsive disorder, and substance dependence are not likely to share a common cause with eating disorders. However, obsessional personality traits may be a specific familial risk factor for anorexia nervosa.

Br J Clin Pract 1990 Dec;44(12):630-1
Anorexia nervosa in the elderly: a case report and review of the literature.
White A, Harries D, Allen SC.
Department of Medicine for the Elderly, Christchurch Hospital, Dorset.
Anorexia nervosa is a rare disorder in the elderly but should be thought of in the differential diagnosis of extreme weight loss, especially if there are accompanying psychological features and normal baseline investigations. Psychiatric opinion should be obtained and treatment, although of unproven value, considered, since improvement may increase mobility and reduce morbidity and mortality.
Publication Types: Review; Review, tutorial

Br J Med Psychol 1978 Dec;51(4):375-7
Anorexia nervosa in late life.
Launer MA.

Br J Psychiatry 1976 Jun;128:555-8
Anorexia nervosa after the menopause.
Kellett J, Trimble M, Thorley A.
A patient is described who developed the classical syndrome of anorexia nervosa at the age of 52. Her illness

occurred in relation to the marriages of her daughters and showed an extreme preoccupation with her body shape and a determination to slim by diet, purging and vomiting, and the hiding of food to the extent of rendering herself too weak to cope with the demands of her life. It is suggested that anorexia nervosa, though predominantly a disease of onset in adolescence, may present at any age and should be considered in the differential diagnosis of anorexia in patients over the age of 50.

Br J Psychiatry 1991 Aug;159:296-7
Comment on: Br J Psychiatry. 1991 May;158:716-7
Anorexia nervosa in the elderly.
Cosford P, Arnold E.
Publication Types: Comment Letter

Br J Psychiatry 1991 May;158:716-7
Comment in: Br J Psychiatry. 1991 Aug;159:296-7
Comment on: Br J Psychiatry. 1991 Feb;158:286-7
Anorexia nervosa in the elderly.
O'Shea B.
Publication Types: Comment Letter

Can J Psychiatry 1998 May;43(4):367-74
The meaning of body image for women with eating disorders.
Jarry JL.
Department of Psychology, University of Toronto, Ontario.
OBJECTIVE: A theoretical model accounting for the meaning and function of body image disturbances for individuals with eating disorders is proposed. This model departs from available conceptualizations of body image focused on attractiveness and emphasizes the role of body image preoccupations in the regulation of self-esteem and affect. This model is designed to be a therapeutic tool within body image therapy. Body image therapy can be most effective when focused on the unique meaning of body image for each individual patient.
Publication Types: Review; Review, tutorial

Clin Nurse Spec 1992 Spring;6(1):50
Comment on: Clin Nurse Spec. 1991 Summer;5(2):79-85
Anorexia nervosa in the older adult: a case study.
DiMaria RA.
Publication Types: Comment Letter

Compr Psychiatry 1987 Jul-Aug;28(4):323-8
Late onset bulimia.
Mitchell JE, Hatsukami D, Pyle RL, Eckert ED, Soll E.

Drugs Aging 1996 Feb;8(2):134-55
Anorexia in older persons: epidemiology and optimal treatment.
Morley JE.
Geriatric Research, Education and Clinical Center, St Louis University Medical School, Missouri, USA 63104.
Anorexia and weight loss are common findings in older persons. Over a life-time, normal persons decrease their food intake to counterbalance the decrease in physical activity and resting metabolic rate that occurs with aging. This physiological anorexia of aging increases the propensity to develop pathological anorexia and weight loss when an older person

develops either a medical or psychological illness. Early screening for malnutrition is a cornerstone of the management of anorexia; the Mini Nutritional Assessment is a well validated screening tool available for this purpose. Aggressive use of caloric supplements, enteral tube feeding and peripheral parenteral nutrition all have a role in the early management of anorexia. Numerous drugs (growth hormone, megestrol, cyproheptadine, tetrahydrocannabinol, anabolic steroids, prokinetic agents and antidepressants) have been utilised to treat the anorexia of aging with varying success.
Publication Types: Review; Review, academic

Focus Crit Care 1985 Aug;12(4):32-41
Eating disorders in women.
Worthington-Roberts B.

Int J Eat Disord 1993 Dec;14(4):497-9
Anorexia in the elderly--an annotation.
Hall P, Driscoll R.
Eating Disorders Programme, Woodbourne Clinic, Birmingham, United Kingdom.
Genuine anorexia nervosa starting in the elderly is thought relatively uncommon. Two illustrative patients are briefly reported. Some possible psychological mechanisms in this syndrome are discussed in the context of the relatively small total number of previously reported single cases.

Int J Eat Disord 1993 Dec;14(4):501-4
Anorexia nervosa in an elderly man.
Riemann BC, McNally RJ, Meier A.
Center for the Study and Treatment of Anxiety Disorders, Oconomowoc, WI 53066.
Anorexia nervosa (AN) rarely develops after the age of 30 years, and rarely occurs in men. Reported here is the a case of chronic AN in a 72-year-old man, who reported a 20-year history of extreme low body weight, persistent fears of obesity, and feelings of being fat even at 93 lb. Also reported were episodes of self-induced vomiting, laxative abuse, and excessive exercising. Patient's scores on a battery of questionnaires were also consistent with a diagnosis of AN

Int J Eat Disord 1995 Apr;17(3):251-61
Temperament in eating disorders.
Bulik CM, Sullivan PF, Weltzin TE, Kaye WH.
Department of Psychology, University of Canterbury, Christchurch, New Zealand.
This study examined dimensional personality and temperamental characteristics in women with eating disorders. Clinical symptoms, personality, and temperament were examined in 30 women with anorexia nervosa (AN), 32 women with bulimia nervosa with no history of anorexia nervosa (BN), and 20 women with comorbid anorexia and bulimia nervosa (AB). Temperament differed markedly across the groups on the Tridimensional Personality Questionnaire (TPQ) with AN women showing greater reward dependence, BN women scoring higher on novelty seeking subscales, and AB women showing high harm avoidance.

Int J Eat Disord 1995 Sep;18(2):135-43
An age-matched comparison of subjects with binge eating disorder

and bulimia nervosa.
Raymond NC, Mussell MP, Mitchell JE, de Zwaan M, Crosby RD.
Department of Psychiatry, University of Minnesota Hospital and Clinic, Minneapolis 55455, USA.
The purpose of this study was to compare data from a group of obese subjects with binge eating disorder (BED) with data from a group of normal weight bulimia nervosa (BN) subjects. Subjects were compared using the Eating Disorder Questionnaire (EDQ), the Eating Disorder Inventory (EDI), the Personality
Disorders Questionnaire for DSM-III-R (PDQ-R), the Hamilton Anxiety and Depression Rating Scales, and the Beck Depression Inventory. A group of 35 age-matched subjects were selected retrospectively from treatment study subjects.

Int J Eat Disord 1998 Dec;24(4):395-403
Eating disturbances in white and minority female dieters.
le Grange D, Stone AA, Brownell KD.
University of Chicago, Department of Psychiatry, Illinois 60637, USA.
OBJECTIVE: This study examined disordered eating, attitudes about weight and appearance, self-esteem, weight loss, and reasons for weight regain in a sample of white, black, Asian, and Hispanic female dieters. This study suggests that unhealthy eating attitudes and practices may be similar for women who diet, irrespective of ethnic background. However, the generalizability of these findings is limited by the inherent sampling bias.

Int J Eat Disord 1998 Nov;24(3):285-98
Shape- and weight-based self-esteem and the eating disorders.
Geller J, Johnston C, Madsen K, Goldner EM, Remick RA, Birmingham CL.
University of British Columbia, Vancouver, Canada.
Determining the psychometric properties of the Shape- and Weight-Based Self-Esteem (SAWBS) Inventory in women with eating disorders, and to compare SAWBS scores in women who have eating disorders with women from psychiatric and normal control groups. The psychometric properties of the SAWBS Inventory were established in women with eating disorders. As expected, SAWBS scores were higher in women with eating disorders than in the control groups. Clinical implications of these findings are discussed.

Int J Eat Disord 1999 May;25(4):415-24
More males seek treatment for eating disorders.
Braun DL, Sunday SR, Huang A, Halmi KA.
Department of Psychiatry, New York Presbyterian Hospital, White Plains 10605, USA.
OBJECTIVE: This study compares males and females with DSM-IV-defined eating disorders who were admitted to the inpatient eating disorders service at The New York Hospital, Cornell between 1984 and 1987. The similarities of core eating disorder psychopathology and comorbid illness in male and female patients encourage the continued use of similar detection and treatment

strategies with both groups.

Int J Eat Disord 2000 Apr;27(3):353-7
Personality disorders among subjects recovered from eating disorders.
Matsunaga H, Kaye WH, McConaha C, Plotnicov K, Pollice C, Rao R.
Western Psychiatric Institute and Clinic, University of Pittsburgh Medical Center, Pittsburgh, PA, USA.
OBJECTIVE: Personality disorders are common in symptomatic eating disorders subjects. Because personality symptoms could be exaggerated by malnutrition or Axis I disorders, we studied women who had recovered from eating disorders for at least 1 year to see if personality disorder symptoms persisted in the well state. Fourteen of 54 subjects (26%) met the criteria for at least one personality disorder, such as self-defeating, obsessive-compulsive, or borderline personality disorder. While a recovery from eating disorders may have an attenuating influence on the symptoms of personality disorders, such personality disorder diagnoses persist after recovery in some recovered subjects.

Int J Eat Disord 2000 Jan;27(1):83-9
Effect of Western culture on women's attitudes to eating and perceptions of body shape.
Lake AJ, Staiger PK, Glowinski H.
School of Psychology, Deakin University, Melbourne, Australia.
This study investigated the effect of culture on two factors implicated in the development of eating disorders, negative attitudes toward eating and dissatisfaction with body shape. Main implications center around the need for a cross-culturally sensitive definition of eating disorders, the effect of level of ethnic identity on eating attitudes and body image, and the importance of developing culturally appropriate measures. Copyright 2000 by John Wiley & Sons, Inc.

Int J Eat Disord 2001 Apr;29(3):358-62
Parental medical neglect in the treatment of adolescents with anorexia nervosa.
Fornari V, Dancyger I, Schneider M, Fisher M, Goodman B, McCall A.
Division of Child and Adolescent Psychiatry, Department of Psychiatry, North Shore University Hospital, New York University School of Medicine, Manhasset, New York.
Although childhood sexual abuse has been a frequent focus of research on eating disorders, other forms of maltreatment have been less commonly reported. Clinicians who treat minors with anorexia nervosa must consider parental compliance with treatment. Indications for the involvement of CPS are outlined. Optimally, this notification can ensure that the patient and family receive the requisite treatment. Copyright 2001 by John Wiley & Sons, Inc.

J Adv Nurs 1998 Jun;27(6):1158-64
The phenomenon of compulsive overeating in a selected group of professional women.
Lyons MA.
The University of Alabama, Capstone College of Nursing, Tuscaloosa 35487-0358, USA. Many data have been generated concerning individuals with eating disorders such as anorexia

and bulimia. However, few data exist that have explored the phenomenon of compulsive overeating or binge eating. The purpose of this study was to determine the meaning of compulsive overeating, or binge eating, in the lives of adult professional women. Recurrent themes that emerged from data collection included those pertaining to childhood experiences with food, descriptions of the types of food most often eaten during the adult years, eating behaviours in the adult years, perceptions of loss of control, reasons for overeating, emotional consequences of overeating, compensatory behaviours, and prevention strategies.

J Clin Psychol 1991 Jan;47(1):53-7
Gender role and risk patterns for eating disorders in men and women.
Cantrell PJ, Ellis JB.
Department of Psychology, ETSU, Johnson City 37614.
The relationship between gender role and at-risk patterns for eating dysfunction was examined in this study of 206 men and women. The Bem Sex Role Inventory (Bem, 1974) and the Eating Disorders Inventory (EDI; Garner, Olmsted, & Polivy, 1983) were the measures used. An interaction between gender and gender role was found across factors associated with eating disorders: different gender role identities contributed differentially to specific risk factors. The data contribute to a growing body of literature that suggests that the relationship between gender role and eating dysfunction is complex and requires multidimensional conceptualizations.

J Psychol 1999 Jul;133(4):357-68
Gender and ethnic differences in the relationship between body esteem and self-esteem.
Henriques GR, Calhoun LG.
Department of Psychology, University of North Carolina-Charlotte, USA.
Gender and ethnic differences in the relationship between body esteem and self-esteem were examined to assess the degree to which these variables change in relation to each other over time. Difference scores (between Time 1 and Time 2, 1 week apart) were obtained using the Self-Esteem Scale (M. Rosenberg, 1979) and the Body Esteem Scale (S. L. Franzoi & S. A. Shields, 1984) for 163 White women, 140 White men, 55 Black women, and 37 Black men. The results indicated that the correlation of the difference scores was stronger for the group of White women than for the other 3 groups, suggesting that changes in self-esteem parallel changes in body esteem more for White women than for White men, Black men, and Black women. The findings are discussed in relation to the prevalence of bulimia nervosa among White women.

Kans Med 1985 Jan;86(1):13-4
Anorexia nervosa/bulimia in a male.
Reith P, Lee K, Kyner JL.

Neurobiol Aging 1988 Jan-Feb;9(1):9-16
Anorexia in the elderly.
Morley JE, Silver AJ.
Geriatric Research, Education and Clinical Center, Sepulveda VA Medical Center, CA 91343.

Weight loss and anorexia occur commonly in the elderly. While in many cases the anorexia can be attributed to associated disease processes, it does appear that a true anorexia of aging exists. Other older persons develop anorexia in association with depression. In these subjects, excess corticotropin-releasing factor may be the neurotransmitter involved in the pathogenesis of the anorexia. In Alzheimer's disease, decreases in norepinephrine and neuropeptide Y may be involved in the anorexia seen in the these patients.
Publication Types: Review; Review, tutorial

Postgrad Med 1989 Feb 15;85(3):140-4
Anorexia and weight loss in the elderly. Causes range from loose dentures to debilitating illness.
Olsen-Noll CG, Bosworth MF.
Family Practice Center, Good Samaritan Hospital and Health Center, Dayton, OH 45406.
Differentiating between anorexia (loss of appetite) and weight loss (documented loss of pounds) can be difficult, but the same causes and treatments apply to both. Although the physician may find assessment of anorexia or weight loss in the elderly a challenge, it usually responds well to corrective measures.
Publication Types: Review; Review, tutorial

Psychopharmacol Bull 1998;34(3):267-9
Recognizing eating disorders in women.
Casper RC.
Department of Psychiatry and Behavioral Sciences, Stanford University School of Medicine 94305, USA.
Anorexia nervosa (AN) and bulimia nervosa (BN) are currently classified as eating disorders. Both disorders are the product of a complex interaction between psychological and physiological processes and both show considerable comorbidity with other psychiatric disorders. Physiological and endocrine abnormalities, including primary or secondary amenorrhea and menstrual dysfunction, are common and for the most part a function of the severity of weight loss, malnutrition and/or abnormal eating habits. Therefore, assessment needs to include several steps: (1) Clinical evaluation to ascertain the diagnosis, including weight and height measurements; (2) Determination of co-existing psychiatric illnesses; and (3) Physical examination and evaluation of the physiological and endocrine status.
Publication Types: Review; Review, tutorial

Psychosom Med 1992 Jan-Feb;54(1):59-69
A three-year prospective study of life events and course for adults with anorexia nervosa/bulimia nervosa.
Sohlberg S, Norring C.
Department of Clinical Psychology, Uppsala University, Sweden.
Attempts to understand the pathogenesis and course of eating disorders have increasingly included investigation of stressful life events. Reported was a prospective study in which major life events were assessed 1, 2, and 3 years after the patient's

initial presentation to a university hospital psychiatric department. Events explained a substantial 30% of the variability in follow-up status, with analyses taking potential confounds into consideration unable to explain the finding. Also, significant correlations between events and self-rated variables (Eating Disorder Inventory and Beck Depression Inventory) were obtained at one of the follow-ups, but in all, the data did not consistently imply that life events affect the patients' course.

Psychosomatics 1986 Mar;27(3):209-12
Rumination: its significance in adults with bulimia nervosa.
Larocca FE, Della-Fera MA.

Singapore Med J 1997 Aug;38(8):332-5
Anorexia nervosa and bulimia--a Singapore perspective.
Ung EK, Lee S, Kua EH.
Department of Psychological Medicine, National University Hospital, Singapore.
A study of the clinical characteristics of patients with anorexia nervosa and bulimia. The clinical characteristics of anorexics and bulimics were found to be more striking for their similarities rather than differences to that described in the West

ANOREXIA NERVOSA

Acta Psychiatr Scand 1988 Nov;78(5):550-4
Anorexia nervosa in two Nigerians.
Famuyiwa OO.
Department of Psychiatry, College of Medicine, University of Lagos, Nigeria.
The general belief that anorexia nervosa is rare among non-whites should be cautiously accepted based on some very recent reports of the occurrence of the disorder in individuals of African descent. The relatively low prevalence of the disorder that has been observed might be due to: the protective influence of the Nigerian extended kinship system, the customary passion for plumpness as an attribute of physical attractiveness, carbohydrate diet "resistance" and the non-inclusion of cases in hospital records because of consultation with unorthodox healers. The general trend of increasing prevalence calls for more diagnostic vigilance, particularly among doctors serving populations with Third World background.

Acta Psychiatr Scand Suppl 1968;203:113-16
Anorexia nervosa.
Jensen L.

Adolescence 1984 Winter;19(76):839-46
Anorexia nervosa: adolescent starvation by choice.
Gilbert EH, DeBlassie RR.
Anorexia nervosa is an eating disorder which affects people of all classes and ages but in particular adolescent girls. The symptoms, characteristics, family, and modes of treatment of the typical anorectic patient are discussed.

Adolescence 1992 Summer;27(106):381-6
Predisposition factors in anorexia nervosa.
Nagel KL, Jones KH.
Home Economics Education, University of Georgia, Athens 30602.
Since its first recognition, a number of researchers have endeavored to link anorexia nervosa to underlying pathology. This article reviews the literature concerned with investigating psychiatric disturbances and genetic variables hypothesized as predisposing factors in the etiology of anorexia nervosa. Particular emphasis is given to research which discusses the association between anorexia

nervosa and depression. Psychopharmacological evidence and family genetics studies are reviewed. Suggestions for future research are also made.
Publication Types: Review; Review, tutorial

Am Correct Ther J 1970 Mar-Apr;24(2):34-42
Anorexia nervosa: a new approach.
Ziemer RR, Ross JL.

Am Fam Physician 1976 Apr;13(4):121-6
Anorexia nervosa.
Reece RM.
Anorexia nervosa occurs predominantly in white, middle-class, adolescent females with perfectionistic tendencies. Their solution to the intense guilt induced by any sensory pleasure is to deny themselves the pleasure of eating. Amenorrhea is universal. Diagnostic criteria include a 25 percent weight loss. Therapies are long and involved different approaches. All recognize that food is the medicine for the body and that some form of supportive psychotherapy is the medicine forthe mind.

Am J Psychiatry 1969 Jul;126(1):85-90
The insignificant difference: discordant incidence of anorexia nervosa in monozygotic twins.
Bruch H.

Am J Psychiatry 1973 Dec;130(12):1394-7
Family structure in three cases of anorexia nervosa: the role of the father.
Wold P.

Am J Psychiatry 1980 May;137(5):631-2
Social attitudes toward patients with anorexia nervosa.
Branch CH, Eurman LJ.

Am J Psychiatry 1988 Oct;145(10):1287-8
Pattern of onset of bulimic symptoms in anorexia nervosa.
Kassett JA, Gwirtsman HE, Kaye WH, Brandt HA, Jimerson DC.
Laboratory of Clinical Science, NIMH, Bethesda, MD 20892.
Among patients with anorexia nervosa in a research program, the proportion of those who had developed bulimia before anorexia increased between 1976 and 1987.
These preliminary results may reflect a new symptom pattern with important clinical and research implications.

Am J Psychiatry 1995 Jul;152(7):1073-4
Mortality in anorexia nervosa.
Sullivan PF.
University Department of Psychological Medicine, Christchurch School of Medicine, New Zealand.
OBJECTIVE: The author's goal was to shed light on the debate regarding the mortality rate over time associated with anorexia nervosa. METHOD: He conducted a meta-analytic study using weighted linear regression to combine crude mortality proportions from 42 published studies to estimate the mortality associated with anorexia nervosa over time. The aggregate estimated mortality rate for subjects with anorexia nervosa is substantially greater than that reported for female psychiatric inpatients and for the

general population.
Publication Types: Meta-analysis

Am J Psychiatry 1997 Jul;154(7):1041
Anorexia nervosa in eighteenth century.
Gordon AG.
Publication Types: Historical article; Letter

Am J Psychiatry 1998 Jul;155(7):939-46
Outcome of anorexia nervosa: a case-control study.
Sullivan PF, Bulik CM, Fear JL, Pickering A.
Department of Psychiatry, Virginia Institute for Psychiatric and Behavioral Genetics, Virginia Commonwealth University, Richmond 23298-0126, USA.
sullivan@psycho.psi.vcu.edu
OBJECTIVE: Although there have been many studies of the outcome of anorexia nervosa, methodological weaknesses limit their interpretation. The authors used a case-control design to try to improve knowledge about the outcome of anorexia nervosa. All new female patients referred to an eating disorders service between Jan. 1, 1981, and Dec. 31, 1984, who had probable or definite anorexia nervosa were eligible for inclusion. Of these women, 86.4% (N = 70) were located and agreed to participate. A minority of the patients (10%) continued to meet the criteria for anorexia nervosa a mean of 12 years after initial referral. In the managed care/brief treatment era, therapeutic approaches with an excessive focus on weight gain that neglect the detection and treatment of associated psychological features and comorbidity may be inappropriate. Anorexia nervosa is a serious psychiatric disorder with substantial morbidity.

Am J Psychiatry 2000 Dec;157(12):2060
Anorexia nervosa and body mass index.
Russell J, Gross G.
Publication Types: Letter

Am J Public Health 1998 Aug;88(8):1206-7
Is anorexia nervosa associated with elevated rates of suicide?
Coren S, Hewitt PL.
Department of Psychology, University of British Columbia, Vancouver.
OBJECTIVES: The purpose of this study was to ascertain whether individuals with anorexia nervosa are more likely to commit suicide, as suggested by previously noted associations between anorexia nervosa and mood disorders. These findings suggest that the suicide rate is not elevated among individuals currently suffering from anorexia nervosa.

Ann Intern Med 1973 Jun;78(6):907-9
Prognosis in anorexia nervosa.
Halmi K, Brodland G, Loney J.

Ann Intern Med 1981 Mar;94(3):371-81
Anorexia nervosa.
Schwabe AD, Lippe BM, Chang RJ, Pops MA, Yager J.
The clinical and physiologic features of anorexia nervosa seem to be consequences of a complex interaction among psychologic abnormalities, endocrine disturbances, and malnutrition. Although a spectrum of psychologic disorders has been observed, distortion of body image, weight phobia, disordered perception

of hunger and satiety, and a sense of ineffectiveness are encountered most frequently. Because most of the endocrine abnormalities are reversible with improved nutrition, they are probably secondary to malnutrition rather than to hypothalamic dysfunction. Hypercarotenemia observed in 16 of 21 patients studied recently seems useful in differentiating anorexia nervosa from other forms of malnutrition and weight loss. A combined medical and psychiatric approach has been successful in drastically reducing the mortality of this disorder.
Publication Types: Review

Ann N Y Acad Sci 2000 May;904:614-6
Longitudinal study of patients with anorexia nervosa 6 to 10 years after treatment. Impact of adequate weight restoration on outcome.
Gross G, Russell JD, Beumont PJ, Touyz SW, Roach P, Aslani A, Hansen RD, Allen BJ.
Department of Psychology, University of Trier, Germany.
gaby@psy.rpa.cs.nsw.gov.au

Annu Rev Med 2000;51:299-313
Anorexia and bulimia nervosa.
Kaye WH, Klump KL, Frank GK, Strober M.
University of Pittsburgh, School of Medicine, Department of Psychiatry, Western Psychiatric Institute and Clinic, Pennsylvania 15213, USA.
kayewh@msx.upmc.edu
Anorexia nervosa (AN) and bulimia nervosa (BN) are disorders characterized by abnormal patterns of weight regulation and eating behavior and by disturbances in attitudes and perceptions toward weight and body shape. Etiologic research has indicated substantial genetic influence on these disorders, suggesting significant biological contributions to their development. Obsessional, perfectionistic, and anxious personality styles may be premorbid traits that contribute to this pathogenesis. Studies of neuroendocrine, neuropeptide, and neurotransmitter functioning in patients with AN and BN indicate that disturbances of these systems may contribute to the maintenance as well as the etiology of these sometimes fatal disorders. The efficacy of psychological treatments and pharmacotherapy has been more clearly established for BN than for AN.
Publication Types: Review; Review, tutorial

Arch Gen Psychiatry 1974 Mar;30(3):279-86
Behavior modification of anorexia nervosa.
Agras WS, Barlow DH, Chapin HN, Abel GG, Leitenberg H.

Aust N Z J Psychiatry 1977 Dec;11(4):251-7
Prevalence and prognosis in anorexia nervosa.
Kalucy RS, Crisp AH, Lacey JH, Harding B.

Aust N Z J Psychiatry 1993 Dec;27(4):708-9, 713-4, 717
Comment in: Aust N Z J Psychiatry. 1994 Mar;28(1):147-8
Comment on: Aust N Z J Psychiatry. 1993 Sep;27(3):512-7

Male patients with anorexia nervosa.
Lee S.
Publication Types: Comment Letter

Behav Res Ther 1999 Jan;37(1):1-13
A cognitive behavioural theory of anorexia nervosa.
Fairburn CG, Shafran R, Cooper Z.
Oxford University Department of Psychiatry, Warneford Hospital, UK.
A cognitive behavioural theory of the maintenance of anorexia nervosa is proposed. It is argued that an extreme need to control eating is the central feature of the disorder, and that in Western societies a tendency to judge self-worth in terms of shape and weight is superimposed on this need for self-control. It is suggested that the theory has important implications for treatment.
Publication Types: Review; Review, tutorial

BMJ 1989 Jul 15;299(6692):139-40
The course of anorexia nervosa.
Patton G.
Publication Types: Review; Review, tutorial

Br J Clin Pract 1972 Nov;26(11):509-12
Anorexia nervosa.
Dally P.

Br J Clin Pract 1977 Jun;31(6):80-1
Anorexia nervosa in a male identical twin.
Dowson JH.

Br J Clin Psychol 2000 Jun;39 (Pt 2):193-203
Differential environmental factors in anorexia nervosa: a sibling pair study.
Murphy F, Troop NA, Treasure JL.
Eating Disorders Unit, Institute of Psychiatry, London, UK.
F.M.Murphy@rhbnc.ac.uk
OBJECTIVES: Previous studies have explored differences in psychosocial and familial factors between women who develop anorexia nervosa and those who do not. However, these studies have generally used between-group comparisons. This study looks at the environmental factors which may be antecedents of anorexia nervosa looking at sister pairs where one had anorexia nervosa and the other did not. These results confirm the perceived differences in background environment between women with and women without anorexia nervosa. These issues are discussed in relation to behavioural genetics, family dynamics and psychosexual development.

Br J Clin Psychol 2000 Jun;39 (Pt 2):215-8
Underlying assumptions and core beliefs in anorexia nervosa and dieting.
Cooper M, Turner H.
Isis Education Centre, Warneford Hospital, Oxford, UK.
myra.cooper@oxmhc-tr.anglox.nhs.uk
OBJECTIVE: To investigate assumptions and beliefs in anorexia nervosa and dieting. DESIGN AND METHOD: The Eating Disorder Belief Questionnaire (EDBQ), was administered to patients with anorexia nervosa, dieters and female controls. The cognitive content of anorexia nervosa (both assumptions and negative self-beliefs) differs from that found in dieting. Assumptions about weight and shape may also distinguish

dieters from female controls.

Br J Med Psychol 1969 Jun;42(2):109-18
Anorexia nervosa.
Goodsitt A.

Br J Med Psychol 1974 Dec;47(4):349-61
Aspects of the perceptual disorder in anorexia nervosa.
Crisp AH, Kalucy RS.

Br J Med Psychol 1998 Jun;71 (Pt 2):175-84
Subjective body-image dimensions in normal and anorexic adolescents.
Gila A, Castro J, Toro J, Salamero M.
Section of Child and Adolescent Psychiatry, Corporacio Sanitaria Clinic, Barcelona, Spain.
The subjective body dimensions of adolescent anorexic patients and adolescents from the general population were studied by means of a new technique that combines certain characteristics of the 'body-site estimation' and the 'whole-image adjustment' procedures. The technique used (Subjective Body Dimensions Apparatus-SBDA) reveals the individual's idea of the size of the different parts of his/her body, and produces a life-size global silhouette. Eighty-five female anorexic patients (ages 12 to 18) were compared with 427 adolescents from the general population. For all parts of the body, the anorexic group showed greater overestimation ($p < .0001$) than the comparison group.

Br J Med Psychol 2000 Mar;73 (Pt 1):53-65
The personal construction of death in anorexia nervosa.
Warren B, Beumont PV.
Department of Education, University of Newcastle, NSW, Australia.
edwgw@cc.newcastle.edu.au
This paper reports a study concerned with an attempt to understand the manner in which individuals at high objective risk of death through their own behaviour, understand the phenomenon of death, and their own death.

Br J Psychiatry 1969 Jul;115(524):827-31
Anorexia nervosa: a discriminant function analysis.
Wright WS, Manwell MK, Merrett JD.

Br J Psychiatry 1973 Dec;123(577):711-2
An increase of anorexia nervosa in a university population.
Duddle M.

Br J Psychiatry 1973 Jan;122(566):83-5
A short anorexic behaviour scale.
Slade PD.

Br J Psychiatry 1975;Spec No 9:150-8
Anorexia nervosa.
Crisp AH.
Publication Types: Review

Br J Psychiatry 1987 Jul;151:80-3
Anorexia nervosa in males. A comparison with female patients.
Margo JL.
Oxford Higher Training Scheme in Psychiatry, Warenford Hospital.
The demographic features, clinical picture, antecedent events and family background in 13 male patients with anorexia nervosa are compared with those in a control group of 39 adolescent female anorectics; the

general picture of the illness in males is similar to that in females. Focusing on a group of males, usually less vulnerable to anorexia nervosa, can highlight possible predisposing factors.

Br J Psychiatry 1988 Dec;153:847-8
Anorexia nervosa.
Publication Types: Letter

Br J Psychiatry 1991 Feb;158:284-6
Comment on: Br J Psychiatry. 1990 Apr;156:565-8
Br J Psychiatry. 1990 Nov;157:783-4
Anorexia nervosa across cultures.
Publication Types: Comment Letter

Br J Psychiatry 1991 Feb;158:286-7
Comment in: Br J Psychiatry. 1991 May;158:716-7
Comment on: Br J Psychiatry. 1990 Nov;157:754-7
Anorexia nervosa in the elderly.
Cosford P, Arnold E.
Publication Types: Comment Letter

Br J Psychiatry 1993 Nov;163:697-8
Comment on: Br J Psychiatry. 1993 Aug;163:195-200
How well are 'cured' anorexic nervosa patients?
Hsu LK.
Publication Types: Comment Letter

Br J Psychiatry 1994 Feb;164(2):268-9
Anorexic siblings.
Hall P.
Publication Types: Letter

Br J Psychiatry 1998 Feb;172:189
Comment on: Br J Psychiatry. 1997 Apr;170:381-6
Anorexia and the overvalued idea.
Jones E, Watson JP.
Publication Types: Comment Letter

Br J Psychiatry 1999 Oct;175:306-9
Providing specialised services for anorexia nervosa.
Palmer RL, Treasure J.
Publication Types: Editorial

Br J Psychiatry 2000 Mar;176:298-9
Compulsory treatment in anorexia nervosa.
Beumont PJ.
Publication Types: Letter

Br J Psychiatry Suppl 1988 Jul;(2):20-2
Body image in anorexia nervosa.
Slade PD.
Department of Psychiatry, Liverpool University Medical School, UK.
Publication Types: Review; Review, tutorial

Br J Psychiatry Suppl 1988 Jul;(2):23-6
Body size estimation in anorexia nervosa.
Whitehouse AM, Freeman CP, Annandale A.
Department of Psychiatry, University of Cambridge, Addenbrooke's Hospital.

Br Med J (Clin Res Ed) 1988 Jun 18;296(6638):1736-7
Anorexia nervosa.
Publication Types: Letter

Br Med J 1969 Mar 1;1(643):529-30
Anorexia nervosa.

Br Med J 1972 Dec 23;4(842):686
Anorexia nervosa males.

Br Med J 1973 Apr 21;2(859):158-63
A case of anorexia.

Br Med J 1973 Sep 15;3(880):556
Epidemiology of anorexia nervosa.

Br Med J 1978 Aug 12;2(6135):500
Prevalence of anorexia nervosa.
Crisp AH.
Publication Types: Letter

Can Med Assoc J 1978 Feb 4;118(3):230
Prognosis in anorexia nervosa.
Feldman W.
Publication Types: Letter

Child Care Health Dev 1985 Nov-Dec;11(6):355-73
Anorexia nervosa.
Elston T, Thomas JB.
This paper, following a brief historical note, reviews the literature on anorexia nervosa. The authors are eclectic in their literature survey and also present some experience collected in a hospital school. The paper isintended as a teaching synthesis for clinicians new to this area or for those seeking a brief introduction to the present 'state of the art' in theory and practice.
Publication Types: Review

Clin Endocrinol Metab 1976 Jul;5(2):517-35
Anorexia nervosa: behavioural and hypothalamic aspects.
Vigersky RA, Loriaux DL, Andersen AE, Lipsett MB.
Publication Types: Review

Clin Pediatr (Phila) 1970 Feb;9(2):115-7
Functional anorexia in school-age children.
Poznanski E.

Clin Psychol Rev 1998 Jun;18(4):447-75
Long-term course of anorexia nervosa: response, relapse, remission, and recovery.
Pike KM.
Department of Psychiatry, Columbia University College of Physicians and Surgeons, New York, NY 10032, USA.
There is no predictable or normative long-term course associated with anorexia nervosa. Some Individuals achieve complete recovery; others are ravaged by a chronic disorder; and some die from it. Predicting course and outcome of anorexia nervosa is complicated by the intrinsic complexity of the disorder; a lack of shared terminology in studying the disorder; and a paucity of controlled clinical treatment studies. Based on existing studies, a discussion of treatment outcome and prognostic factors is provided. Clinical recommendations are provided for the clinician who is responsible for the long-term care of an individual with anorexia nervosa.
Publication Types: Review; Review literature

Compr Psychiatry 1968 Nov;9(6):644-51
A naturalistic study of patients with anorexia nervosa admitted to a university medical center.
Ziegler R, Sours JA.

Compr Psychiatry 1993 Nov-Dec;34(6):406-9
Anorexia nervosa and "reverse anorexia" among 108 male bodybuilders.

Pope HG Jr, Katz DL, Hudson JI.
Biological Psychiatry Laboratory, McLean Hospital, Belmont, MA 02178.
Two disorders of body image encountered in a study of 108 bodybuilders are described. In a study of the psychiatric effects of anabolic steroids, structured interviews were administered to 55 bodybuilders who had used anabolic steroids and 53 non-user controls. Nine (8.3%) of the subjects, two of whom were former anorexics, described a "reverse anorexia" syndrome, where they believed that they appeared small and weak even though they were actually large and muscular. Disorders of body image, including both anorexia nervosa and its reverse form, may occur frequently in men who lift weights regularly. Reverse anorexia may precipitate or perpetuate the use of anabolic steroids in some individuals.

Compr Ther 1978 May;4(5):44-50
Anorexia nervosa.
Brooks MH, Braithwaite SS, Barbato AL.

Compr Ther 1987 Sep;13(9):16-21
Anorexia nervosa: a syndrome of starvation dependence.
Luby ED, Marrazzi MA, Sperti S.
Department of Psychiatry, Harper-Grace Hospitals, Detroit, MI 48201.
Publication Types: Review; Review, tutorial

Compr Ther 1990 Dec;16(12):24-34
Anorexia nervosa: evaluation and treatment.
Powers PS.
University of South Florida College of Medicine, Tampa 33613.
Publication Types: Review; Review, tutorial

Compr Ther 1997 Oct;23(10):664-71
Anorexia nervosa.
Beresin EV.
Harvard Medical School, Boston, Massachusetts, USA.
Publication Types: Review; Review, tutorial

Curr Concepts Nutr 1982;11:139-49
Anorexia nervosa.
Baker L, Lyen KR.
Publication Types: Review

Curr Concepts Nutr 1988;16:125-35
Appetite regulation in anorexia nervosa.
Halmi KA.
Cornell University Medical College, New York Hospital-Westchester Division, White Plains.

Eat Weight Disord 1998 Mar;3(1):1-6
Outpatient group therapy for anorexia nervosa: a preliminary study.
Fernandez-Aranda F, Bel M, Jimenez S, Vinuales M, Turon J, Vallejo J.
Department of Psychiatry, University Hospital of Bellvitge, c/Feixa Llarga s/n, 08907 Barcelona, Spain.
Group therapy is generally recognized as an important form of psychotherapy for anorexia nervosa patients, but there are few controlled studies of its effectiveness. The aim of the current study was to determine the effectiveness of cognitive-behavioural therapy (CBT) for the treatment of anorexia nervosa in outpatients. Further research should assess the

effectiveness of therapeutic groups more intensively because of their economic advantages.
Publication Types: Evaluation studies

Eur J Clin Nutr 1998 Sep;52(9):655-62
Body composition changes in anorexia nervosa.
Polito A, Cuzzolaro M, Raguzzini A, Censi L, Ferro-Luzzi A.
National Institute of Nutrition, Rome, Italy.
To assess the body composition changes in anorexia nervosa and after medium term recovery. This study shows that AN is a condition of reduced body fat as well as of muscle mass, with a slightly reduced bone mass. In the course of rehabilitation, most of the weight regained is represented by fat, while the muscle mass appears to lag behind, at least in the medium term.

Fam Process 1977 Dec;16(4):455-65
A systems theory approach to a case of anorexia nervosa.
Caille P, Abrahamsen P, Girolami C, Sorbye B.
Systems theory views mental and psychosomatic illness as the natural consequences of a dysfunctional human interactional group. The symptom chosen isaffected by the symptom carrier's age, sex, and unique individual characteristics. However, the reason the symptom develops and is maintained is to be found in the system(s) of which the symptom carrier is a part. There is a hope that this article's description of a typical treatment situation will demonstrate how a systems theory approach differs from other forms of family therapy in its evaluations and techniques.

Geriatrics 1990 Dec;45(12):59-62, 65-6
Anorexia in older patients: its meaning and management.
Morley JE.
Geriatric Research, Education, and Clinical Center, Department of Veterans Affairs, St. Louis, Missouri.
In the elderly, clinically significant weight loss is closely related to malnutrition, the causes of which can proliferate in this age group. Clinicians must therefore keep a wide range of possible etiologies in mind when evaluating these patients. These fall into the general categories of social, psychological, medical, and age-related. Isolating the cause will direct what is often simple, effective, and, perhaps, life-saving therapy.
Publication Types: Review; Review, tutorial

Gut 1968 Aug;9(4):370-2
Primary anorexia nervosa.
Crisp AH.
Publication Types: Review

Hosp J 1993;9(2-3):73-83
Appetite stimulants in terminal care: treatment of anorexia.
Grauer PA.
Anorexia is a common problem in terminally ill patients. The loss of appetite brings with it physical, psychological, and social problems. Effective treatment, therefore, should be multidimensional. Total parenteral nutrition can also sustain meaningful life for many terminally ill patients, but it is rarely successful in alleviating the anorexia associated with terminal

illness.

Hosp Pract (Off Ed) 1996 Apr 15;31(4):16
Anorexia nervosa.
Cheng TO.
Publication Types: Letter

Int J Eat Disord 1993 Nov;14(3):297-304
Anorexia nervosa and total parenteral nutrition.
Mehler PS, Weiner KL.
Columbine Hospital, Colorado.
Anorexia nervosa can have a devastating outcome. There is a high rate of treatment failures and recidivism among anorectic patients. Further, it isgenerally accepted that unless one can effectuate a significant weight gain in these patients, treatment is even more likely to fail. Total parenteral nutrition (TPN) offers an alternative mode of treatment to be used in the armamentarium to successfully treat anorexia nervosa.
Publication Types: Review; Review, tutorial

Int J Eat Disord 1997 Apr;21(3):261-72
Recovery from anorexia nervosa: a sociological perspective.
Garrett CJ.
Department of Behavioural and Social Science, Faculty of Health Studies, University of Western Sydney, Nepean, Australia.
The focus of this article was on the process of recovery from anorexia nervosa, rather than on its etiology. It seeks for sociological, instead of clinical, reasons for recovery. Anorexia and recovery are conceptualized as two phases in an ascetic rite of passage which involves a confrontation with death and an eventual return to fuller community life. Suggestions are offered concerning the ways this insight can be translated into clinical practice.

Int J Eat Disord 1998 Dec;24(4):381-93
Behavioral activation and lack of concern, core symptoms of anorexia nervosa?
Casper RC.
Department of Psychiatry and Behavioral Sciences, Stanford University School of Medicine, CA 94305, USA.
The core symptoms of anorexia nervosa have remained points of debate. The goal of this paper is a close study of unexpected and paradoxical symptoms in anorexia nervosa which are described in the literature but which, for the most part, have escaped the attention of investigator. Areas of research to test this hypothesis, positing starvation-induced arousal or activation as a physiological dysregulation in anorexia nervosa which would powerfully support food avoidance, are discussed.

Int J Eat Disord 1998 Jan;23(1):77-82
Conscious and preconscious processing of food, body weight and shape, and emotion-related words in women with anorexia nervosa.
Sackville T, Schotte DE, Touyz SW, Griffiths R, Beumont PJ.
School of Psychology, University of New South Wales, Australia.
The present study was conducted to extend prior research on attention toward food and body weight and shape-related stimuli in women with eating disorders. METHOD: A

modified Stroop color-naming task was completed by women with anorexia nervosa and by control females subdivided on a measure of dietary restraint. The findings suggest that both thinness and fatness are especially salient to women with anorexia. The lack of effects for emotion words suggests that these findings do not reflect a valence effect. It was found no evidence for preconscious attentional biases in the masked condition.

Int J Eat Disord 1998 Mar;23(2):207-12
Anorexia nervosa in an Arab culture.
Abou-Saleh MT, Younis Y, Karim L.
Department of Psychiatry and Behavioural Sciences, Faculty of Medicine and Health Sciences, United Arab Emirates University, Al Ain, United Arab Emirates.
The available literature indicates that anorexia nervosa is rare in Arab culture. Reported were 5 cases of anorexia nervosa: 3 female and 2 male patients.
Two are UAE nationals, 2 were Omanis, and 1 was Sudanese. The occurrence of these cases is discussed in the context of sociocultural changes and the increasing westernization of the UAE society.

Int J Eat Disord 1999 Dec;26(4):397-405
The ups and downs of anorexia nervosa.
Lucas AR, Crowson CS, O'Fallon WM, Melton LJ 3rd.
Division of Child and Adolescent Psychiatry, Mayo Clinic, Rochester, Minnesota
55905, USA.
We updated our incidence study by identifying Rochester, Minnesota, residents diagnosed with anorexia nervosa during 1985 through 1989. METHOD: From a community-based epidemiologic resource, 2,806 medical records with diagnoses including anorexia nervosa, eating disorder, bulimia, amenorrhea and other conditions were screened to identify new cases of anorexia nervosa. The disorder remained less frequent among older females. Anorexia nervosa remains a relatively common disorder among young females. While there are short-term fluctuations in incidence, the long-term increasing trend for 15 to 24-year-old females has continued.

Int J Eat Disord 1999 Mar;25(2):135-42
Atypical anorexia nervosa: separation from typical cases in course and outcome in a long-term prospective study.
Strober M, Freeman R, Morrell W.
Neuropsychiatric Institute & Hospital, School of Medicine, University of California at Los Angeles 90024-1759, USA.
Assessing differences in long-term course and outcome between typical and atypical cases of anorexia nervosa. A naturalistic, longitudinal prospective design was used to assess recovery, relapse, and onset of binge eating over 10 to 15 years in patients ascertained through a university-based specialty treatment program. Atypical anorexia nervosa was distinguished from the diagnostically prototypic form of the disorder based on the continuous absence of morbid fear of weight gain and body size distortion during the inpatient phase of

treatment. Patients were assessed semiannually for 5 years then annually thereafter until the final visit. RESULTS: Compared to pure cases of anorexia nervosa, atypical cases were less likely to drop weight after discharge, recovered more rapidly, and had lower cumulative risk for developing binge eating.

Int J Eat Disord 1999 Mar;25(2):177-86
Anorexia nervosa: friend or foe?
Serpell L, Treasure J, Teasdale J, Sullivan V.
Eating Disorders Unit, University of London, United Kingdom.
The aim of this study was to examine anorexics' attitudes towards anorexia nervosa. Anorexic patients were asked to write two letters to their anorexia nervosa, one addressing it as a friend and the other addressing it as an enemy. A coding scheme was developed using a "Grounded Theory" methodology to group recurrent themes. The positive themes found in the letters are important indicators of factors which may maintain anorexia nervosa. The use of the letters to examine these factors has important clinical implications which are outlined.

Int J Eat Disord 2000 Sep;28(2):139-47
Outcome of anorexia nervosa: eating attitudes, personality, and parental bonding.
Bulik CM, Sullivan PF, Fear JL, Pickering A.
Virginia Commonwealth University, Department of Psychiatry, Virginia Institute for Psychiatric and Behavioral Genetics, Richmond, Virginia 23298-0126, USA.
cbulik@hsc.vcu.edu
BACKGROUND: We examined eating attitudes, personality, and parental bonding in women with a history of anorexia nervosa stratified by degree of recovery in comparison to randomly selected controls. We were interested in the distinguishing characteristics of recovery and of chronic anorexia nervosa. The domains of personality, character, and parental bonding differ among categories of recovery in anorexia nervosa. Whether these differences contribute to recovery or emerge during recovery or lack thereof remains an unanswered question.

Int J Psychoanal 1974;55(4):567-79
The anorexia nervosa syndrome.
Sours JA.

Int J Psychoanal 1984;65 (Pt 3):315-22
The problem of anorexia nervosa.
Boris HN.
In anorexia nervosa the pain of hunger or, alternatively (in bulemia), of glut recalls Freud's aphorism that the man with toothache cannot fall in love. But object longing remains and stimulates such envy that the anorectic must project her wishes; she is not be found wanting. The use of projection, in turn, complicates self-other boundaries, with the result that she experiences not only people but even food as overpowering. This, then, excites more envy, indeed an envy so ruinous that self-starvation or compulsive evacuations are employed additionally to make reparation. Because all of this condenses into Less isMore, the anorexic poses particular problems for analytic

treatment, which isthe subject of a companion paper.

Int Psychiatry Clin 1970;7(1):139-228
Anorexia nervosa in one of identical twins.
Gifford S, Murawski BJ, Pilot ML.

Int Psychiatry Clin 1970;7(1):3-24
Changing approaches to anorexia nervosa.
Bruch H.

Int Psychiatry Clin 1970;7(1):37-137
Anorexia nervosa. A survey of the literature and review of 30 cases.
Rowland CV Jr.
Publication Types: Historical article

Ir Med J 1978 Mar 18;71(4):120-2
Marginal anorexia nervosa.
Griffin JA, Hennessy A, Warnes H.

J Adolesc 1988 Dec;11(4):361-71
Anorexia, psychoanalysis, and feminism: fantasy and reality.
Sayers J.
Keynes College, University of Kent, Canterbury, U.K.
Two distinct trends inform current psychoanalytic and feminist approaches to anorexia: one focuses on its roots in the fantasy, the other in the reality of childhood and adolescent deprivation and abuse. In outlining these two approaches, this article shows how both increasingly attend to the place of the mother to the neglect of the father in the genesis of anorexia--a shift of perspective somewhat redressed by systemic family therapy.

J Adv Nurs 2000 Jul;32(1):139-47
Caring for adolescent females with anorexia nervosa: registered nurses' perspective.
King SJ, de Sales Turner.
Deakin University, Burwood, Victoria, Australia.
sking@deakin.edu.au
This phenomenological study was undertaken to explore in depth the experiences of registered nurses caring for adolescent anorexic females within paediatric wards of general hospitals in Victoria, Australia. A qualitative design underpinned by the philosophy of Edmund Husserl was employed for this study.

J Am Acad Child Adolesc Psychiatry 1991 Sep;30(5):853-4
Comment on: J Am Acad Child Adolesc Psychiatry. 1991 Mar;30(2):283-9
Anorexia and family dynamics.
Jacobs W.
Publication Types: Comment Letter

J Am Acad Child Adolesc Psychiatry 1999 Jul;38(7):829-37
Recovery and relapse in anorexia and bulimia nervosa: a 7.5-year follow-up study.
Herzog DB, Dorer DJ, Keel PK, Selwyn SE, Ekeblad ER, Flores AT, Greenwood DN, Burwell RA, Keller MB.
Harvard Medical School, Boston, USA.
To assess the course and outcome of anorexia nervosa (AN) and bulimia nervosa (BN) at a median of 90 months of follow-up in a large cohort of women with eating disorders. The full recovery rate of women with BN

was significantly higher than that of women with AN, with 74% of those with BN and 33% of those with AN achieving full recovery by a median of 90 months of follow-up. The findings suggest that the course of AN is characterized by high rates of partial recovery and low rates of full recovery, while the course of BN is characterized by higher rates of both partial and full recovery.

J Am Acad Child Adolesc Psychiatry
2000 Mar;39(3):378-85
Detection and importance of laxative use in adolescents with anorexia nervosa.
Turner J, Batik M, Palmer LJ, Forbes D, McDermott BM.
Princess Margaret Hospital for Children, Perth, Western Australia.
The frequency of laxative use in adolescents with anorexia nervosa is poorly described. This study of adolescents with anorexia nervosa examined self-report and biochemical screening methods for the detection of laxative use, the pattern of laxative use in this population over time, and the associated medical complications and psychopathology. The frequency of laxative use from self-report alone was 12%; combined with urine screening it was 19%. The frequency of laxative use increased to 32% with prospective follow-up. Medical complications were associated with laxative use at follow-up. Laxative use was associated with longer duration of disease and with higher scores on the Eating Disorders Examination subscale Eating Concern. Laxative use is common among adolescents with anorexia nervosa, and the risk of associated medical complications increases over time. Biochemical screening will improve detection of laxative use. Longer duration of illness and greater Eating Concern scores are associated with increased risk of laxative use, and monitoring patients at increased risk is important.

J Am Acad Child Adolesc Psychiatry
2001 Feb;40(2):129-30
Therapy for anorexia nervosa.
Gelbaugh S, Ramos M, Soucar E, Urena R.
Publication Types: Letter

J Am Acad Child Psychiatry 1976
Summer;15(3):523-34
Identical male twins discordant for anorexia nervosa. A case study.
Wiener JM.

J Am Acad Child Psychiatry 1979
Summer;18(3):527-36
Identical twins simultaneously concordant for anorexia nervosa.
Simmons RC, Kessler MD.

J Am Acad Psychoanal 1989
Spring;17(1):43-64
Infantile anorexia nervosa: a developmental disorder or separation and individuation.
Chatoor I.
Psychiatry and Behavioral Sciences, George Washington University, School of Medicine.
Infantile anorexia nervosa is an eating disorder that has its onset during the early developmental stage of separation and individuation between the ages of six months and three years. Infantile anorexia nervosa is characterized by food refusal and leads to failure to thrive. Treatment is

aimed toward helping the parents understand and promote the developmental process of somatopsychological differentiation. Initially, a behavioral-cognitive approach is used; however, parents who struggle with unresolved issues around dependency and control require further psychotherapy.

J Am Geriatr Soc 1985 Mar;33(3):213-5
Anorexia nervosa in the elderly.
Price WA, Giannini AJ, Colella J.

J Anal Psychol 1976 Jul;21(2):193-207
A psychological study of anorexia nervosa. An account of the relationship between psychic factors and bodily functioning.
Seligman E.

J Child Psychol Psychiatry 1997 Mar;38(3):271-6
Outcome of anorexia nervosa in the younger patient.
Steinhausen HC.
Department of Child and Adolescent Psychiatry, University of Zurich, Switzerland.
Publication Types: Review; Review, tutorial

J Clin Exp Neuropsychol 1998 Aug;20(4):548-64
Neuropsychological consequences of extreme weight loss and dietary restriction in patients with anorexia nervosa.
Mathias JL, Kent PS.
Department of Psychology, University of Adelaide, South Australia.
psyj-mat@psychology.adelaide.edu.au
This study examined the effects of weight loss and nutritional status on the cognitive performance of patients with anorexia nervosa. The intellectual, memory, attentional, verbal fluency and visuospatial abilities of 34 females with anorexia were compared to that of 31 normal weight-for-height females. The failure to find many cognitive deficits in this sample may reflect the fact that few patients with anorexia exhibited frank nutritional deficiencies.
Publication Types: Clinical trial

J Community Health Nurs 1987;4(1):57-60
Anorexia nervosa: case finding of families at risk.
MacMullen NJ, Brucker MC.

J Maine Med Assoc 1980 Feb;71(2):37
Anorexia nervosa.
Tobin HW.

J Nerv Ment Dis 2000 Aug;188(8):537-42
Self-injurious behavior in anorexia nervosa.
Favaro A, Santonastaso P.
Department of Neurological and Psychiatric Sciences, University of Padua, Padova, Italy.
Recent reports have postulated the existence of two different types of self-injurious behavior: impulsive and compulsive. The aim of the present study is to analyze the dimensionality of self-injurious behavior and to study the link between self-injurious behavior and clinical features in anorexia nervosa. The study involved 236 consecutive patients with anorexia nervosa, diagnosed by DSM-IV criteria. Subjects were evaluated by means of a semistructured interview and self-reported

questionnaires, such as the Eating Disorders Inventory and Hopkins Symptom Checklist. A principal component analysis was used to study the dimensionality of different types of self-injurious behavior, including purging. Our findings confirm the distinction between impulsive and compulsive self-injurious behavior. The dimensions appear to be represented as a continuum in both the anorexia nervosa diagnostic subgroups. A third distinct dimension emerged that included self-induced vomiting and laxative/diuretics abuse. Childhood sexual abuse and anxiety significantly predict the presence of impulsive self-injury, whereas obsessionality and age predict compulsive self-injury. The coexistence of a positive score on both dimensions of self-injurious behavior was the strongest predictor of treatment dropout. The present study highlights the importance of self-injurious behavior; it should be given due consideration in future outcome studies on anorexia nervosa

J Nurs Care 1982 Jan;15(1):14-6
Anorexia nervosa: choosing to starve.
Ferrara CB.

J Palliat Care 1994 Spring;10(1):51-3
Anorexia.
Billings JA.
Massachusetts General Hospital, Boston.
Publication Types: Review; Review, tutorial

J Pediatr 1986 Jan;108(1):163-4
Outcome in anorexia nervosa.
Silverman J, Halmi KA.
Publication Types: Letter

J Pediatr Perinat Nutr 1987 Spring-Summer;1(1):13-26
Anorexia nervosa in adolescence: an overview.
Opremcak C.
Publication Types: Review; Review, tutorial

J Psychiatr Nurs Ment Health Serv 1976 Oct;14(10):28, 35-7
Anorexia nervosa.
Dikowitz S.

J Psychiatr Res 1979;15(4):239-51
Attitudinal dimensions in anorexia nervosa.
Goldberg SC, Halmi KA, Eckert ED, Casper RC, Davis JM, Roper M.

J Psychiatr Res 1985;19(2-3):305-13
Anorexic syndromes in the male.
Fichter MM, Daser C, Postpischil F.
Study of forty-two male patients with an anorexic syndrome were assessed personally (n =29) or by the reviewing of the case-notes. Twenty-nine male patients were classified as primary anorexia nervosa and they were compared to our series of atypical male patients and a series of 23 female anorexia nervosa patients. Male and female anorexia nervosa cases were very similar in their personality profile and symptomatology; however, male cases were more preoccupied in their thoughts with food, weight etc., and showed more hyperactivity, more achievement orientation and more sexual anxiety than female cases. Male anorexia nervosa patients were more extraverted and scored "superfeminine" on the masculinity vs

feminity scale (FPI). A continuum from "true" anorexia nervosa to atypical cases and to secondary loss of appetite was observed.

J Psychiatr Res 1985;19(2-3):315-21
Anorexia nervosa in the male: clinical features and follow-up of nine patients.
Hall A, Delahunt JW, Ellis PM.
Nine male patients formed approximately 5% of patients presenting with anorexia nervosa from a population area. Their clinical and family features and outcome at a mean of 5 1/2 yr from onset were similar to those of female patients. All patients lost libido during the syndrome. In four patients at average weight at follow-up the level of libido and sexual activity was related to testosterone level, other hormonal investigations being normal in post pubertal patients. All patients had a history of increased attention to bodily appearance and/or diet before the onset of the illness (e.g. aberrant body size or appearance, close contact with an eating disorder patient).

J Psychiatr Res 1985;19(2-3):449-51
Correcting the eating disorder in anorexia nervosa.
Wilson AJ, Touyz SW, O'Connor M, Beumont PJ.
The aim of the present study was to assess whether direct informational feedback using videotape recordings would improve abnormal eating behaviour in patients with anorexia nervosa. A statistically significant improvement was noted in the occurrence of obsessional eating behaviour and in table manners. However, there was no change in the speed of eating, disposal of food or behaviours which reduce caloric intake. The implications of these findings for the treatment and prognosis of anorexia nervosa are discussed.
Publication Types: Clinical trial; Randomized controlled trial

J Psychosoc Nurs Ment Health Serv 1984 Jan;22(1):11-3, 17-20
Postadolescent onset male anorexia.
Kiecolt-Glaser J, Dixon K.

J Psychosom Res 1988;32(6):561-71
Anorexia nervosa: evidence for a genetic basis.
Holland AJ, Sicotte N, Treasure J.
Department of Psychiatry, Institute of Psychiatry, London, U.K.
This paper reports the preliminary results of a combined twin and family study of anorexia nervosa. Fifty-six per cent of the 25 female monozygotic (MZ) twin pairs and 5% of the 20 female dizygotic (DZ) twin pairs were concordant for anorexia nervosa. Nearly 5% of other female first degree relatives also had a history of anorexia nervosa. Analysis of data from the Eating Disorders Questionnaire (EDI) given to the twins and data as to weight loss, length of amenorrhoea and other characteristics of anorexia nervosa, together with the twin and family data, supports the hypothesis that genetic factors are very significant in the aetiology of anorexia nervosa. Analysis of this data using established techniques of psychiatric genetics suggested that up to 80% of the variance in liability to anorexia nervosa may be accounted for by

genetic factors. The problems of this type of analysis are discussed as is the background to the genetics of weight and appetite control. A genetic/environmental model accounting for the features of anorexia nervosa isproposed.

J R Coll Physicians Lond 1982 Jul;16(3):191-4
The diagnosis of anorexia nervosa.
Mattingly D, Bhanji S.

J Singapore Paediatr Soc 1985;27(3-4):158-65
Anorexia nervosa.
Lyen KR.

J Tenn Med Assoc 1966 Sep;59(9):865-70
Pre-pubertal anorexia nervosa.
Kyger K.

Lancet 1979 Jan;1(8107):61-5
Outcome of anorexia nervosa.
Hsu LK, Crisp AH, Harding B.
100 females with anorexia nervosa were followed up 4-8 years after first presentation. Poor outcome could be positively associated with clinical data such as longer duration of illness, older age of onset and presentation, lower weight during illness and at presentation, presence of symptoms such as bulimia, vomiting, and anxiety when eating with others, poor childhood social adjustment, and poor parental relationships.

Lancet 1979 Sep 15;2(8142):574-5
Anorexia nervosa in males.
Hay GG, Leonard JC.
Five cases of anorexia nervosa in males aged 13--23 years are described. Four patients presented to a general medical outpatient clinic with emaciation, and the fifth was diagnosed retrospectively. Sinus bradycardia was a useful pointer to the diagnosis, which was confirmed by the finding of characteristic psychopathological features of a relentless "pursuit of thinness", along with a fear of becoming obese.

Lancet 1987 Mar 28;1(8535):751-2
Trends in anorexia nervosa.
Publication Types: Letter

Lancet 1988 Apr 23;1(8591):928-30
Anorexia nervosa in 1888.
Silverman JA.
Department of Pediatrics, Columbia University College of Physicians and Surgeons, New York, NY.
Publication Types: Historical article

Lancet 1998 Oct 10;352(9135):1192
Functional anatomy of calorie fear in anorexia nervosa.
Ellison Z, Foong J, Howard R, Bullmore E, Williams S, Treasure J.
Publication Types: Letter

Lancet 1998 Oct 31;352(9138):1445-6
Refeeding of anorexics: wasteful not wilful.
Russell J, Baur L, Beumont P, Byrnes S, Zipfel S.
Publication Types: Letter

Mayo Clin Proc 1988 May;63(5):511-3
Anorexia nervosa: who are you? Where are you?
Andersen AE.
Publication Types: Editorial

Med J Aust 1979 Jun 30;1(13):587-9
Psychosocial dynamics in anorexia

nervosa.
Rickarby GA.
Anorexia nervosa represents a self-destructive struggle for separate identity, and cultural factors play a part in the present increasing incidence. This paper presents a broad view, which embraces family dynamics and the natural history of the disease, to clarify important issues in its management and prevention. Both family and individual psychotherapy may have a place in the patient's personal rehabilitation.

Med J Aust 2001 Feb 5;174(3):155-6
Anorexia nervosa, infertility and pregnancy.
Beumont P, Tam P.
Publication Types: Letter

Med Times 1967 Jan;95(1):98-105
Anorexia nervosa.
Black MM.

Med Times 1976 May;104(5):108-18
The enigma of anorexia nervosa.
Bruch H.

Metabolism 1968 Dec;17(12):1109-18
Aspects of fat metabolism in anorexia nervosa.
Crisp AH, Blendis LM, Pawan GL.

N Engl J Med 1989 Mar 16;320(11):736-7
The prevalence of anorexia nervosa.
Ben-Tovim DI, Morton J.
Publication Types: Letter

N Y State J Med 1968 Jun 1;68(11):1363-9
Clinical studies in anorexia nervosa syndrome.
Sours JA.

N Z Med J 1976 Oct 27;84(574):309-12
Anorexia nervosa: a study of 44 strictly defined cases.
Fox KC, James NM.
Forty-four patients with strictly defined anorexia nervosa were studied. They were found to come from the higher socio-economic levels and to be the early born of older parents. Their families were of average size, but females were over-represented. Premorbid obesity was uncommon, but over two-thirds had secondary depression. The treatment methods used until 1974 showed no great variation in success. Poor prognosis was most commonly linked to use of purgatives. A new treatment programme involving re-feeding to reach ideal weight and followed by psychotherapy shows encouraging results.

Nat Med 1996 Apr;2(4):366-7
Anorexia nervosa--more than an eating disorder.
Russell JD, Hunt GE.
Publication Types: Letter

New Dir Ment Health Serv 1986 Fall;(31):13-9
Anorexia nervosa: an affective disorder.
Munoz RA, Amado H.

Nurs Care 1976 Oct;9(10):28-31
Anorexia nervosa; a self-imposed starvation.
Orr R.

Nurs Mirror Midwives J 1968 Nov 15;127(20):38-41

Anorexia nervosa.
Hatherly F.

Nurs Mirror Midwives J 1974 Mar 22;138(1):84-6
Anorexia nervosa.
Joynes V.

Nurs Stand 1997 Dec 10-16;12(12):41-5; quiz 46-7
Anorexia nervosa.
Halek C.
Annex Nursing Development Unit, Pathfinder NHS Trust, London.

Nurs Times 1975 Jan 23;71(4):134-5
Anorexia nervosa.
Baldwin W.

Nurs Times 1976 Mar 18;72(11):407-8
Anorexia nervosa.
Lacey JH.

Nurs Times 1984 Aug 1-7;80(31):28-32
Anorexia nervosa.
Biley F, Savage S.

Nutr Rev 1968 Sep;26(9):276-7
Anorexia nervosa.
Publication Types: Review

Nutr Rev 1981 Feb;39(2):99-103
Anorexia nervosa.
Schleimer K.
Publication Types: Review

Nutrition 1996 Jan;12(1 Suppl):S48-51
Cancer anorexia: new pathogenic and therapeutic insights.
Cangiano C, Laviano A, Muscaritoli M, Meguid MM, Cascino A, Fanelli FR.
Department of Clinical Medicine, University La Sapienza, Rome, Italy.
During tumor growth, anorexia and reduced food intake markedly contribute to the development of malnutrition, thus worsening overall patients' survival. A better understanding of the pathophysiology of eating behavior may lead to new and more effective therapies, aiming at counteracting the detrimental effects of anorexia and reduced food intake on nutritional status and survival in cancer patients.
Publication Types: Review; Review, tutorial

Obes Res 1997 Sep;5(5):498-502
Comment in: Obes Res. 1997 Sep;5(5):489-91
Anorexia nervosa (apepsia hysterica, anorexia hysterica). 1868.
Gull, WW.
Publication Types: Biography; Classical article; Historical article

Ohio State Med J 1969 Nov;65(11):1107-9
Work and the anorexia nervosa patient.
Miller SI, Browning CH.

Pediatr Ann 1984 Jul;13(7):538-42
Anorexia nervosa and binge vomiting.
Collipp PJ.

Pediatr Nurs 1989 Nov-Dec;15(6):612-3
Comment on: Pediatr Nurs. 1989 Jul-Aug;15(4):380, 389
The management of anorexia.
Mead AF.
Publication Types: Comment Letter

Pediatr Pulmonol Suppl 1997;16:169
Diaphragmatic function in severely malnourished patients with anorexia

nervosa.
Murciano D.
Inserm U 408, Clinique de Pneumologie, Hopital Beaujon, Clichy, France.
Publication Types: Review; Review, tutorial

Physiol Behav 1991 Nov;50(5):945-9
Activity-based anorexia: relationship to gender and activity-stress ulcers.
Doerries LE, Stanley EZ, Aravich PF.
Department of Psychology, Christopher Newport College, Newport News, VA 23606.
The phenomena of activity-based anorexia (ABA) and the activity-stress ulcer (ASU) both involve paradigms in which the food intake of rats is restricted and the animals are allowed voluntary exercise in a running wheel. This study determined the susceptibility of male and female rats to ABA and ASU following 25- and 30-percent losses of their original body weights. It was concluded that ASUs are a consequence rather than a cause of ABA, and that there is a sexually "dimorphic" susceptibility to ABA but not ASUs.

Postgrad Med 1987 Oct;82(5):32, 35
Anorexia nervosa.
Cheng TO.
Publication Types: Letter

Postgrad Med 1990 Jun;87(8):161-5, 168
Anorexia nervosa in males.
Barry A, Lippmann SB.
Department of Psychiatry and Behavioral Sciences, University of Louisville School of Medicine.
Although anorexia nervosa is usually considered a disorder of young women and girls, 5% to 10% of cases occur in men and boys. Onset can range from prepubertal years to adulthood. The unique conflicts that may lead to anorexia nervosa in males must be considered when treating these patients.

Postgrad Med J 1966 Feb;42(484):86-92
Anorexia nervosa in an identical twin.
Crisp A.

Postgrad Med J 1977 Mar;53(617):146-51
Primary anorexia nervosa (weight phobia) in males.
Hasan MK, Tibbetts RW.
Ten cases of primary anorexia nervosa (weight phobia) in males (as against 196 females) have been treated in the United Birmingham Hospitals over 19 years. Six illustrative case histories are described briefly. The heavy loading with consistent abnormalities of psychiatric interest makes it very probable that weight phobia is primarily a psychiatric disorder.

Postgrad Med J 1995 Dec;71(842):712-6
Comment in: Postgrad Med J. 1996 Jun;72(848):383
Anorexia nervosa--diagnosis, aetiology, and treatment.
Hartman D.
Department of Mental Health Sciences, St George's Hospital Medical School, London, UK.
The aetiology, assessment and treatment of anorexia nervosa are reviewed in the light of the classical accounts of Morton, Lasegue and Gull. Psychological theories of aetiology are discussed with reference to Bruch, Crisp, Palazzoli and Minuchin: the common theme is the

reaction of the patient and her family to the physical and social changes of puberty. Individual and/or family psychotherapy is seen as central to the treatment of anorexia nervosa, and the relevant clinical research is reviewed. The roles of general practitioners, general psychiatrists and eating disorder specialists are discussed in the light of recent consensus treatment guidelines.
Publication Types: Review; Review, tutorial

Postgrad Med J 1996 Jun;72(848):383
Comment on: Postgrad Med J. 1995 Dec;71(842):712-6
Anorexia nervosa.
Cheng TO.
Publication Types: Comment Letter

Prim Care 1981 Mar;8(1):19-31
Anorexia nervosa.
Klibanski A.
Publication Types: Review

Prim Care 1987 Mar;14(1):177-201
Anorexia nervosa.
Long TJ.
Anorexia nervosa is a complex neuroendocrine-psychiatric illness that affects adolescents; its origins and pathophysiology are still poorly understood. The typical psychologic and physiologic characteristics of the illness are discussed, and the multidisciplinary team approach to diagnosis and management is outlined.
Publication Types: Review

Prof Care Mother Child 1999;9(5):134-6
Anorexia: the warning signs.
Hartley P.
Department of Psychology, University of Manchester.
Publication Types: Review; Review, tutorial

Prog Cardiovasc Nurs 1999 Spring;14(2):75-6
What is the most serious complication for patients with anorexia nervosa?
Fukoka Y, Ide B, Drew B.
Department of Care Coordination, UCSF Stanford Health Care, UCSF Medical Center 94143-0210, USA.

Psychiatr Dev 1989 Winter;7(4):395-407
Long-term stability of anorexia nervosa treatments: follow-up study of 218 patients.
Engel K, Wittern M, Hentze M, Meyer AE.
Psychosomatic Department, University Clinic Hamburg-Eppendorf, Germany.
We are reporting about the stability of n = 218 female in-patient treatments of Anorexia nervosa carried out at the University Clinic at Hamburg-Eppendorf from 1965 to 1979 mainly by a special program: introductory interview (with the family present), in-patient medical treatment (bed-rest, phenothiazines, tube-feeding), strict regimen and addressing the patients' conflict situation.
The average interval between the end of therapy and the follow-up examination was 9.8 years. Possible interpretations of our results and consequences for therapy are presented.

Psychiatr Genet 1998 Spring;8(1):1-12
Genetics and anorexia nervosa: a review of candidate genes.
Gorwood P, Bouvard M, Mouren-

Simeoni MC, Kipman A, Ades J.
Psychiatric Department, Hospital Louis Mourier, Colombes, France.
pgorwood@imaginet.fr

Anorexia nervosa is a severe disorder which seems likely to have a multifactorial aetiology. However, several studies have stressed that genetic factors play a significant role. Attention is paid to psychological dimensions, clinical symptoms, co-morbidity frequency, pharmacological data, and biological measures that characterize anorexia nervosa.

Publication Types: Review; Review, academic

Psychiatr Med 1989;7(4):293-315
An overview of the treatment of anorexia nervosa.
Eckert ED, Mitchell JE.
University of Minnesota.
Publication Types: Review; Review, tutorial

Psychol Med 1973 May;3(2):200-3
The epidemiology of anorexia nervosa.
Kendell RE, Hall DJ, Hailey A, Babigian HM.

Psychol Med 1973 Nov;3(4):521-4
Monozygotic twins concordant and discordant for anorexia nervosa.
Halmi K, Brodland G.

Psychol Med 1980 Nov;10(4):647-56
Socio-cultural factors in the development of anorexia nervosa.
Garner DM, Garfinkel PE.

A population of professional dance (N = 183) and modelling (N = 56) students, who by career choice must focus increased attention and control over their body shapes, was studied. All but one case developed the disorder while studying dance. Within the dance group those from the most competitive environments had the greatest frequency of anorexia nervosa. These data suggest that both pressures to be slim and achievement expectations are risk factors in the development of anorexia nervosa. The influence of socio-cultural determinants are discussed within the context of anorexia nervosa as a multidetermined disorder.

Psychol Med 1987 Nov;17(4):843-59
Psychobiology of anorexia nervosa.
Ploog DW, Pirke KM.
Max Planck Institute for Psychiatry, Munich, FRG.

The psychobiology of anorexia nervosa is described and explained under four headings; (1) the psychopathology as related to the motivation for fasting; (2) metabolic and somatic consequences of starvation, including brain morphology; (3) endocrine abnormalities in the hypothalamic-pituitary-adrenal and gonadal axis; and (4) the hunger drive and its possible perversions in terms of aspects of neuroethology and the reward system in the brain.

Publication Types: Review; Review, tutorial

Psychol Med 1988 Nov;18(4):807-12
The outcome of anorexia nervosa: a reappraisal.
Hsu LK.
Department of Psychiatry, University of Pittsburgh, Western Psychiatric Institute and Clinic, PA 15213-2593.
Publication Types: Review; Review,

tutorial

Psychol Med 1999 Mar;29(2):407-14
Clinical characteristics in patients with anorexia nervosa and obsessive-compulsive disorder. Matsunaga H, Kiriike N, Iwasaki Y, Miyata A, Yamagami S, Kaye WH.
Department of Neuropsychiatry, Osaka City University Medical School, Osaka, Japan.
BACKGROUND: The purpose of this study was to assess clinical characteristics, including co-morbid personality disorders in patients with both anorexia nervosa (AN) and obsessive-compulsive disorder (OCD) in comparison with age- and sex-matched patients with OCD. The results suggest that there are some differential characteristics of the OCD symptomatology between these disorders, although many patients with AN manifest significant impairment from primary OCD symptoms with similar magnitude in severity to that found in OCD patients.

Psychopathology 1994;27(1-2):29-36
The sociocultural theory in the development of anorexia nervosa.
Iancu I, Spivak B, Ratzoni G, Apter A, Weizman A.
Children & Adolescents Psychiatric Department, Geha Psychiatric Hospital, Beilinson Medical Center, Petah Tikva, Israel.
The relationship between anorexia nervosa (AN) and sociocultural factors is examined. Anorexia nervosa was first described in the West and was reported as particularly rare or absent in Eastern cultures. However, the frequency of its presentation has increased worldwide over the past two decades, probably as a consequence of changes in cultural norms and concepts of feminine beauty and an increasing inflow of Western values into other countries.
Publication Types: Review; Review, tutorial

Psychopathology 1997;30(1):49-52
Three cases of severe early-onset eating disorder: are they cases of anorexia nervosa?
Nielsen GB, Lausch B, Thomsen PH.
Psychiatric Hospital for Children and Adolescents, Risskov, Denmark.
3 cases of early onset, severe eating disorder are described. These young children did not present a distorted body image even though they had suffered a great weight loss, were somatically distressed and in all other aspects fulfilled the criteria for anorexia nervosa. The criteria for anorexia nervosa are discussed for this group of young patients.

Psychosom Med 1970 Mar-Apr;32(2):201-8
The mother-daughter relationship in anorexia nervosa.
Ehrensing RH, Weitzman EL.

Psychosom Med 1974 Jan-Feb;36(1):18-26
Anorexia nervosa: demographic and clinical features in 94 cases.
Halmi KA.

Psychosomatics 1967 Sep-Oct;8(5):281-6
Anorexia nervosa.
Offord DR.

Psychother Psychosom 1970;18(1):365-71
Anorexia nervosa in male subjects.
Beumont PJ.

Psychother Psychosom 1988;49(3-4):137-44
Prognostic factors in anorexia nervosa.
Engel K.
Department of Psychosomatics and Psychotherapy of the Medical Clinic, University Hospital, Hamburg, FRG.
Preclinical inpatient therapy and postclinical prognostic factors concerning 113 cases were empirically scrutinized and hierarchically classified in accordance with their importance, especially in light of the relative weight of somatic, psychologic, or social variables. The criterion is the state of health at the time of follow-up, after 6.4 years. The results thus obtained are the basis of therapy recommendations.

Q J Med 1992 Jul;83(303):507-22
Anorexia nervosa as a compulsive behaviour disease.
Mills IH, Medlicott L.
Department of Medicine, University of Cambridge, Addenbrooke's Hospital.
A number of anorexic young women develop bulimia, a condition in which binge eating is driven so intensely they cannot resist it. Although this drive has the character of a compulsion the patients do not as a rule suffer from obsessional-compulsive neurosis. A questionnaire was developed and used to determine whether similar compulsive drives manifest themselves in restricting anorexics and whether there are compulsive features resembling patients with compulsive personality disorder (as described in DSM-III) in eating disorders. It was found that many of the factors which underlie compulsive personality disorder are present in primary eating disorders and the compulsive nature of anorexia could not be ignored when treatment was considered. The difference between compulsive behaviour and addiction is discussed in the light of the failure of long-term naloxone infusion to cure severe anorexia, even though some patients had dramatic weight gains associated with the antilipolytic action of naloxone.

R I Med J 1977 Sep;60(9):419-22, 455-6
Anorexia nervosa.
Reilly PP.

S Afr Med J 1970 Aug 15;44(32):911-5
Anorexia nervosa: a review.
Beumont PJ.
Publication Types: Historical article; Review

S Afr Med J 1977 Jul 2;52(1):2-3
Anorexia nervosa.
Publication Types: Editorial

Theor Med 1997 Dec;18(4):401-20
Cultural and historical aspects of eating disorders.
Bemporad JR.
Department of Psychiatry, New York Medical College, Valhalla 10595, USA.
A review of cultural and historical accounts of anorexia nervosa indicates that this disorder is found primarily in Westernized societies during periods of relative affluence and greater social

opportunities for women. Some hypotheses regarding the vulnerability to eating disorders are proposed to the basis of these data.
Publication Types: Historical article

Tijdschr Gastroenterol 1970;13(1):44-53
Anorexia nervosa.
Crisp AH.

Vet Med Small Anim Clin 1967 Nov;62(11):1075-80
A new solution to the problem of anorexia.
Morris ML Jr, Collins DR.

West J Nurs Res 1994 Feb;16(1):69-80
Anorexia as symbolic expression of a woman's rejection of her mother's life.
Korb M.
Montana State University, Missoula.
Studies have failed to find consistent pathologic characteristics of mothers of women with anorexia nervosa. Yet the anorexic woman's perception of her mother remains implicated in the illness (Brumberg, 1988). Literature based on anecdotal and clinical reports of anorexia nervosa has questioned anorexic women's views of their mothers and their mothers' lives. Comparison of symptomatic and asymptomatic college women found that women with anorexia nervosa described more negative impressions of their mothers' lives. Perception of maternal role model may be related to anorexia nervosa.

World Ir Nurs 1978 Sep;7(8):8
Anorexia nervosa.
McDonnell M.

World Rev Nutr Diet 1970;12:452-504
Anorexia nervosa 'feeding disorder', 'nervous malnutrition' or 'weight phobia'?
Crisp AH.

BULIMIA

Acta Psychiatr Scand 1999 Jul;100(1):33-9

Bulimia and bulimic behaviour in middle adolescence: more common than thought?

Kaltiala-Heino R, Rissanen A, Rimpela M, Rantanen P.

University of Tampere, Tampere School of Public health and Tampere University Hospital, Finland.

Studies on the prevalence of bulimia and bulimic behaviour have focused on female populations from their late teens. This study assesses the prevalence of bulimia and bulimic behaviour in 14- to 16-year-old adolescents. Bulimia and bulimic eating behaviour appear to be more common than was previously thought in middle adolescence, and also among boys. Bulimia deserves more attention in younger age groups than main risk groups so far considered.

Publication Types: Review; Review, tutorial

Addict Behav 1988;13(4):359-68

Bulimics and restrained eaters: a personality comparison.

Ruderman AJ, Grace PS.

Dept. of Psychology, University of Illinois, Chicago 60680.

This study compared the psychological characteristics of restrained eaters and bulimics. One hundred and thirty six female undergraduates completed the Restraint Scale, the Bulimia Test, the Narcissistic Personality Disorder Scale, a borderline personality disorder scale, the Body Cathexis Scale, and the Tennessee Self-Concept Scale which yields six measures of self-esteem (physical self, moral-ethical self, personal self, family self, social self, and total self-esteem) and four measures of psychopathology (general maladjustment, psychosis, personality disorder, and neurosis). Stepwise regression analyses were done using restraint and bulimia as dependent measures and the other measures as predictor variables. The results indicate that both bulimics and restrained eaters are dissatisfied with their bodies and have narcissistic qualities. However, bulimics show an element of psychopathology which restrained eaters do not and restrained eaters perceive themselves as morally virtuous, whereas bulimics do not.

Addict Behav 1993 Nov-Dec;18(6):671-80
The abstinence violation effect in bulimia nervosa.
Ward T, Hudson SM, Bulik CM.
Department of Psychology, University of Canterbury, Christchurch, New Zealand. Bulimia nervosa often follows a chronic and relapsing course. To understand relapse in this disorder, we highlight cognitive processes underlying the binge/purge cycle. Links are drawn between cognitions, causal perceptions, and the binge/purge cycle in a reformulation of the abstinence violation effect with a special focus on attributions. This reformulation is then applied to the lapse-relapse transition in bulimia nervosa. Finally, theoretical and clinical implications of the reformulation are presented.
Publication Types: Review; Review, tutorial

Addict Behav 1993 Nov-Dec;18(6):681-9
Parental factors related to bulimia nervosa.
Moreno A, Thelen MH.
Psychology Department, University of Missouri-Columbia 65211.
The purpose of the present study was to examine the relationship between parental factors and bulimia nervosa. Subjects were female undergraduate students (classified as bulimic, subclinical bulimic, or normal) and their parents. Daughters and their parents were administered a questionnaire which assesses attitudes about being overweight, radical dieting, and parental pressure to lose weight. Limitations of these findings were discussed as well as implications for further research.

Adolesc Psychiatry 1986;13:428-36
Is bulimia an affective disorder?
Herzog DB.

Am Fam Physician 1981 Jul;24(1):141-3
Bulimia.
Johnson RE, Sinnott SK.
Bulimia, also known as compulsive eating, has recently been recognized as a disease. Although bulimia is thought to be common, especially among young women, little is known about it. Theorized causes are primary neurologic dysfunction (epileptiform), disturbance in the appetite/satiety center of the hypothalamus, learned abnormal behavior or unsuppressed oral drive. Diagnosis rests primarily on the symptoms. Possible treatment measures include phenytoin, aversion therapy, psychotherapy and self-help groups.

Am Fam Physician 1998 Jun;57(11):2743-50
Assessment and treatment of bulimia nervosa.
Mcgilley BM, Pryor TL.
University of Kanasas School of Medicine, Wichita.
Bulimia nervosa is characterized by binge eating and inappropriate compensatory behaviors, such as vomiting, fasting, excessive exercise and the misuse of diuretics, laxatives or enemas. Although the etiology of this disorder is unknown, genetic and neurochemical factors have been implicated. Treatment strategies are based on medication, psychotherapy or a combination of these modalities.
Publication Types: Review; Review,

tutorial

Am J Orthopsychiatry 1985 Jul;55(3):384-96
Assessment of the bulimic patient.
Swift WJ.
A comprehensive method of assessing the bulimic patient founded on the biopsychosocial model is outlined. Particular emphasis is given to the behavioral, biological, and psychological levels of organization. Case material is used to illustrate the marked heterogeneity of the bulimic syndrome and the need for thorough assessment.

Am J Psychiatry 1985 Jul;142(7):851-4
Prevalence of bulimia in working and university women.
Hart KJ, Ollendick TH.
The authors determined the prevalence of binge eating and bulimia in samples of 139 working women and 234 women who were university students. Results are discussed in terms of factors that might be associated with bulimia in these two samples of women.

Am J Psychiatry 1987 Nov;144(11):1456-60
Perceptual and cognitive abnormalities in bulimia.
Powers PS, Schulman RG, Gleghorn AA, Prange ME.
Department of Psychiatry and Behavioral Medicine, University of South Florida College of Medicine.
The authors compared 55 bulimic subjects and 55 normal control subjects using the Beck Depression Inventory, a new scale designed to detect cognitive distortions (the Bulimia Cognitive Distortion Scale), and several perceptual and attitudinal measures of body image. There were significant differences between the bulimic and control groups on all measures except estimates of face width. These findings are discussed in terms of a multifactorial theory of the psychopathogenesis of bulimia.

Am J Psychiatry 1994 May;151(5):738-43
Rate and prediction of relapse in bulimia nervosa.
Olmsted MP, Kaplan AS, Rockert W.
Eating Disorder Day Centre, Toronto Hospital, Ont., Canada.
The purpose of this study was to provide an estimate of the rate of relapse in patients with bulimia nervosa and to attempt to identify indexes of functioning before or after treatment that predicted subsequent relapse. The subjects were 48 fmeale patients with bulimia nervosa who achieved symptom control while attending a specialized day hospital treatment program for eating disorders. Vomiting frequency, even at subthreshold levels, appears to be an important prognostic indicator and may be one of the best barometers of residual symptoms in these patients.

Am J Psychiatry 1997 Mar;154(3):313-21
Comment in: Am J Psychiatry. 1997 Dec;154(12):1791; discussion 1791-2
Outcome in bulimia nervosa.
Keel PK, Mitchell JE.
Department of Psychology, University of Minnesota, Minneapolis 55455, USA.
The authors sought to synthesize existing data on outcome forindividuals diagnosed with bulimia

nervosa in order to better understand long-term outcome and prognostic factors. It was found that treatment interventions may speed eventual recovery but do not appear to alter outcome more than 5 years following presentation. Long-term outcome for women diagnosed with bulimia nervosa remains unclear. However, this disorder may be chronic for at least a subset of women.
Publication Types: Review; Review, tutorial

Am J Psychiatry 2001 Mar;158(3):503-4
Obsessive-compulsive disorder and bulimia.
Fava GA, Raffi AR.
Publication Types: Letter

Ann Intern Med 1987 Jul;107(1):71-7
Medical complications and medical management of bulimia.
Mitchell JE, Seim HC, Colon E, Pomeroy C.
The syndrome of bulimia is a common disorder and can be associated with serious psychological and physical morbidity. Unfortunately, many patients are reluctant to discuss their symptoms with their physicians and few clues can be found on physical examination to aid in the diagnosis. Medical management including monitoring of fluid and electrolyte balance is essential during treatment.
Publication Types: Review

Ann Med 1992 Aug;24(4):297-302
The treatment of bulimia nervosa.
Fairburn CG, Hay PJ.
University Department of Psychiatry, Warneford Hospital, Oxford, U.K.
Bulimia nervosa is a significant source of morbidity amongst young women. There has been a considerable body of work on its treatment since it was first described in 1979. At present, too little is known about the factors that predict response to particular forms of treatment to allow the matching of patients with treatments.
Publication Types: Review; Review, tutorial

Arch Gen Psychiatry 1997 Jun;54(6):509-17
Risk factors for bulimia nervosa. A community-based case-control study.
Fairburn CG, Welch SL, Doll HA, Davies BA, O'Connor ME.
Department of Psychiatry, Oxford University, Warneford Hospital, United Kingdom.
Many apparently disparate risk factors have been implicated as causes of eating disorders. This study was designed to test the hypothesis that 2 broad classes of risk factors exist for bulimia nervosa: those that increase the risk for development of a psychiatric disorder in general and those that increase the risk of dieting. The findings support the hypothesis that bulimia nervosa is the result of exposure to general risk factors for psychiatric disorder and risk factors for dieting. An unexpected finding was the particularly high rates of premorbid negative self-evaluation and certain parental problems among those with bulimia nervosa.

Arch Gen Psychiatry 1999 Jan;56(1):63-9
Long-term outcome of bulimia nervosa.
Keel PK, Mitchell JE, Miller KB, Davis TL, Crow SJ.

Department of Psychology, Harvard University, Cambridge, Mass 02138, USA.

Since bulimia nervosa's introduction to the psychiatric nomenclature in 1979, data concerning long-term outcome have been largely unavailable. Women with the diagnosis of bulimia nervosa between 1981 and 1987 who participated in 1 of 2 studies were located and invited to participate in follow-up assessments. The findings suggest that the number of women who continue to meet full criteria for bulimia nervosa declines as the duration of follow-up increases; approximately 30%, however, continued to engage in recurrent binge eating or purging behaviors (incidence rate, 0.026 cases per person-years). A history of substance use problems and a longer duration of the disorder at presentation predicted worse outcome.

Arch Gen Psychiatry 2000 Jul;57(7):659-65

The natural course of bulimia nervosa and binge eating disorder in young women.

Fairburn CG, Cooper Z, Doll HA, Norman P, O'Connor M.

Department of Psychiatry, Oxford University, England.

BACKGROUND: Little is known about the relative course and outcome of bulimia nervosa and binge eating disorder. METHODS: Two community-based cohorts were studied prospectively over a 5-year year period. One comprised 102 participants with bulimia nervosa and the other 48 participants with binge eating disorder (21% [9/42] of whom had comorbid obesity). All participants were female and aged between 16 and 35 years at recruitment. The assessments were at 15-month intervals and addressed eating disorder features, general psychiatric symptoms, and social functioning. RESULTS: Both cohorts showed marked initial improvement followed by gradual improvement thereafter. Between half and two thirds of the bulimia nervosa cohort had some form of eating disorder of clinical severity at each assessment point, although only a minority continued to meet diagnostic criteria for bulimia nervosa. Each year about a third remitted and a third relapsed. The outcome of the binge eating disorder cohort was better, with the proportion with any form of clinical eating disorder declining to 18% (7 of 40) by the 5-year follow-up. The relapse rate was low among this cohort. There was little movement of participants across the 2 diagnostic categories and few sought treatment. Both groups gained weight, with 39% of the binge eating disorder cohort (14 of 36) meeting criteria for obesity at 5-year follow-up. CONCLUSIONS: These findings suggest that, among young women in the community, bulimia nervosa and binge eating disorder have a different course and outcome. Whereas the prognosis of those with bulimia nervosa was relatively poor, the great majority of those with binge eating disorder recovered.

Arch Psychiatr Nurs 2000 Apr;14(2):81-92

Symptom development in bulimia

nervosa: a comparison of women with and without a history of anorexia nervosa.
White JH.
School of Nursing, Catholic University of America, Washington, DC 20064, USA.
Identifying women at risk for developing bulimia nervosa (BN) is an important area of study for psychiatric-mental health nurses. Of those who develop BN, a large proportion of women have been diagnosed earlier with anorexia nervosa (AN). It has been posited that women who are treated for AN are often only partially recovered. Findings from this study have implications for early detection of and extended follow-up care after treatment for AN.

Aviat Space Environ Med 1988 May;59(5):462
Bulimia.
Hoffman K.
Publication Types: Letter

Behav Genet 1999 Jan;29(1):1-10
Erratum in: Behav Genet 1999 May;29(3):205
A genetic analysis of the eating and attitudes associated with bulimia nervosa: dealing with the problem of ascertainment in twin studies.
Wade T, Neale MC, Lake RI, Martin NG.
Department of Psychology, Flinders University of South Australia, Australia.
tdwade@hsc.vcu.edu
Little is known about the etiology of bulimia nervosa and the attitudes. The analysis undertaken was a study of selected (45 pairs) and unselected (106 pairs) female twins to elucidate the broad causes of individual differences in these behaviours and attitudes.
Publication Types: Twin study

Behav Res Ther 1995 Nov;33(8):875-85
A comparison of two psychological treatments for bulimia nervosa: implications for models of maintenance.
Cooper PJ, Steere J.
Department of Psychology, University of Reading, England.
In an effort to elucidate the role of cognitive factors in the maintenance of bulimia nervosa, the efficacy of two psychological treatments was examined in a randomised control trial: cognitive behaviour therapy in the absence of explicit exposure instructions was compared with exposure and response prevention treatment in the absence of cognitive restructuring procedures. In the short term both treatments were successful at effecting substantial improvement in both the specific and the non-specific psychopathology of the disorder. However, at a one year follow up, whilst improvements were well maintained for those who had received the cognitive-behavioural treatment, virtually all of those who had responded to the purely behavioural treatment had relapsed. This provides some support for the cognitive model of the maintenance of bulimia nervosa.
Publication Types: Clinical trial; Randomized controlled trial

Behav Res Ther 1998 Oct;36(10):931-44
Modeling of eating pathology and

social reinforcement of the thin-ideal predict onset of bulimic symptoms.
Stice E.
Stanford University, Department of Psychiatry, CA 94305-5542, USA.
estice@stanford.edu
Although social influences are thought to promote bulimic pathology, little research has examined the effects of multiple socialization agents, or considered both modeling and social reinforcement processes. Accordingly, these two studies tested whether social reinforcement of the thin-ideal, and modeling of abnormal eating behavior by family, peers, and the media, (i) correlated with bulimic symptoms in a sample of young adult female (N = 114) and (ii) predicted the onset of bulimic behavior in a sample of adolescent females (N = 218). Results suggest that both social reinforcement and modeling processes may promote bulimic pathology, but imply that the effects are limited to family and peer influences.

Behav Res Ther 1998 Sep;36(9):895-8
Core beliefs and underlying assumptions in bulimia nervosa and depression.
Cooper M, Hunt J.
Isis Education Centre, Warneford Hospital, Oxford, UK.
In a pilot study, core beliefs and underlying assumptions were investigated in patients with bulimia nervosa, patients with depression and female controls, using a new self-report measure. The findings support recent developments in cognitive theories of eating disorders. Treatment implications are briefly discussed.

BMJ 1990 Feb 24;300(6723):485-7
Bulimia nervosa.
Fairburn CG.
Publication Types: Review; Review, tutorial

Bol Asoc Med P R 1991 Jan;83(1):22-4
Bulimia nervosa.
Mitchell JE.
Eating Disorders Program, University of Minnesota, Medical School, Minneapolis55455.
Bulimia nervosa is a disorder affecting the eating patterns of women in industrialized societies. Medical and dental consequences of the illness often lead patients to seek treatment after about six years. Controlled treatment studies to date utilize outpatient therapy instead of hospitalization. Published literature suggests that the illness is most effectively treated with psychotherapy and antidepressant medications; however, including nutritional intervention in the treatment regimen shows promise. Clearly more studies are necessary.
Publication Types: Review; Review, tutorial

Br Dent J 1986 Apr 19;160(8):290-1
Bulimia nervosa in a male.
Negus TW, Todd JO.

Br J Clin Psychol 1987 Sep;26 (Pt 3):223-4
Prognostic factors in bulimia nervosa.
Fairburn CG, Kirk J, O'Connor M, Anastasiades P, Cooper PJ.
Department of Psychiatry, University of Oxford, Warneford Hospital, UK.
Factors predictive of outcome were sought from the data from a controlled

study of the treatment of bulimia nervosa. Four different indices of outcome were used, and outcome was assessed at four points during a 12-month, treatment-free follow-up period. It was found that the pre-treatment level of self-esteem was a consistent predictor of outcome with those patients having low self-esteem responding least well to treatment. There were no other consistent predictors of outcome.

Br J Med Psychol 1992 Mar;65 (Pt 1):59-66
Possible effects of the popular and medical recognition of bulimia nervosa.
Habermas T.
Institute for Medical Psychology, Freie Universitat Berlin, Germany.
Historical changes in psychological symptoms are analysed not only from a social causation approach but also from a labelling perspective. Modern eating disorders lend themselves to such an analysis because of their historical variability. Data of an exploratory interview study with 39 bulimic patients evaluated along these lines (a) indicate that the recognition of bulimia has facilitated seeking of professional and non-professional help, (b) invite categorization of bulimic behaviour implying less self-blame, (c) render imitation of bulimia more probable, and (d) covary with less secretive illness behaviour indicating a broadening of underlying motivations.

Br J Psychiatry 1984 Jul;145:93
Complications of bulimia nervosa.
Healy K.
Publication Types: Letter

Br J Psychiatry 1984 Mar;144:238-46
The clinical features of bulimia nervosa.
Fairburn CG, Cooper PJ.
The clinical features of 35 patients with bulimia nervosa are described. All the patients came from the Oxford area and each fulfilled conservative operational diagnostic criteria. Standardised assessment procedures were used including a structured interview designed to assess the psychopathology characteristic of patients with eating disorders. It was confirmed that these patients have grossly disturbed eating habits accompanied by morbid beliefs and values concerning their shape and weight. Although the majority had a weight within the normal range, a history of weight disturbance was common. There was a high degree of psychiatric morbidity with depressive symptoms being particularly prominent.

Br J Psychiatry 1987 Nov;151:684-6
The prevalence of bulimia nervosa. A replication study.
Cooper PJ, Charnock DJ, Taylor MJ.
Department of Psychiatry, University of Cambridge, Addenbrooke's Hospital.
There have been reports of a high prevalence of bulimic episodes and the syndromes of bulimia nervosa and DSM-III bulimia in community samples. The present study replicates a community survey conducted four years ago in Britain. The prevalence of bulimic episodes, self-induced vomiting and bulimia nervosa found

in the present survey was very similar to that found in the earlier study.

Br J Psychiatry 1991 Dec;159:882
Sibling sex and bulimia nervosa.
Publication Types: Letter

Br J Psychiatry Suppl 1988 Jul;(2):32-6
Body image disturbance in bulimia nervosa.
Cooper PJ, Taylor MJ.
Department of Psychiatry, University of Cambridge, Addenbrooke's Hospital, UK.
Publication Types: Review; Review, tutorial

Clin Neuropharmacol 1986;9(1):14-36
The bulimic disorders.
Robinson PH.
Publication Types: Review

Compr Psychiatry 1983 Nov-Dec;24(6):546-54
Bulimia: concept and therapy.
Lowenkopf EL.
Publication Types: Review

Compr Psychiatry 1990 Mar-Apr;31(2):171-5
Bulimia nervosa with and without a history of anorexia nervosa.
Mitchell JE, Pyle RL, Eckert ED, Hatsukami D, Soll E.
Eating Disorders Program, Department of Psychiatry, Minneapolis, MN.
This study compared two subgroups of women of normal weight with bulimia nervosa: those with a history of anorexia nervosa and those without such a history. Those with a history of anorexia nervosa indicated a desired body weight significantly lower than those without the history. Those with a history of anorexia nervosa were more likely to abuse laxatives and less likely to self-induce vomiting. Both groups reported feeling fat and worrying a great deal about weight and shape issues.

Compr Psychiatry 1999 Jan-Feb;40(1):57-60
Different types of self-injurious behavior in bulimia nervosa.
Favaro A, Santonastaso P.
Department of Neurological and Psychiatric Sciences, University of Padua, Italy.
In a previous study, we demonstrated the validity of the distinction, in bulimia nervosa (BN), between compulsive self-injurious behavior (SIB), such as hair pulling and onycophagia, and impulsive SIB, such as skin cutting and burning. In our sample, impulsive SIB appeared to be associated with suicide attempts, a history of sexual abuse, and depression. On the other hand, compulsive SIB seemed to be related to a lack of awareness towards emotions and body sensations, greater obsessionality, and a shorter duration of illness.

Compr Psychiatry 1999 May-Jun;40(3):229-33
A preliminary report on pain thresholds in bulimia nervosa during a bulimic episode.
Raymond NC, Eckert ED, Hamalainen M, Evanson D, Thuras PD, Hartman BK, Faris PL.
Department of Psychiatry, University of Minnesota Medical School, Minneapolis55455, USA.

In this preliminary study, pressure pain thresholds were assessed in nine subjects with BN on 3 consecutive days during a binge-eating and vomiting (B/V) episode, during a normal meal, and after an overnight fast. A significant time versus condition effect was found with a significant change in the pain threshold in BN subjects under the B/V condition only. These data are consistent with the hypothesis that vagal afferent activation by a B/V episode also activates the descending pain inhibitory pathway.

Compr Ther 1987 Sep;13(9):12-5
Bulimia: diagnosis and treatment.
Humphries LL. Eating Disorders Service, University of Kentucky, Lexington.
Publication Types: Review Review, tutorial

Curr Concepts Nutr 1988;16:137-49
Appetite regulation in bulimia.
Walsh BT.
College of Physicians & Surgeons, Columbia University, New York, New York.
Publication Types: Review; Review, tutorial

Drug Ther Bull 1992 Feb 17;30(4):13-4
Bulimia nervosa--common in women.
Publication Types: Review; Review, tutorial

Eat Weight Disord 1999 Dec;4(4):157-64
Body weight in bulimia nervosa.
Gendall KA, Bulik CM, Sullivan PF, Joyce PR, Mcintosh VV, Carter FA.
Western Psychiatric Institute and Clinic, University of Pittsburgh Medical Center, PA, USA.
The objectives of this study were to determine: 1) factors associated with body mass index (BMI) in women with bulimia nervosa prior to treatment; 2) changes in BMI during cognitive behavioral therapy (CBT) for bulimia nervosa; and 3) predictors of weight change during CBT treatment. A significantly lower BMI prior to treatment was independently associated with a history of anorexia nervosa, substance use, cigarette smoking, and a high frequency of vomiting. Reductions in binge eating, purging, and food restriction after treatment did not result in significant changes in BMI. Identification of women at risk of significant weight gain or loss during CBT may enable therapists to focus on its aspects that help to prevent excessive body weight changes.
Publication Types: Clinical trial; Randomized controlled trial

Holist Nurs Pract 1988 Nov;3(1):56-66
Bulimia nervosa and gender identity: symbols of a culture.
Miles MW.

Hong Kong Med J 2000 Jun;6(2):227-30
Three different presentations of bulimia nervosa.
Lam M, Lee S.
Department of Psychiatry, The Chinese University of Hong Kong, Prince of Wales Hospital, Shatin.
This case report describes the different presentations of three women with bulimia nervosa, all of whom demonstrated purging behaviour. Two of the patients also had hypokalaemia, whereas the third exhibited Russell's

sign-that is, calluses on the dorsum of each hand. Drug treatment and psychosocial intervention improved the condition of all three patients. The report emphasises the need for both health care professionals and the public to recognise this potentially dangerous but treatable disorder.

Hosp Pract (Off Ed) 2001 Mar 15;36(3):71-2
Eating disorders: 2. Bulimia nervosa.

Int J Clin Exp Hypn 1990 Apr;38(2):101-11
The use of hypnosis in the treatment of bulimia nervosa.
Vanderlinden J, Vandereycken W.
University Psychiatric Center, Kortenberg, Belgium.
Promising research data, relating hypnotizability and the possible presence of a dissociative mechanism in bulimic individuals, stimulated the present authors to incorporate hypnosis in their directive and multidimensional treatment of bulimic patients. Important strategies and how and when they can be applied in the different phases of treatment are described.
Publication Types: Review; Review, tutorial

Int J Eat Disord 1993 May;13(4):359-68
Survival analysis of response to group psychotherapy in bulimia nervosa.
Crosby RD, Mitchell JE, Raymond N, Specker S, Nugent SM, Pyle RL.
Department of Psychiatry, University of Minnesota Medical School, Minneapolis55455.
This reanalysis of treatment response and relapse was performed using survival analysis in a 12-week clinical trial of cognitive behavioral group psychotherapy for the treatment of bulimia nervosa. "Initial" and "maintained" response to treatment based on "total" and "near" abstinence criteria were determined using self-reported binge eating, vomiting, and laxative use data. Results suggest that an emphasis on abstinence appears important in achieving initial abstinence, whereas intensity of treatment may be important in maintaining abstinence.
Publication Types: Clinical trial; Randomized controlled trial

Int J Eat Disord 1996 Jan;19(1):99-103
Treating bulimia nervosa in primary care: a pilot study.
Waller D, Fairburn CG, McPherson A, Kay R, Lee A, Nowell T.
Developing and evaluating a simplified and condensed cognitive behavioral treatment for bulimia nervosa suitable for use in primary care are examined here. It was discussed that this form of treatment may benefit a significant proportion of those patients with bulimia nervosa who are seen in primary care. It can be administered by nonspecialist therapists.

Int J Eat Disord 1997 Jul;22(1):35-41
Drop-out and failure to engage in individual outpatient cognitive behavior therapy for bulimic disorders.
Waller G.
Department of Psychology, University of Southampton, Highfield, UK.
OBJECTIVE: It was the aim of this study to explore the characteristics of

bulimics who fail to complete therapy. Noncompleters were divided into those who failed to engage and those who dropped out, so that these groups could be directly compared. The noncompleting groups both had high levels of borderline psychopathology and more severe perceived bulimic characteristics than the completers. However, the "drop-out" and "failures to engage" had very different patterns of perceived family emotional involvement, with the failures to engage reporting relatively healthy functioning.

Int J Eat Disord 1997 May;21(4):361-5
Body dissatisfaction and sexuality among women with bulimia nervosa.
Wiederman MW, Pryor T.
Department of Psychological Science, Ball State University, Muncie, IN 47306-0520, USA.
Past research and clinical observations have implicated sexuality as a factor involved in eating disorders. Yet little research has been conducted on possible links between body image and sexuality. Investigated were relationships within a large sample of women with bulimia nervosa. After controlling for age, age of onset of menses, and current body size, body dissatisfaction was unrelated to coital experience. Results are discussed with regard to past research, directions for future research, and clinical implications.

Int J Eat Disord 1998 Nov;24(3):323-7
Very early-onset bulimia nervosa: report of two cases.
Stein S, Chalhoub N, Hodes M.
Northgate Clinic, London, United Kingdom.
Bulimia nervosa is very rare in children below the age of 14 years, and no reliable reports of prepubertal bulimia nervosa have been published. We describe two cases of early-onset bulimia nervosa who presented before the age of 14 years, and with premenarchal onset in one patient. Implications of these cases regarding the etiology and occurrence of bulimia nervosa in younger adolescents are discussed.

Int J Eat Disord 1998 Sep;24(2):193-205
Accounts of experiences of bulimia: a discourse analytic study.
Brooks A, LeCouteur A, Hepworth J.
Department of Psychology, Flinders University, Adelaide, South Australia.
To identify the variety of versions of bulimia constructed by participants, to suggest functions and consequences of these constructions, and to examine the sociocultural ideologies evident in participants' discourse.
Five dominant ways of talking about bulimia were identified:
Individuals were constructed as victims of bulimia, women were constructed as victims of social stereotypes, bulimia was constructed as a damaging action one performs on oneself, bulimia was constructed as a personality trait of individuals, and bulimia was marginalized as abnormal and disgusting.

Int J Eat Disord 1999 Jul;26(1):1-12
Social support, social adjustment, and recovery status in bulimia nervosa.
Rorty M, Yager J, Buckwalter JG, Rossotto E.
Department of Graduate Psychology,

Azusa Pacific University, California 91702, USA.
To examine recovery status in bulimia nervosa (BN) and its relation to social support and social adjustment. Using a cross-sectional design we administered the modified Social Support Questionnaire and the Social Adjustment Scale-Self-Report (SAS-SR) to 40 women, each of whom was actively bulimic (ABN), were in remission from BN (RBN), or had no history of eating disturbance (comparison). The results suggest that the social functioning of RBN women lies between ABN women and non-eating-disordered women, indicating both gains relative to the active phase and residual deficits.

Int J Eat Disord 1999 Sep;26(2):145-51
Self-verification and bulimic symptoms: do bulimic women play a role in perpetuating their own dissatisfaction and symptoms?
Joiner TE Jr.
Department of Psychology, Florida State University, Tallahassee 32306-1270, USA.
It is suggested that self-verification theory may provide insight as to why bulimic symptoms often persist for years, sometimes even despite intervention. In an effort to meet basic needs for self-confirmation, bulimic women may invite the very responses they fear (e.g., negative feedback about appearance), and thus propagate their symptoms.

Int J Eat Disord 2000 May;27(4):428-34
Duration of illness predicts outcome for bulimia nervosa: a long-term follow-up study.
Reas DL, Williamson DA, Martin CK, Zucker NL.
Department of Psychology, Louisiana State University, Baton Rouge, LA 70808, USA.
The purpose of this study was to investigate long-term outcome and prognosis in a bulimic and subthreshold bulimic sample. This finding suggests that early identification of bulimia nervosa may be a very important factor in preventing a chronic eating disorder.

Int J Eat Disord 2000 May;27(4):435-45
Influence of shape and weight on self-evaluation in bulimia nervosa.
Goldfein JA, Walsh BT, Midlarsky E.
Department of Psychiatry, Columbia University, College of Physicians and Surgeons, New York, NY 10032, USA.
Comparing three related but different measures of excessive concerns about shape and weight in bulimia nervosa (BN): influence of shape and weight (influence; DSM-IV Criterion D), overconcern with shape and weight (overconcern; DSM-III-R Criterion E), and dissatisfaction with shape and weight (dissatisfaction). Influence and overconcern, but not dissatisfaction, successfully discriminated BNs from NCs but not from REs. Influence and overconcern are equally valid measures of the excessive concerns about shape and weight characteristic of BN.

Int J Eat Disord 2000 Nov;28(3):259-64
Which comes first in the pathogenesis of bulimia nervosa: dieting or bingeing?
Brewerton TD, Dansky BS, Kilpatrick

DG, O'Neil PM.
Department of Psychiatry and Behavioral Sciences, Medical University of South Carolina, Charleston, South Carolina 29425, USA.
OBJECTIVE: Clinical experience has indicated that dieting usually precedes the onset of binge eating in the development of bulimia nervosa (BN). These data confirm that dieting is more likely to precede binge eating, although binge eating precedes significant dieting in a substantial proportion of bulimic respondents. Copyright 2000 by John Wiley & Sons, Inc.

Int J Psychosom 1989;36(1-4):58
Treatment of bulimia with hypnosis involving awareness and control in clients with high dissociative capacity.
Barabasz M.
The details of an easily replicable intervention using hypnosis in the treatment of bulimia are presented. Follow-up data at one month, three months, six months, and one year indicated that the intervention appeared to be effective in two out of the three cases presented. Factors affecting treatment outcomes are discussed.

J Abnorm Psychol 1993 May;102(2):297-303
The social self in bulimia nervosa: public self-consciousness, social anxiety, and perceived fraudulence.
Striegel-Moore RH, Silberstein LR, Rodin J.
Department of Psychology, Wesleyan University, Middletown, Connecticut 06459-0408.
Bulimic women appear preoccupied not only with their physical presentation but also with their "social self"--how others perceive them in general. This study examined the relationship of the social self to body esteem and to bulimia nervosa. The findings strongly support the hypothesized link of social-self concerns to body dissatisfaction and bulimia nervosa.
Publication Types: Review; Review, tutorial

J Abnorm Psychol 1999 Nov;108(4):695-700
Perfectionism, perceived weight status, and self-esteem interact to predict bulimic symptoms: a model of bulimic symptom development.
Vohs KD, Bardone AM, Joiner TE Jr, Abramson LY, Heatherton TF.
Department of Psychological and Brain Sciences, Dartmouth College, Hanover, New Hampshire 03755, USA. vohs@dartmouth.edu
An interactive model of perfectionism, perceived weight status, and self-esteem was tested on 342 female undergraduates to predict bulimic symptoms. Using a longitudinal design, the authors tested the model on data collected at 2 points: the spring of participants' senior year of high school and during participants' first year of college. The authors hypothesized and found that self-esteem moderates the interaction between perfectionism and perceived weight status in predicting bulimic symptoms.

J Am Acad Child Adolesc Psychiatry 1999 Feb;38(2):109-10

Comment on: J Am Acad Child Adolesc Psychiatry. 1998 Apr;37(4):352-9
Review of anorexia and bulimia.
Lask B, Bryant-Waugh R.
Publication Types: Comment Letter

J Am Acad Psychoanal 1989 Spring;17(1):131-40
Bulimia: the construction of a symptom.
Hamburg P.
Eating Disorders Unit, Massachusetts General Hospital.

J Am Coll Health 1991 Nov;40(3):107-12
Using the health belief model for bulimia prevention.
Grodner M.
Department of Health Service, William Paterson College, Wayne, New Jersey.
The author discusses application of the Health Belief Model to bulimia prevention (reduction of bulimic-like behaviors of food obsessions, bingeing, and various forms of purging). She considers the individual's beliefs about bulimia and bulimic-like behaviors as a means of predicting the likelihood of behavior change to prevent clinically diagnosable bulimia. Includes a description of each Health Belief Model component, and offers implications forfurther research.

J Am Diet Assoc 1990 Apr;90(4):576-8
Dietary intake and dieting practices of bulimic and non-bulimic female college students.
Greene GW, Achterberg C, Crumbaugh J, Soper J.
Nutrition Department, Pennsylvania State University, University Park 16802.

J Behav Med 2000 Feb;23(1):37-57
Bulimia interventions via interpersonal influence: the role of threat and efficacy in persuading bulimics to seek help.
Smalec JL, Klingle RS.
University of Hawaii at Manoa, USA.
The causes and medical consequences of bulimia are well established in the literature, yet prevalence rates for bulimia continue to be quite high. Eating disorder books and popular magazines have offered a variety of ways in which individuals can communicatively influence bulimics to seek the help they need to treat their disorder. Unfortunately, many of the recommended influence strategies have been atheoretically derived and sorely lack empirical data affirming their effectiveness. The study investigates and empirically tests the effectiveness of interpersonal intervention messages aimed at getting bulimic individuals to seek medical help.

J Behav Ther Exp Psychiatry 1987 Jun;18(2):165-9
Bulimia: a case illustration of the superiority of behavioral over cognitive treatment.
Morin CM, Winter B, Besalel VA, Azrin NH.
The present study compared the relative efficacy of two major clinical procedures previously used in multicomponent cognitive-behavioral programs for treating bulimia. A single-subject experimental design was used and the results showed that

the behavioral procedure of exposure plus response prevention was more effective than the cognitive procedure in reducing binge and vomit episodes as well as the urges to binge-vomit. These results suggest that the exposure plus response prevention component is more relevant for cognitive as well as behavioral changes in treating bulimia.

J Behav Ther Exp Psychiatry 1987 Mar;18(1):41-9
Bulimia: an individual behavioral analysis.
Chiodo J.
This transcript is taken from the initial interview with a 24-year-old woman presenting with the problems of depression related to episodic binge eating, and anxiety concerning her difficulty to control her weight. Behavior analysis of the problem indicates that while the patient's binge eating was a means to cope with feelings of anxiety and emotional distress, her struggle to exert strict dietary control and maintain a thin body shape was in order to avoid negative evaluation, criticism and social rejection. Predisposing factors and precipitating events were examined to help explain the development of this behavioral pattern.

J Clin Psychol 1988 Jul;44(4):491-8
Bulimia: an entity in search of definition.
Shapiro S.
University of Southern California.
A review of research literature that addresses personality correlates of bulimia revealed a major problem which affects that research and its interpretation:
Criteria used to define this disorder have not been consistent across investigators. This very basic issue needs to be resolved if the findings in bulimia research are to be cumulative and generalizable across studies. Suggestions are offered as to how this resolution should occur.
Publication Types: Review; Review, academic

J Consult Clin Psychol 1987 Oct;55(5):668-76
Symptom management of bulimia.
Johnson C, Connors ME, Tobin DL.

J Consult Clin Psychol 2000 Jun;68(3):432-7
Commitment to treatment goals in prediction of group cognitive-behavioral therapy treatment outcome for women with bulimia nervosa.
Mussell MP, Mitchell JE, Crosby RD, Fulkerson JA, Hoberman HM, Romano JL.
Graduate Department of Professional Psychology, University of St. Thomas, Minneapolis, Minnesota 55403, USA. mpmussell@stthomas.edu
The purpose of this study was to investigate potential client variables that predict favorable response to group cognitive-behavioral therapy in a sample of women (N = 143) seeking treatment for bulimia nervosa. The primary variable found to predict longer term outcome was symptom remission at the end of treatment and at the 1-month follow-up.
Publication Types: Clinical trial; Randomized controlled trial

J Fam Pract 1988 May;26(5):495, 498
Bulimia in family practice.
Wells JE.
Publication Types: Letter

J Gt Houst Dent Soc 1997 Aug;69(1):31-4
Oral signs and symptoms of bulimia nervosa.
Zachariasen RD.
University of Texas, Houston, Health Science Center-Dental Branch, Department of Basic Science, USA.
Publication Types: Review; Review, tutorial

J Nerv Ment Dis 1988 Apr;176(4):246-8
Bulimia in a pair of monozygotic twins.
Kaminer Y, Feingold M, Lyons K.
Western Psychiatric Institute and Clinic, Pittsburgh, Pennsylvania 15213.
Bulimia was diagnosed in a pair of monozygotic twins and was manifested in both sisters concurrently through their adolescent years. After a later separation only one continued to manifest the disorder with additional associated features of the bulimic syndrome. The case is presented and suggestions regarding the roles of environmental and genetic factors in the development and course of the disorder are discussed.

J Nerv Ment Dis 1990 May;178(5):324-7
Bulimia nervosa in overweight individuals.
Mitchell JE, Pyle RL, Eckert ED, Hatsukami D, Soll E.
Department of Psychiatry, University of Minnesota Hospitals, Minneapolis.
Patients who have bulimia nervosa and are overweight have received little attention in the medical literature. The authors identified 25 patients who weighed greater than or equal to 130% of their ideal body weight out of a series of 591 patients with bulimia nervosa. This subgroup was contrasted with a sample of 25 patients with bulimia nervosa who were 90% to 110% of their ideal body weight. Members of the overweight bulimia nervosa group were binge-eating and vomiting less frequently than the comparison group but were more likely to be abusing laxatives, and to report a history of self-injurious behavior and suicide attempt(s). Both groups reported frequent binge-eating.

J Nerv Ment Dis 1998 Mar;186(3):157-65
Impulsive and compulsive self-injurious behavior in bulimia nervosa: prevalence and psychological correlates.
Favaro A, Santonastaso P.
Department of Neurological and Psychiatric Sciences, University of Padua, Padova, Italy.
A specific link between self-injurious behavior and bulimia nervosa has been observed. In affective spectrum disorders, some authors propose a distinction between impulsive and compulsive self-injurious behavior. One of the aims of the present study is to examine how different kinds of self-injurious behavior, including purging behavior, may be classified in bulimia nervosa. The clinical impact of the different types of self-injury are studied.

J Psychosoc Nurs Ment Health Serv 1992 Feb;30(2):23-7
Bulimia nervosa. Associated physical

problems.
Hofland SL, Dardis PO.
College of Nursing, South Dakota State University, Brookings 57007
Bulimia involves more serious problems than previously thought. Bulimia nervosa is a psychiatric disorder characterized by binge eating followed by some form of combination of purging, including laxative or diuretic use, strenuous exercise, and self-induced vomiting to eliminate unwanted calories. Physical problems of bulimia include oral and neck problems, metabolic acid-base imbalances, volume depletion, hypochloremia, hypokalemia, hyponatremia, hypomagnesia, hypocalcemia, hyperuricemia, gastrointestinal problems, and edema. The physical problems of bulimia are less well known than those of anorexia.
Nurses must be alert for clues, act on suspicions, use a nonjudgmental approach, and be knowledgeable of all assessment factors, including psychological parameters.
Publication Types: Review; Review, tutorial

J Psychother Pract Res 1998 Spring;7(2):102-18
Guided imagery treatment to promote self-soothing in bulimia nervosa. A theoretical rationale.
Esplen MJ, Garfinkel PE.
Department of Psychiatry, Mount Sinai Hospital, Toronto, Ontario, Canada.
Bulimia nervosa (BN) has been described as involving impairment in affect regulation and in self-soothing. A model of guided imagery therapy suggests that imagery therapy has multiple levels of action and can assist these individuals in the regulation of affect by providing an external source of soothing and also by enhancing self-soothing. The authors illustrate the model with a case example and report the results of a study in a clinical sample of BN.
Publication Types: Review; Review, tutorial

J Subst Abuse 1990;2(3):369-74
Bulimia nervosa with and without a history of overweight.
Mitchell JE, Pyle RL, Eckert E, Hatsukami D, Soll E.
Department of Psychiatry, University of Minnesota, Minneapolis.
In a review of the records of 454 patients with bulimia nervosa, 87 (19.2%) reported having a history of weight greater than 130% ideal body weight, although they were normal weight at evaluation. As contrasted to patients who had no history of having been overweight, this group of patients had a later onset of bulimia symptoms, weighed more and were more likely to be very dissatisfied with their current weight and to fear becoming overweight. The eating problems were similar in both groups.

Med J Aust 1998 Nov 2;169(9):488-91
Eating disorders revisited. II: Bulimia nervosa and related syndromes.
Hay PJ, Gilchrist PN, Ben-Tovim DI, Kalucy RS, Walker MK.
Department of Psychiatry, University of Adelaide, SA.
Bulimia nervosa and related syndromes are common, and occur in up to 5% of women who attend

general practitioners. Only a minority of those with these disorders present for treatment. General practitioners play a key role in primary and secondary prevention. About 50% of patients make a complete recovery, but the long term outcome is unknown.
Publication Types: Review; Review, tutorial

Miss Dent Assoc J 1988 Fall;44(3):10
Case presentation: bulimia nervosa.
Krolls SO.

Nervenarzt 2000 Jul;71(7):552-8
[Prevalence of eating disorders among students].
[Article in German]
Thiels C, Garthe R.
Fachbereich Sozialwesen, Fachhochschule Bielefeld. thiels@sozialwesen.fh-bielefeld.de A sample of 507 social work students completed the Bulimic Investigatory Test Edinburgh (BITE). In light of the association between weight discontent and eating disorders, suggestions are made for the management of overweight patients and both normal and underweight clients with eating disorders.

Nurs Times 1984 Aug 8-14;80(32):42-5
Bulimia nervosa.
Savage S, Biley F.

Pediatr Ann 1984 Dec;13(12):908-9, 912, 914
Bulimia: a modern epidemic among adolescents.
DuPont RL.

Percept Mot Skills 1998 Aug;87(1):108-10
Body perceptions of bulimic and nonbulimic groups.
Harden AJ, Butler S, Scheetz M.
Department of Family and Consumer Sciences, Ball State University, Muncie, IN 47306, USA.
A brief survey measuring satisfaction with the body, concern for physical appearance, and motivations for selection of clothing was administered to 30 women in a university-sponsored support group for bulimic students and 30 women randomly selected from a college campus. No mean differences were found between the groups on concern for physical appearance when in a social setting, but mean differences were significant on satisfaction with weight, satisfaction with body image, and concern for physical appearance when alone.

Postgrad Med 1988 Aug;84(2):119-23
Bulimia nervosa. Uncovering a secret disorder.
Fitzgerald BA, Wright JH, Atala KD.
Norton Psychiatric Clinic, Louisville, KY 40232-5070.
Bulimia nervosa is a common eating disorder among women. Sociocultural and interpersonal pressures are thought to be highly influential in the development of the syndrome. An association with depression has also been suggested.
Recognizing bulimia nervosa is usually difficult, because patients are hesitant to reveal their symptoms. If the condition is diagnosed early in its course, the prognosis is more favorable. Use of tricyclic

antidepressants and psychotherapy is the accepted treatment regimen.

Practitioner 1991 May;235(1502):396-9
Advances in bulimia nervosa.
Kent A.
Bulimia Research Clinic, St Georges' Hospital Medical School, London.
Publication Types: Review; Review, tutorial

Psychiatry Res 1999 Jul 30;87(1):77-82
Bulimia nervosa and autoimmunity.
Corcos M, Atger F, Levy-Soussan P, Avrameas S, Guilbert B, Cayol V, Jeammet P.
Department of Psychiatry (Adolescents and Young Adults), Institute Mutualiste Montsouris, Paris, France. jeammet@ext.jussieu.fr
The autoantibodies that react with dopamine and serotonin are of interest in the study of bulimia nervosa. These neurotransmitters play an important role in appetite control, sexual and social behavior, and stress responses, all of which form a part of the clinical picture of bulimia nervosa. The study of specific autoantibodies provides information about the immunological characteristics that may be related to brain disturbances.

Psychol Med 1987 Nov;17(4):891-8
Comparison of bulimic and non-bulimic anorexia nervosa patients during treatment.
Eckert ED, Halmi KA, Marchi P, Cohen J.
University of Minnesota Hospitals, Minneapolis.
Bulimic and non-bulimic anorexics were compared on psychological variables during a hospital treatment study. Although before treatment bulimic anorexics displayed more overall psychopathology than non-bulimics, many of the differences disappeared with treatment. There was no difference in severity of depression or body size estimation in these groups both before and with treatment. There was no difference in treatment response as measured by rate of weight gain. More expression of discomfort by bulimic anorexics during the acute phase of illness may in part account for some described differences in these two groups.

Psychol Med 1994 Aug;24(3):591-604
Course of multi-impulsive bulimia.
Fichter MM, Quadflieg N, Rief W.
Department of Psychiatry, University of Munich, Germany.
Thirty-two consecutively admitted females with bulimia nervosa (purging type) according to DSM-IV and additional impulsive behaviours (multi-impulsive bulimia (MIB)) and 32 age-matched female controls with DSM-IV bulimia nervosa (purging type) (uni-impulsive bulimia (UIB)) were assessed longitudinally on admission and at discharge following in-patient therapy and at a 2-year follow-up.
Multi-impulsive bulimics were defined as presenting at least three of the six of the following impulsive behaviours in their life-time in addition to their bulimic symptoms at admission: (a) suicidal attempts, (b) severe autoaggression, (c) shop lifting (other than food), (d) alcohol abuse, (e) drug abuse, or (f) sexual promiscuity. Multi-impulsive bulimics were more frequently separated or

divorced, had less schooling and held less-skilled jobs. Except forinteroceptive awareness (EDI), which was more disturbed in multi-impulsive bulimics, there were no differences concerning scales measuring eating disturbances and related areas. The data support the notion that 'multi-impulsive bulimia' or 'multi-impulsive disorder' should be classified as a distinct diagnostic group on axis I or that an 'Impulsive Personality Disorder' should be introduced on axis II. The development of more effective treatment for multi-impulsive bulimia is warranted.

Psychol Med 1998 Jul;28(4):761-71
Genetic and environmental risk factors for the weight and shape concerns characteristic of bulimia nervosa.
Wade T, Martin NG, Tiggemann M.
School of Psychology, Flinders University of South Australia, Brisbane, Australia.
This study seeks to identify the genetic and environmental risk factors for the overvalued ideas that are characteristic of bulimia nervosa, using a biometrical model fitting approach with twin data. With the exception of the Shape Concern subscale, environmental factors make a greater contribution than genetic factors to the development of the overvalued ideas that are seen to be one of the triggers for the development of bulimia nervosa. Given this substantial role of the environment influences, it seems likely that environmental manipulation can be effective in the prevention of bulimia nervosa.
Publication Types: Twin study

Psychol Rep 1994 Aug;75(1 Pt 1):51-6
Bulimia: an empirical analysis of psychodynamic theory.
Herkov MJ, Greer RA, Blau BI, McGuire JM, Eaker D.
Department of Psychiatry, College of Medicine, University of Florida, Gainesville 32610-0256.
This study examined two aspects of psychodynamic theory concerning bulimia nervosa, that bulimic patients ascribe to a traditionally feminine sex-role and that bulimic women have difficulty differentiating emotional from visceral sensations. 18 bulimic and 18 control women were administered the Bem Sex-role Inventory and the Eating Disorder Inventory. Contrary to dynamic theory, bulimic women were not more likely classified as traditionally feminine than control subjects; however, significantly more controls than bulimic women were classified as androgynous. Analysis of scores on the Eating Disorder Inventory's Interoceptive Awareness scale indicated a significant difference between bulimic persons and controls, providing strong support for the hypothesis that bulimic women have a difficult time differentiating emotional from visceral sensations.

Psychol Rep 1994 Feb;74(1):27-32
Bulimic women's perceptions of interaction within their families.
Waller G.
School of Psychology, University of Birmingham, Edgbaston, UK.
The association between women's perceptions of the interaction within

their families and symptomatology related to eating was investigated in a case series of 81 women suffering from bulimic disorders. Bingeing was more frequent when the family was perceived to have poor problem-solving skills but was less frequent when the women perceived their families as having a more cohesive style. In contrast abnormal restriction of intake was linked, although not significantly, to the converse pattern of perceived interaction within the family--greater when the family was relatively cohesive and lower when the family had good problem-solving skills.

Psychol Rep 1998 Aug;83(1):355-63
Femininity, bulimia, and distress in college women.
Brazelton EW, Greene KS, Gynther M, O'Mell J.
Haley Center, Auburn University, AL 36849, USA.
brazene@mail.auburn.edu
This study investigated differences in the scores on perceived Distress and Bulimia among college women with varying scores on the Behavioral Self-report of Femininity. Distress was assessed using The Psychological Distress Inventory and Bulimia was measured using the Bulimia Cognitive Distortions Scale. Distress scores were not significantly different between women scoring high and low on Bulimic Cognitive Distortions, and Bulimic Cognitive Distortion scores did not vary as a function of scores on Distress and Femininity.

Psychopathology 1998;31(4):197-205
Psychopathological considerations on the relationship between bulimia and obsessive-compulsive disorder.Aragona M, Vella G.
Ist Psychiatric Clinic, University La Sapienza, Rome, Italy.
The relationship between eating disorders, impulse control disorders and obsessive-compulsive disorder as part of a so-called 'obsessive-compulsive spectrum' is discussed, with particular emphasis on the relationship between eating disorders (particularly bulimia) and obsessive-compulsive disorder. The empirical studies on comorbidity, personality and familiarity are briefly reviewed. In particular the importance of distinguishing between obsessive thoughts and prevalent (dominant) thoughts is underlined.
Publication Types: Review; Review, tutorial

Psychosomatics 1984 Dec;25(12):909-13
Bulimia in male patients.
Mitchell JE, Goff G.

Psychosomatics 1985 Mar;26(3):252-3
Bulimia: a potentially fatal syndrome.
Ferguson JM.

Psychother Psychosom 1991;56(1-2):64-9
Everyday addictive behavior of bulimic women.
Jager B, Liedtke R, Kunsebeck HW, Seide L, Lempa W.
Department of Psychosomatics, Hannover Medical School, FRG.
The comorbidity of bulimia nervosa and other forms of drug use or dependence isfrequently reported, but statistical comparison as well as reference to a theoretical background is rare to be found. In order to assess

the associated dependencies of bulimia, 105 bulimic women participated in a structured interview with a focus on their everyday drug use. The results suggest that there is little evidence of other forms of related addicting drugs among bulimics.

Semin Gastrointest Dis 1998 Oct;9(4):176-82
Diagnosis and treatment of bulimia nervosa.
Caruso D, Klein H.
Department of Psychiatry, Saint Louis University School of Medicine, MO 63104, USA.
Bulimia nervosa often has an obscure presentation that requires a high level of suspicion by physicians. Awareness of subtle signs and knowledge of important questions to pursue are critical to a physician's ability to diagnose this disorder. Although the prognosis can be variable, the majority of bulimic patients have a serious chronic illness with remissions and exacerbations.
Publication Types: Review; Review, tutorial

South Med J 1983 Feb;76(2):181-4
Bulimia: the binge eating syndrome.
Humphries LL, Wrobel S.
Bulimia occurs in roughly half of obese and anorexic patients. Reported here is a case illustrating the bulimic's distorted body image, review alternative treatment methods, and suggest needed areas of research, particularly those elucidating the relationship between bulimia and affective disorders.
Publication Types: Review

Understanding bulimia. Signs, symptoms and the human experience.

Va Med 1984 Jul;111(7):397-8
Bulimia.
Kiernan K, Dove H, Wise TN.

West J Med 1991 Nov;155(5):523-4
Bulimia nervosa.
Yager J.

BINGEING

Addict Behav 1982;7(1):47-55
The assessment of binge eating severity among obese persons.
Gormally J, Black S, Daston S, Rardin D.
The purpose of this study was to conduct an assessment of binge eating severity among obese persons. A 16-item Binge Eating Scale was constructed describing both behavioral manifestations and feeling/cognitions surrounding a binge episode An 11-item Cognitive Factors Scale was developed measure two cognitive phenomena thought to be related to binge eating: the tendency to set unrealistic standards for a diet and low efficacy expectations for sustaining a diet. The results showed that the Binge Eating Scale successfully discriminated among persons judged by trained interviewers to have either no, moderate or severe binge eating problems. Significant correlation between the scales were obtained such that severe bingers tended to set up diets which were unrealistically strict while reporting low efficacy expectations to sustain a diet.
Publication Types: Clinical trial; Randomized controlled trial

Addict Behav 1989;14(5):503-11
Emotional and somatic consequences of binge episodes.
Lingswiler VM, Crowther JH, Stephens MA.
Kent State University, OH 44242.
The present study investigated emotional and somatic consequences of the daily eating episodes of 19 bulimics, 15 bingers, and 20 normal control subjects. For1 week, subjects rated 21 emotional and somatic states immediately following all eating episodes and 1 h later. Results indicated that bulimics and bingers reported significantly greater negative and somatic consequences immediately following their binge episodes than normal eaters following all of their eating episodes. Comparisons of the binge and nonbinge episodes of the bulimics and bingers indicated that binge episodes are followed by greater immediate and delayed negative and somatic consequences than nonbinge episodes. Theoretical and clinical implications of these findings are discussed.

Addict Behav 2000 Mar-Apr;25(2):205-16
Differences in daily stress, mood, coping, and eating behavior in binge

eating and nonbinge eating college women.
Wolff GE, Crosby RD, Roberts JA, Wittrock DA.
Mayo Medical Center, Rochester, MN 55905, USA.
wolff.gretchen@mayo.edu
This study investigated differences between binge eaters and controls on measures of daily stress, mood, coping, and eating behavior. The same measures were also used to compare binge days to nonbinge days for the binge group. Participants included 20 college women who reported binge eating at least two times per week and 20 women who reported no disturbance in their eating behavior.

Am J Psychiatry 1991 Aug;148(8):1097-8
Comment on: Am J Psychiatry. 1990 Nov;147(11):1509-13
Nonpurging bulimia nervosa and binge eating disorder.
Spitzer RL.
Publication Types: Comment Letter

BMJ 2001 Feb 10;322(7282):343
Binge eating.
Waller D.
Publication Types: Review; Review, tutorial

Can J Psychiatry 1998 Dec;43(10):1052-3
Body image alterations in binge eating disorder.
Adami GF, Bressani A, Marini P.
Publication Types: Letter

Clin Psychol Rev 1999 Jan;19(1):25-44
The role of dieting in binge eating disorder: etiology and treatment implications.
Howard CE, Porzelius LK.
Pacific University, School of Professional Psychology, Forest Grove, OR 97116-1797, USA.
Dieting has been implicated as a potential contributor in the development of binge eating problems in binge eating disorder (BED). If dieting plays a causal role in the etiology of BED, this could have major implications for understanding and treating individuals with the disorder. Although the literature is inconclusive as to the exact role that dieting plays in the etiology of BED, recommendations for future research and suggestions for treatment are given.
Publication Types: Review; Review, tutorial

Eat Weight Disord 1999 Jun;4(2):76-80
Gender differences among those exhibiting characteristics of binge eating disorder.
DiGioacchino RF, Sargent RG, Sharpe PA, Miller P.
Department of Health Promotion and Kinesiology, University of North Carolina at Charlotte, 9201 University City Boulevard, Charlotte, NC 28223, USA.
One hundred and eighty-seven former residential weight control participants exhibiting binge eating traits were assessed for gender differences regarding demographics, diet, exercise, weight control techniques, behavior modification techniques and binge eating characteristics. Results from this study suggest that males and females differ in regard to the diet/binge cycle and additionally, males appear to have a different or less emotional response subsequent to

a binge.

Harv Rev Psychiatry 1994 Mar-Apr;1(6):310-25
Binge eating disorder: clinical features and treatment of a new diagnosis.
de Zwaan M, Mitchell JE, Raymond NC, Spitzer RL.
Department of Psychiatry, University of Vienna, Austria.
This review will describe the diagnostic criteria for the recently proposed diagnosis of binge eating disorder and provide an overview of its prevalence, clinical characteristics, and treatment approaches. Studies indicate that binge eaters represent a substantial proportion (18-46%) of the obese in weight control programs. Preliminary findings indicate that obese binge eaters may be more likely than nonbinge eaters to drop out of treatment when treated by conventional weight loss programs, although weight losses achieved by binge eaters and nonbinge eaters who finish treatment do not differ significantly.
Publication Types: Review; Review, tutorial

Int J Eat Disord 1993 Dec;14(4):427-31
Eating behavior in binge eating disorder.
Goldfein JA, Walsh BT, LaChaussee JL, Kissileff HR, Devlin MJ.
Department of Psychiatry, Columbia University, College of Physicians and Surgeons, New York, NY 10032.
In order to examine the eating behavior of individuals with the newly proposed diagnosis, binge eating disorder (BED), standardized meals were served to 20 obese women, 10 with BED and 10 without BED. When asked to binge eat from a multiple-item array of foods, obese subjects with BED consumed significantly more calories than did obese subjects without BED. Significant differences between the two groups were also found on several of the self-report measures.

Int J Eat Disord 1993 Jan;13(1):25-33
Assessment of binge eating in obese patients.
Wilson GT, Nonas CA, Rosenblum GD.
Rutgers University, Piscataway, NJ 08854.
Obese patients entering a weight control program were classified as binge eaters if they reported uncontrolled consumption of what others would regard as an unusually large amount of food at least once a week for the previous month. Binge eaters differed significantly from nonbingers across a broad range of eating and weight-related characteristics assessed using a self-report version of the Eating Disorder Examination. Attitudinal differences were marked. The results provided no support for the view that obese binge eaters have a pattern of general "addictiveness" to psychoactive substances or other activities.

Int J Eat Disord 1995 Nov;18(3):199-208
Interrupting the binge-purge cycle in bulimia: the use of planned binges.
Steel ZP, Farag PA, Blaszczynski AP.
Academic Mental Health Unit, School of Psychiatry, University of New South Wales, Liverpool Hospital, Australia.

Research investigating the specific effects of the various cognitive and behavioral components of the standard cognitive-behavioral treatment (CBT) approach for bulimia nervosa is examined in combination with comprehensive reviews of the treatment outcome literature. RESULTS: These reviews suggest that while treatment has largely been effective at reducing binge-purge frequencies, it does not result in the elimination of the presenting problem for a significant proportion of participants. These cases in combination with the analysis of the potential deficits of the standard behavioral procedures employed in CBT provide tentative support for the use of planned binges as an addition to the strategies currently used in the treatment of binge and purge behavior. In conclusion the paper explores some of the ethical implications raised by asking subjects to engage in their problematic behavior.

Publication Types: Review; Review, tutorial

Int J Eat Disord 1997 Jul;22(1):77-81

Skills training treatment for adaptive affect regulation in a woman with binge-eating disorder.

Telch CF.

Department of Psychiatry and Behavioral Sciences, Stanford University School of Medicine, CA 94305-5542, USA.

This case study describes a skills training treatment for binge eating which focused on teaching adaptive affect regulation. A 36-year-old obese woman with a long history of severe binge eating received individual treatment specifically aimed at enhancing her emotion regulation abilities. By treatment end she no longer met criteria for binge eating disorder.

Int J Eat Disord 1998 Jan;23(1):17-26

A comparison of two approaches to the assessment of binge eating in obesity.

Gladis MM, Wadden TA, Foster GD, Vogt RA, Wingate BJ.

Department of Psychiatry, University of Pennsylvania, Philadelphia, USA.

Comparison of two different methods of assessing binge eating in a sample of 128 obese women enrolled in a weight loss protocol. Prior to treatment, participants completed the Binge Eating Scale (BES) and the Questionnaire on Eating and Weight Patterns (QEWP), as well as measures of other relevant constructs. The relative merits of these two approaches to classifying binge eaters and implications for the design of new methods are discussed.

Int J Eat Disord 1998 May;23(4):390-7

Variability in self-esteem, moods, shame, and guilt in women who binge.

Sanftner JL, Crowther JH.

Department of Psychology, Kent State University, OH 44242, USA.

Variability in self-esteem, moods, shame, and guilt was explored in a sample of 78 women (37 who binge and 41 who do not binge) attending a large university. Results indicated that women who binge reported significantly greater fluctuations than women who do not binge in state self-esteem, negative affect, shame, and guilt.

Int J Eat Disord 1998 Nov;24(3):251-7
Binge eating disorder with and without a history of purging symptoms.
Peterson CB, Mitchell JE, Engbloom S, Nugent S, Mussell MP, Crow SJ, Miller JP.
Department of Psychiatry, University of Minnesota, Minneapolis, USA.
The purpose of this study was to evaluate whether a history of purging behaviors in individuals with binge eating disorder (BED) is associated with increased comorbid psychopathology, dietary restraint, severity of eating pathology, and attitudinal disturbance in self-esteem and body image. The findings indicate that a history of purging behavior in BED is not associated with increased rates of comorbid psychopathology, severity of eating problems, dietary restraint, or attitudinal disturbance. Purging history does not appear to be a clinically meaningful variable with which to subclassify individuals with BED.

Int J Eat Disord 1998 Nov;24(3):307-12
Does the size of a binge matter?
Pratt EM, Niego SH, Agras WS.
Department of Psychology, Rutgers University, Piscataway, New Jersey, USA.
OBJECTIVE: The aim of this study was to examine whether objective and subjective binges differ significantly from each other in relation to measures of psychopathology in a sample of women who meet DSM-IV diagnostic criteria forbulimia nervosa. The lack of significant findings questions the diagnostic validity of the "large amount of food" criterion used to define binge eating in the DSM-IV.

Int J Eat Disord 1998 Sep;24(2):185-92
Bulimia nervosa, restrained, and unrestrained eaters: a comparison of non-binge eating behavior.
Bourne SK, Bryant RA, Griffiths RA, Touyz SW, Beumont PJ.
Psychiatric Unit, Prince of Wales Hospital, Sydney, New South Wales, Australia.
This study investigated non-binge eating behavior in bulimia nervosa, restrained and unrestrained eaters. Bulimic subjects display aberrant eating behavior, and the extent to which subjects engage in maladaptive eating behavior isrelated to the degree of eating pathology. These results support the utility of the EBRS as a useful index of eating behaviors in clinical and nonclinical populations.

Int J Eat Disord 1999 Apr;25(3):287-92
Binge eating disorder in females: a population-based investigation.
Kinzl JF, Traweger C, Trefalt E, Mangweth B, Biebl W.
Department of Psychiatry, Innsbruck University Clinics, Austria.
The authors investigated the prevalence of binge eating behavior in a general female Austrian population. The findings indicate that binge eating appears to be a fairly common behavior in women. Dieting, chronic restrained eating, and excessive exercise may be important triggers for BED (binge eating disorder) and bulimia nervosa.

Int J Eat Disord 1999 Jan;25(1):45-54
Natural course of a community sample of women with binge eating disorder.
Cachelin FM, Striegel-Moore RH, Elder KA, Pike KM, Wilfley DE, Fairburn CG.
Department of Psychology, Wesleyan University, Middletown, Connecticut 06459-0408, USA.
A community sample of women with binge eating disorder (BED) was followed for a period of 6 months, in order to examine the natural course of the disorder. It appears that for some women with BED, the eating disorder improves with a decrease in binge eating and importance of weight or shape. For others, the eating disorder symptoms remain constant.

Int J Eat Disord 1999 Mar;25(2):215-8
Differences between binge eating disorder and nonpurging bulimia nervosa.
Santonastaso P, Ferrara S, Favaro A.
Department of Neurological and Psychiatric Sciences, University of Padua, Italy.
A comparisonn of the pathway to binge eating and clinical characteristics of binge eating disorder patients (BED) and nonpurging bulimics. Unlike nonpurging bulimics, BED patients appear to form a more heterogeneous group.

Int J Eat Disord 1999 Nov;26(3):295-300
Binge eating severity, self-concept, dieting self-efficacy and social support during treatment of binge eating disorder.
Goodrick GK, Pendleton VR, Kimball KT, Carlos Poston WS, Reeves RS, Foreyt JP.
Behavioral Medicine Research Center, Baylor College of Medicine, Houston, Texas, USA.
OBJECTIVE: In treatment of binge eating, measures of self-concept, eating self-efficacy, and social support were examined at 0, 6, and 18 months to determine if improvements in these variables were associated with reductions in binge eating severity. This study showed that self-concept and eating self-efficacy were associated with improvement in binge eating severity. Improvement in self-concept and eating self-efficacy may be processes leading to clinical improvement in this eating disorder, or they may result from changes in binge eating. Copyright 1999 by John Wiley & Sons, Inc.

Int J Eat Disord 2000 Mar;27(2):238-43
Binge eating disorder and bulimia nervosa: differences in the quality and quantity of binge eating episodes.
Fitzgibbon ML, Blackman LR.
Department of Psychiatry, Northwestern University Medical School, Chicago, Illinois, USA.
mlf056@nwu.edu
This study sought to examine the differences in the quantity and quality of binges between binge eating disorder (BED) and bulimia nervosa. Results suggest no differences in binge quantity with BED and bulimia, but there were differences in the binge quality. The importance of increasing our knowledge of the continuum of weight and binging is discussed.

Int J Eat Disord 2000 May;27(4):471-9
What is a binge? The influence of amount, duration, and loss of control

criteria on judgments of binge eating.
Johnson WG, Boutelle KN, Torgrud L, Davig JP, Turner S.
Department of Psychiatry and Human Behavior, University of Mississippi Medical Center, Jackson, MS 39216, USA. triwill@fiona.umsmed.edu
We investigated the influence of amount of food eaten, duration of eating episode, and loss of control in judgments of eating episodes as binges.
METHOD: Participants rated the degree to which the eating behavior of a female actress qualified as a "binge" after observing eight videotaped vignettes in which the amount of food eaten, apparent duration of eating episode, and loss of control were varied. The results are consistent with the definitional criteria of a binge, underscore the independence of loss of control, and highlight the importance of the violation of dietary standards in judgments of binges. Moreover, they illustrate the reliability and sensitivity of the methodology, and its potential for further investigations of binge eating.
Copyright 2000 by John Wiley & Sons, Inc.

Int J Eat Disord 2000 Sep;28(2):131-8
Predictors of treatment outcome for binge eating disorder.
Peterson CB, Crow SJ, Nugent S, Mitchell JE, Engbloom S, Mussell MP.
Eating Disorders Research Program, Department of Psychiatry, University of Minnesota, Minneapolis, Minnesota 55414, USA. peter161@tc.umn.edu
OBJECTIVE: The purpose of this study was to identify predictors of short-term treatment outcome for individuals with binge eating disorder (BED). This study indicates that the frequency of binge eating episodes at baseline is predictive of outcome status at the end of treatment, suggesting that meaningful prognostic factors in BED are identifiable.
Copyright 2000 by John Wiley & Sons, Inc.
PMID: 10897074 [PubMed - indexed for MEDLINE]

J Abnorm Psychol 1998 May;107(2):263-71
On the relation of dieting and bingeing in bulimia nervosa.
Lowe MR, Gleaves DH, Murphy-Eberenz KP.
Department of Clinical and Health Psychology, Allegheny University of the Health Sciences, Philadelphia, Pennsylvania 19102-1192, USA. lowem@wpo.auhs.edu
The continuum model of bulimia nervosa suggests that dieting plays a major role in the etiology and maintenance of bulimia. However, a previous study (M. R. Lowe et al., 1996) recently found no relationship between dieting intensity and binge eating problems in nonclinical participants differing widely in eating and weight concerns. The present study extended these findings by examining the relationship between dieting and bingeing among individuals with bulimia. The results raise new questions about the continuum model of bulimia and suggest that weight-loss dieting may not play as prominent a role in the maintenance of bulimia as it does in

its initiation.

J Abnorm Psychol 1998 Nov;107(4):671-5
Age of onset for binge eating and purging during late adolescence: a 4-year survival analysis.
Stice E, Killen JD, Hayward C, Taylor CB.
Department of Psychiatry, Stanford University, USA.
stice@psy.utexas.edu
This prospective study examined age of onset for binge eating and purging among girls during late adolescence and tested whether dieting and negative affectivity predicted these outcomes. Findings suggest that late adolescence is a high-risk period for onset of bulimic behaviors and identify modifiable risk factors for these outcomes.

J Am Diet Assoc 1998 Apr;98(4):446-50
Dieting and binge eating among adolescents: what do they really mean?
Neumark-Sztainer D, Story M.
Division of Epidemiology, School of Public Health at the University of Minnesota, Minneapolis 55454, USA.
The study objectives were to gain insight into how the terms "dieting" and "binge eating" are understood and used by adolescents and to assess whether interpretations of these terms are consistent across age and gender. The findings suggest that prevalence rates of self-reported dieting and binge eating behaviors should be interpreted with caution and it should not be assumed that the majority of adolescents who self-report dieting are engaging in unhealthful behaviors. In providing nutrition counseling to youth, and in assessing dieting and binge eating behaviors in clinical settings and in research studies, specific behaviors should be defined.

J Am Diet Assoc 2001 Feb;101(2):209-15
Nutrient intake of obese female binge eaters.
To compare the 6-month change in selected nutrients and number of binge days (from 7-day food records) between obese binge eaters randomly assigned to either a behavioral self-management (BSM) or waiting list control (WLC) group. Our results suggest that collecting dietary information from participants identified with binge eating disorder is challenging. Dietitians who conduct behavioral weight management programs may require additional training in identifying and understanding the psychological characteristics of participants with binge-eating disorder.

J Behav Med 1987 Jun;10(3):287-99
Emotional reactivity and eating in binge eating and obesity.
Lingswiler VM, Crowther JH, Stephens MA.
The present study investigated daily mood fluctuations and moods during eating in normal and overweight binge and nonbinge eaters (N = 56) and moods during binge and nonbinge episodes of individuals who binge eat (N = 29). The results indicated that bingers experience greater fluctuations of anxiety and depression than nonbingers and overweight individuals experience greater fluctuations in anxiety, hostility, and depression than normal-weight

individuals. In addition, for bingers, negative mood states are experienced during a significantly greater proportion of binge episodes than nonbinge episodes, although the intensity of the negative mood state was not related to the severity of the binge-eating episode. Theoretical and clinical implications of these findings are discussed.

J Pers Soc Psychol 1988 Oct;55(4):588-98
Social contagion of binge eating.
Crandall CS.
Department of Psychology, Yale University, New Haven, Connecticut 06520.
A social psychological account of the acquisition of binge eating, analogous to the classic social psychological work, "Social Pressures in Informal Groups" (Festinger, Schachter, & Back, 1950), is suggested and tested in two college sororities. In these sororities, clear evidence of group norms about appropriate binge-eating behavior was found; in one sorority, the more one binged, the more popular one was. In the other, popularity was associated with binging the right amount: It is argued that there is no great mystery to how bulimia has become such a serious problem for today's women. Binge eating seems to be an acquired pattern of behavior, perhaps through modeling, and appears to be learned much like any other set of behaviors. Like other behaviors, it is under substantial social control.

JAMA 1988 Jan 1;259(1):45
Bulimia: when is a binge a binge?
Dilsaver SC.
Publication Types: Letter

Obes Surg 1998 Oct;8(5):517-9
Body image in binge eating disorder.
Adami GF, Marinari GM, Bressani A, Testa S, Scopinaro N.
Dipartimento di Discipline Chirurgiche e Metodologie Integrate, Facolta di Medicina, Universita di Genova, Genoa, Italy. adami@unige.it
BACKGROUND: The purpose of this study was to evaluate the impairment of body image in patients with binge eating disorder (BED). A 3-year longitudinal study was undertaken in 25 BED obese patients and 26 non-BED obese patients who had undergone biliopancreatic diversion (BPD) for obesity. Over the long term following BPD, binge eating disappears, which suggests that the loss of control over food intake is mainly dependent on dieting and on the preoccupation with food and body shape.

Psychol Med 1981 Nov;11(4):697-706
Binge-eating and vomiting: a survey of a college population.
Halmi KA, Falk JR, Schwartz E.
A survey of 355 college students was carried out to determine the prevalence of the psychiatric disorder bulimia (the binge-eating syndrome). Results of the survey indicate that, within the normal college population, 13% experienced all of the major symptoms of bulimia as outlined in the DSM-III.

Psychol Rep 1991 Oct;69(2):527-32
Bulimics' perceptions of emotional responding during binge-purge episodes.

Mizes JS, Arbitell MR.
Department of Psychiatry, MetroHealth Medical Center, Case Western Reserve University School of Medicine, Cleveland, OH 44109.
The concept of changes in emotional arousal during the binge-purge cycle plays a principal role in bulimia theory. Female bulimic patients (n = 29) retrospectively rated the intensity of several emotions during their binge-purge cycle. When collapsed into positive versus negative emotion categories, both categories showed significant changes in emotions over the course of the binge-purge episode. Negative emotion increased after a binge and decreased during the purge. Positive emotion decreased after binging and increased during and after purging.

Res Nurs Health 1996 Oct;19(5):389-98
The relationship between binge eating severity and body fat in nonpurge binge eating women.
Timmerman GM, Stevenson JS.
School of Nursing, University of Texas at Austin, 78701-1499, USA.
The relationship between binge eating severity, measured by caloric intake, and amount of body fat, measured by percent of body fat and body mass index (BMI) was examined in nonpurge binge eating women. Although there was a low, but significant, relationship between binge eating severity and BMI, the relationship was not significant between binge eating severity and percent of body fat. Age and weight cycling were the best predictors for percent of body fat, while weight cycling alone was the best predictor for BMI.

South Med J 1987 Jul;80(7):937
Binge-purge syndrome.
Burket RC, Hodgin JD.
Publication Types: Letter

OBESITY

Adolescence 1988 Spring;23(89):155-69
Determinants of adolescent obesity: a comparison with anorexia nervosa.
Brone RJ, Fisher CB.
Graduate Program in Developmental Psychology, Fordham University, Bronx, New York 10458.
This report investigates childhood and adolescent obesity through a comparison with anorexia nervosa, an eating disorder typically associated with the opposite end of the eating behavior spectrum. Many similarities in the etiologies of the two conditions are discussed, particularly with regard to the influence of family interactional patterns.
Publication Types: Review; Review, tutorial

Am J Psychiatry 2000 Jun;157(6):851-3
Comment on: Am J Psychiatry. 2000 Jun;157(6):854-66
Am J Psychiatry. 2000 Jun;157(6):886-95
Weighty perspectives: contemporary challenges in obesity and eating disorders.
Yager J.
Publication Types: Comment; Editorial

Ann Clin Res 1987;19(2):143-6
Psychosocial factors in obesity.
Mustajoki P.
Third Department of Medicine, Helsinki University Central Hospital, Finland.
Obese people as a group have similar mental health as normal weight people, and there are no psychiatric features characteristic of obesity in general. However, small subgroups of obese individuals may have psychiatric abnormalities which are specific for obesity, such as body image disturbance or periodic compulsive overeating (bulimia). Obesity is strongly related to sociocultural factors. In western countries obesity is commoner in lower than in higher social classes. Thus, the development of obesity is influenced by social status. However, also the converse is true: recent observations suggest that obese people lose social status. This is probably due to prejudice and discrimination against obese persons in the modern western society.

Ann Intern Med 1985 Dec;103(6 (Pt 2)):1062-7
Social and psychological consequences of obesity.
Wadden TA, Stunkard AJ.
The strong prejudice in this country against obese persons is evident in children as young as 6 years of age. There is discrimination against obese persons in both academic and work settings. Despite this discrimination, overweight persons in the general population show no greater psychological disturbance than do non-obese persons. Similarly, obese patients seen for medical or surgical procedures generally show no more psychopathology than do non-obese patients. Women, adolescent girls, and the morbidly obese appear to suffer the most deleterious consequences of society's contempt for the obese.

Ann Intern Med 2000 Nov 21;133(10):840
The Management of Eating Disorders and Obesity.
Freund KM.
Boston University Medical Center, Boston, Massachusetts.

Ann Med 1992 Aug;24(4):303-8
Binge eating in the obese.
de Zwaan M, Mitchell JE.
Department of Psychiatry, University of Minnesota, Minneapolis 55455.
This review describes problems in the definition of the term binge eating, especially in the absence of purging (vomiting, laxative abuse). Despite differences in the definitions of binge eating and variability among the samples investigated, there is strong evidence that binge eaters represent a distinct subgroup among the obese. Binge eating obese exhibit significantly more eating and weight-related pathology, as well as more psychopathology compared to their non-binge eating obese counterparts.
Publication Types: Review; Review, tutorial

Arch Intern Med 2000 Sep 25;160(17):2581-9
Dieting and the development of eating disorders in overweight and obese adults.
We reviewed articles evaluating the relations among dieting, weight loss treatment, weight cycling, eating disorders, and psychological functioning in overweight and obese adults. Concerns that dieting induces eating disorders or other psychological dysfunction in overweight and obese adults are generally not supported by empirical studies. Such concerns should not preclude attempts to reduce caloric intake and increase physical activity to achieve modest weight loss or prevent additional weight gain.

Can Psychiatr Assoc J 1978 Jan;23(4):249-63
Perceptual experiences in anorexia nervosa and obesity.
Garner DM, Garfinkel PE, Moldofsky H.
There is increasing evidence suggesting that the perceptual-cognitive experiences of people with anorexia nervosa and juvenile onset obesity may differ from those of people without eating disorders. The research related to several perceptual-cognitive dimensions is critically examined. The relative efficacy of

some behavioural and medical therapies may be related, in part, to their effects on perceptual-cognitive parameters. Recommendations are also made for investigations to further delineate the role of perceptual-cognitive difficulties in people with eating problems.

Compr Ther 1994;20(1):3-5
A second look at obesity.
Bellows RT, Franke AL.
Publication Types: Review; Review, tutorial

Curr Concepts Nutr 1975;3:163-75
Behavioral correlates of the obese condition.
Greenwood MR.
Publication Types: Review

Curr Concepts Nutr 1975;3:73-80
Obesity during childhood.
Mayer J.

Curr Concepts Nutr 1975;3:81-8
Juvenile obesity.
Heald FP.

Diabetes Metab 2001 Feb;27(1):71-7
[Behavioural and cognitive approach to obese persons].
[Article in French]
Golay A, Fossati M, Volery M, Rieker A.
Division d'enseignement therapeutique pour maladies chroniques, Departement de Medecine Interne, Hopitaux Universitaires de Geneve, CH-1211 Geneve 14. Alain.Golay@hcuge.ch
We present a description of basic concepts of the cognitive-behavioural approach in obese patients with binge eating disorders. We also give practical advice to the health care providers.
Publication Types: Review; Review, tutorial

Health Psychol 1993 Sep;12(5):339-41
Whether obesity should be treated.
Brownell KD.
Antidieting sentiment is strengthened in part by the assumption that all diets fail, which in turn is based on data from university-based treatment programs. A small percentage of overweight people attempt to lose weight in these programs, and they differ in important ways from overweight people in general. Generalizing from the treatment of this group to all programs is highly questionable. Hence, little is known about the effectiveness of approaches used by most people. There is a pressing need for research on this topic, and a need for treatments that address the specific needs of those who seek clinical treatments.
Publication Types: Editorial Review; Review, tutorial

Int J Eat Disord 1994 Jan;15(1):53-61
Obesity, binge eating and psychopathology: are they related?
Telch CF, Agras WS.
Department of Psychiatry, Stanford University School of Medicine, CA 94305-5542.
Obese female subjects with binge eating disorder BED; (N = 107) completed the Beck Depression Inventory, Symptom Checklist-90, Inventory of Interpersonal Problems, and Rosenberg Self-Esteem Scale. Subjects were divided into moderate

or severe binger on the basis of scores on the Binge Eating Scale, Spearman correlational analyses were performed to determine the relationship between psychopathology and obesity and psychopathology and binge eating. Analyses of variance (ANOVAs) were then performed using scores on the psychological measures with subjects grouped both by severity of obesity and severity of binge eating. The results indicated that in our sample, obesity and scores on the measures of psychiatric symptomatology were unrelated. However, a significant positive relationship was found between binge eating severity and degree of psychiatric symptomatology.

Int J Eat Disord 1998 Jan;23(1):27-37
Binge eating in an obese community sample.
Striegel-Moore RH, Wilson GT, Wilfley DE, Elder KA, Brownell KD.
Department of Psychology, Wesleyan University, Middletown, Connecticut 06459-0408, USA.
The present study sought to examine the validity and utility of diagnostic criteria for binge-eating disorder (BED) by replicating and extending a study reported by de Zwaan and colleagues. Individuals with BED were distinguishable from overeaters and normal controls on a number of psychological and behavioral variables. Few differences were found between subthreshold and full-syndrome BED, raising questions about the diagnostic validity of the frequency threshold. Our findings support the view of BED as a distinct syndrome.

Int J Eat Disord 1998 Nov;24(3):313-7
Obese women with binge eating disorder define the term binge.
Telch CF, Pratt EM, Niego SH.
Department of Psychiatry and Behavioral Sciences, Stanford University School of Medicine, CA 94305-5722, USA.
The purpose of this study was to provide information regarding the criteria used by women with binge eating disorder (BED) to classify an eating episode a binge. The findings from this study are important to consider in an evaluation of the proposed DSM-IV research criteria for BED.

Int J Eat Disord 1999 Sep;26(2):205-10
The gender specificity of emotional, situational, and behavioral indicators of binge eating in a diet-seeking obese population.
Costanzo PR, Musante GJ, Friedman KE, Kern LS, Tomlinson K.
Center for Weight Control and Lifestyle Change, Durham, North Carolina, USA.
This study investigated the unique gender correlates of binge eating severity in a diet-seeking population. METHOD: This sample consisted of 288 self-admitted patients enrolled in a residential weight loss program between 1996 and 1997. Subjects were administered several questionnaires including (a) the Binge Eating Scale, (b) the Beck Depression Inventory, (c) the Rosenberg Self-Esteem Scale, (d) 5-point scales of eating related foci, and (e) 7-point scales of subject confidence in

controlling their eating under various circumstances. Regression results revealed that while men and women share some common predictors of binge eating severity, there are also some gender-specific correlates. The strength of the distinctive gender-specific regressions for binge eating severity suggests that the problems of binging in obese males and females are derivatives of differential sex role expectations.

Int J Obes Relat Metab Disord 1998 Aug;22(8):778-85
Erratum in: Int J Obes Relat Metab Disord 1999 Jan;23(1):106
The Eating Inventory in obese women: clinical correlates and relationship to weight loss.
Foster GD, Wadden TA, Swain RM, Stunkard AJ, Platte P, Vogt RA.
University of Pennsylvania School of Medicine, Philadelphia, USA.
OBJECTIVES: Describe the physical and psychological correlates of the Eating Inventory (EI) (also known as the Three-Factor Eating Questionnaire) factors in an obese sample, and determine the relationship between the three EI factors and weight loss. The three factors of the EI showed clinical utility in a sample of women receiving treatment for obesity.

Ir Med J 1975 May 10;68(9):227-31
Obesity and anorexia nervosa. A study of growth hormone release.
Devlin JG.

J Am Diet Assoc 1996 Jan;96(1):58-61
Comment in: J Am Diet Assoc. 1996 Sep;96(9):854
Binge eating among the overweight population: a serious and prevalent problem.
Bruce B, Wilfley D.
Stanford Center for Research in Disease Prevention, Stanford University, Palo Alto, Calif 94304, USA.
This article provides an overview of current knowledge about obese persons who binge eat and recommends that dietitians who treat patients for weight-related conditions take a proactive role by screening them for binge eating problems or, at a minimum, screen those who are suspected of binge eating and then refine treatment approaches accordingly.
Publication Types: Review; Review, tutorial

J Behav Med 1992 Apr;15(2):155-70
Binge eating among the obese: a descriptive study.
Arnow B, Kenardy J, Agras WS.
Department of Psychiatry, Stanford University School of Medicine, California 94305.
In this study nineteen obese females applying for treatment for binge eating were administered a semistructured interview assessing the presence or absence of food restrictions, thoughts, feelings and physical sensations associated with binges, typical precipitants to binges, and factors identified as useful in avoiding binge eating. Both negative mood and abstinence violations emerged as important precipitants. The results also suggested that these precipitants constitute separate, independent pathways to binge eating. Implications

of these findings with respect to restraint theory are discussed.

J Consult Clin Psychol 1988 Jun;56(3):433-9
Obese binge eaters: affect, cognitions, and response to behavioural weight control.
Marcus MD, Wing RR, Hopkins J.
Publication Types: Clinical trial; Randomized controlled trial

J Nerv Ment Dis 1988 Mar;176(3):144-52
Bulimia in obese individuals. Relationship to normal-weight bulimia.
Hudson JI, Pope HG Jr, Wurtman J, Yurgelun-Todd D, Mark S, Rosenthal NE.
Epidemiology Laboratory, McLean Hospital, Belmont, Massachusetts 02178.
We compared 23 obese subjects meeting DSM-III criteria for bulimia with 47 obese nonbulimic subjects and 47 normal-weight bulimic subjects using structured diagnostic interviews. The results suggest that obese individuals with bulimic symptoms may constitute a sizable but little-recognized population. Further studies will be required, however, to assess whether the syndrome of bulimia in obesity represents a valid diagnostic entity.

J Psychosom Res 1998 Mar-Apr;44(3-4):375-84
Behavioral treatment of obese binge eaters: do they need different care?
Gladis MM, Wadden TA, Vogt R, Foster G, Kuehnel RH, Bartlett SJ.
University of Pennsylvania School of Medicine, Philadelphia 19104, USA.
This study investigated the relationship between binge eating and the outcome of weight loss treatment. On the basis of these findings, and a review of the recent literature, we conclude that obese binge eaters respond as favorably to standard dietary and behavioral treatments as do obese nonbingers.
Publication Types: Clinical trial; Randomized controlled trial

JAMA 1973 Feb 5;223(6):627-30
Physiology and natural history of obesity.
Nelson RA, Anderson LF, Gastineau CF, Hayles AB, Stamnes CL.

Life Sci 1988;43(2):93-110
Obesity: thermodynamic principles in perspective.
Rampone AJ, Reynolds PJ.
Department of Physiology, School of Medicine, Oregon Health Sciences University, Portland 97201.
The energy balance equation applicable to all living organisms was used as a framework on which to construct a critical review of some of the more controversial aspects of the obesity problem. The equation matches energy intake against all the known forms of work that the body does in utilizing that energy, including external and internal work and the work of adipose tissue synthesis(stored energy). Equations representing everyday living conditions, resting, fasting and basal conditions were constructed. Creating these models gave us the added advantage of enabling us better to evaluate the scientific literature because the data we generated,

although theoretical, served as excellent standards against which to compare the real data that have emanated from research laboratories.(ABSTRACT TRUNCATED AT 400 WORDS)
Publication Types: Review; Review, tutorial

Med Sci Sports Exerc 1991 Mar;23(3):292-7
Factors common to successful therapy for the obese patient.
Foreyt JP, Goodrick GK.
Department of Medicine, Baylor College of Medicine, Houston, TX 77030.
The majority of patients treated for obesity regain lost weight after treatment. Speculated upon were what might be done to improve long-term success rates by examining the factors associated with success or relapse. An emphasis on exercise and prescribing more gradual changes in diet and exercise appears to be associated with better outcomes. There may be a need to conceptualize obesity as a food dependency disorder not amenable to self-control strategies. External social control through peer support groups may be indicated to help patients through temptations.
Publication Types: Review; Review, tutorial

Minerva Pediatr 2000 Oct;52(10):521
[Obesity and binge eating: prevalence, significance, therapeutic possibilities in a selected population of obese adolescents].
[Article in Italian]
Biondi M, Spinosa E.
Servizio di Auxo-Endocrinologia e Diabetologia del bambino e dell'adolescente, U.O. di Pediatria A.O. G. Rummo di Benevento.

Nahrung 1977;21(3):193-7
Short-term fasting in the treatment of obesity.
Rath R, Vondra K.
Short-term fasting (five days) accompanied by negative nitrogen balance induced protein sparing effect in the realimentation period at obese persons on the hypocaloric diet. The results of repeated estimations of body composition (densitometry) revealed, that at this regimen the losses of the body fat were in a marked preponderance over the lean body mass (63% versus 37% of the weight decrease). The repeated periods of starvation are well tolerated and appeared to be effective and safe (provided that states with contraindication of starvation are excluded).

Nursing (Lond) 1982 Sep;2(5):117-20
Obesity and anorexia nervosa.
Parsonage SR.

Obes Res 1999 Jul;7(4):379-86
Binge eating, body image, depression, and self-efficacy in an obese clinical population.
Cargill BR, Clark MM, Pera V, Niaura RS, Abrams DB.
Cape Psych Center, Cape Cod Hospital, Hyannis, MA 02601, USA. CAP.MD-CB@CCH.CAPECOD.NET
OBJECTIVE: Binge eating disorder appears to be an important factor in obesity treatment. Researchers have proposed that specialized treatment

programs be developed to address chronic binge eating behavior. This study was conducted to examine the relationships between binge eating, depression, body image, and self-efficacy. Based on related research, it was hypothesized that depression and negative body image would be greater for binge eaters whereas weight self-efficacy would be lower. The findings extend current understanding of the relationships between binge eating, body image, depression, and self-efficacy. The significance of body image, especially in relation to negative social consciousness, was determined when comparing several psychological and behavioral factors thought to influence binge eating. Further research is needed to determine the causal relationships between binge eating and the other factors examined in this study.

Psychosomatics 1978 Apr;19(4):208-12
Obesity and anorexia nervosa.
Bruch H.

Psychother Psychosom 1975;26(2):101-17
Elements of resistance to a combined medical and psychotherapeutic program in anorexia nervosa. An overview.
Pierloot RA, Wellens W, Houben ME.
According to several follow-up studies in the literature, anorexia nervosa has to be considered as an affection with a grave prognosis. We have studied the outcome in a group of 32 female patients who could be considered as homogeneous in a number of aspects. The following five criteria, on which the delineation of the syndrome is based, were realized in all the patients: considerable weight loss; limited food intake; amenorrhea; juvenile age of onset; absence of primary organic or specific psychotic disorder. In order to circumscribe some prognostic elements, we have compared a number of clinical, family and personality variables in these groups. As favorable clinical factors can be mentioned: younger age at admission and shorter duration of the illness. Manifestations of impulsive behavior (automutilation, kleptomania, fugues, etc. ...) and sucide attempts are unfavorable. No definite family factors can be defined, although the absence of psychological interaction with the father seems to be unfavorable. A better prognostic outcome is offered by the following personality characteristics, determined by psychological testing: lower neuroticism and higher self-defensiveness on the ABV; a lower general profile and especially a lower score on the schizophrenia scale of the MMPI; less pronounced tendencies to infantile regression, passivity and sexual repression as these are expressed in the TAT.

Psychother Psychosom 1980;33(4):205-13
A biobehavioral model of obesity.
Hartman LM.
Recent research contributing to an increased understanding of human feeding isreviewed and implications for obesity discussed. Hyperphagia may represent the manifestation of diverse origins requiring different therapeutic strategies. A biobehavioral model of obesity designed to promote increased efficacy of treatment interventions with the overweight is

proposed.

THERAPY

Acta Paedopsychiatr 1968 Oct;35(10):294-301
Treatment problems in adolescents with anorexia nervosa. Preliminary observations on the second phase.
Blackwell A, Rollins N.

Acta Psychiatr Scand 1999 May;99(5):385-7
Assessment of ego state in anorexia nervosa and bulimia nervosa.
Nakao M, Kumano H, Nomura S, Kuboki T, Murata K.
Department of Psychosomatic Medicine, School of Medicine, University of Tokyo, Japan.
To clarify the effects of ego states on anorexia nervosa (AN) and bulimia nervosa (BN), the questionnaire of the Tokyo University Egogram (TEG) with critical parent, nurturing parent, adult, free child and adapted child scales was administered to 32 female AN patients aged 14 to 32 years (mean age 20 years) and 49 female BN patients aged 14 to 33 years (mean age 23 years). The adaptive ego state is suggested for differentiating between the two disorders.

Acta Psychiatr Scand Suppl 1990;361:44-9
Anorexia nervosa. Treatment and triggering factors.
Nygaard JA.
Department of Child Psychiatry, University of Bergen, Norway.
In the period from 1976 to 1983, 84 anorexia nervosa (AN) patients were treated in the Medical and Child Psychiatry Units of the University Hospital of Bergen.
Five were men, 79 women. The criteria used for diagnosis are DSM-III (1) A,B,D and E, but not C. All the patients in this study were treated according to the methods of Bassoe & Eskeland (2) and Bassoe (3) in order to give the patients the necessary insight into the pathophysiology of hunger and to inform them about the symptoms. It was found to be of great importance that the patients received treatment in the early stages of the condition. Also that the patient, as a part of the prophylaxis of the condition, was informed about the dangers of slimming. A short survey of other methods of treatment found in the literature is given.

Adolesc Med 1992 Oct;3(3):541-558
Nutrition Management in Adolescents with Eating Disorders.

Schebendach J, Nussbaum MP.
Associate Professor of Pediatrics, Health Sciences Center, State University of New York at Stony Brook, USA.
Nutritional education and rehabilitation of the adolescent with an eating disorder is based on dietary history and analysis of eating behavior as well as laboratory tests and metabolic and anthropometric assessments. Treatment as well as diagnosis must take into account the distinctions between anorexia and bulimia nervosa.

Adolesc Psychiatry 1985;12:219-32
The etiology and treatment of anorexia nervosa.
Miller D, Carlton BS.

Adolesc Psychiatry 1986;13:358-90
Cognitive therapy for bulimia nervosa.
Garner DM.

Adolesc Psychiatry 1986;13:391-404
Group therapy for bulimia.
Dixon KN.

Adolescence 1993 Summer;28(110):393-422
Male or female therapists for eating-disordered adolescents: guidelines suggested by research and practice.
Bilker L.
Grove School, Madison, Connecticut 06443.
The question of whether male or female therapists are best for female patients has sparked controversy for decades. This paper explores which therapist-patient gender matches facilitate the most patient growth and avoid detriment to female patients. Advantages and disadvantages for male and female therapists are discussed, and suggestions made for variables to be used in future studies.
Publication Types: Review; Review, tutorial

Adv Nurse Pract 1998 Apr;6(4):25
For your patients: recognizing eating disorders.
Ricchini W.

Am J Nurs 1980 Aug;80(8):1471-2
Anorexia nervosa: a behavioral approach.
Claggett MS.

Am J Psychiatry 1970 Feb;126(8):1093-8
Behavior therapy of anorexia nervosa: effectiveness of activity as a reinforcer of weight gain.
Blinder BJ, Freeman DM, Stunkard AJ.

Am J Psychiatry 1974 Apr;131(4):432-6
An integrated treatment program for anorexia nervosa.
Liebman R, Minuchin S, Baker L.

Am J Psychiatry 1976 Sep;133(9):1034-8
The treatment of anorexia nervosa.
Lucas AR, Duncan JW, Piens V.
The authors report on their treatment of 32 young patients with severe anorexia nervosa who had lost an average of 37% of their original body weight. The therapeutic approach, conceived to meet both the physiological and the psychological needs of the patients, was carried out in a psychiatric unit foradolescents in a general hospital and involved separation of the patient from his or her family, treatment of the

malnutrition, individually planned psychotherapy, and concurrent work with the family. The importance of accepting the patient's uniqueness, maintaining long-term contact, and encouraging the patient's striving toward constructive growth and autonomy is emphasized.

Am J Psychiatry 1978 May;135(5):621
Treatment in anorexia nervosa.
Solomon JG.
Publication Types: Letter

Am J Psychiatry 1982 Dec;139(12):1531-8
Anorexia Nervosa: therapy and theory.
Bruch H.
The reciprocal interaction between psychotherapy and theoretical assumptions isillustrated through observations of anorexia nervosa. Traditional psychoanalysis, with its emphasis on interpretation of unconscious processes, was found to be rather ineffective, whereas an approach evoking active participation on the part of the patient led to better treatment results.

Am J Psychiatry 1983 May;140(5):668-9
Alternative theories and treatment for anorexia nervosa.
Publication Types: Letter

Am J Psychiatry 1986 May;143(5):573-81
The treatment of anorexia nervosa.
Hsu LK.
The author reviews recent advances in the treatment of anorexia nervosa. In addition to the usual areas of weight restoration and psychotherapy, he focuses on difficult issues such as how to engage the patient in treatment, the evaluation of the patient, treatment goals, outpatient treatment, and treatment of bulimic and chronic patients. Where expert opinions differ, the author attempts to give a balanced view while acknowledging the relative lack of research data.
Publication Types: Review

Am J Psychiatry 1987 Feb;144(2):260-1
Treatment of anorexia nervosa.
Leichner P.
Publication Types: Letter

Am J Psychiatry 1990 Jul;147(7):871-5
Maintenance treatment and 6-month outcome for bulimic patients who respond to initial treatment.
Pyle RL, Mitchell JE, Eckert ED, Hatsukami D, Pomeroy C, Zimmerman R.
Department of Psychiatry, University of Minnesota Medical School, Minneapolis55455.
Bulimic subjects who responded to intensive group psychotherapy plus imipramine or placebo or to imipramine alone (N = 68) were assigned to 4-month maintenance with weekly support groups and/or medication (placebo or imipramine) and were evaluated 6 months after initial treatment (N = 61). Thirty percent of the subjects relapsed during the 6 months. Initial treatment with group psychotherapy plus placebo or imipramine was associated with a lower relapse rate than initial treatment with imipramine alone. Neither attendance at the maintenance group sessions nor imipramine maintenance was associated with better outcome.

Publication Types: Clinical trial; Randomized controlled trial

Am J Psychiatry 1994 May;151(5):744-50
A controlled study of light therapy for bulimia nervosa.
Lam RW, Goldner EM, Solyom L, Remick RA.
Department of Psychiatry, University of British Columbia, Vancouver, Canada.
Winter worsening of mood and eating symptoms, similar to that of seasonal affective disorder, has recently been reported in patients with bulimia nervosa. To assess the effectiveness of light therapy for treatment of bulimia nervosa, the authors conducted a study of light therapy during winter comparing an active (bright white light) condition to a control (dim red light) condition in bulimic patients who were not selected for a seasonal pattern of bulimia.
Although pretreatment expectation ratings were similar for each condition, the bright white light condition was superior to the dim red light condition for all mood and eating outcome measures. These data suggest that bright white light therapy is an effective short-term treatment for both mood and eating disturbances associated with bulimia nervosa, although the therapeutic effect may be greater in those patients with a seasonal pattern.
Publication Types: Clinical trial; Randomized controlled trial

Am J Psychiatry 1995 Nov;152(11):1630-4
Comment in: Am J Psychiatry. 1997 Jan;154(1):132
Persistent perfectionism, symmetry, and exactness after long-term recovery from anorexia nervosa.
Srinivasagam NM, Kaye WH, Plotnicov KH, Greeno C, Weltzin TE, Rao R.
Department of Psychiatry, Western Psychiatric Institute and Clinic, University of Pittsburgh School of Medicine, PA 15213, USA.
It is well recognized that patients with anorexia nervosa have perfectionistic and obsessive behaviors. This study investigated whether such behaviors persist after recovery. It was learned that using the Eating Disorder Inventory using the Frost Multidimensional Perfectionism Scale, and the Yale-Brown Obsessive Compulsive Scale. Certain characteristics of anorexia nervosa, such as a need for order and precision, persist after good outcome and recovery, raising the question of whether these behaviors are traits that contribute to the pathogenesis of this illness.

Am J Psychiatry 1998 Jul;155(7):947-53
Guided self-change for bulimia nervosa incorporating use of a self-care manual.
Thiels C, Schmidt U, Treasure J, Garthe R, Troop N.
Bielefeld Polytechnic, Germany.
The aim of this study was to evaluate the effectiveness of guided self-change for bulimia nervosa. Guided self-change incorporating use of a self-care manual offers an approach that can be as effective as standard cognitive behavior therapy in the long term and can considerably reduce the amount of therapist contact required.

Publication Types: Clinical trial; Randomized controlled trial

Am J Psychiatry 2000 Nov;157(11):1806-10
Involuntary treatment of eating disorders.
Watson TL, Bowers WA, Andersen AE.
Department of Psychiatry, University of Iowa College of Medicine, Iowa City 52242-1057, USA.
OBJECTIVE: Involuntary treatment of any psychiatric disorder has always been controversial, especially for eating disorders. Patients with an eating disorder of life-threatening severity frequently refuse hospitalization. In this study, the authors compared individual characteristics and treatment outcomes of patients admitted to an inpatient program for voluntary or involuntary treatment of their eating disorder. This study suggests that a substantial minority of patients with severe eating disorders will not seek treatment unless legally committed to an inpatient program. Despite the involuntary initiation of treatment, the short-term response of the legally committed patients was just as good as the response of the patients admitted for voluntary treatment. Further, the majority of those involuntarily treated later affirmed the necessity of their treatment and showed goodwill toward the treatment process. Only a long-term follow-up study will indicate whether these two populations differ in the enduring nature of their treatment response.

Am J Psychother 1972 Oct;26(4):480-9
Anorexia nervosa: dual transference therapy.
Solomon AP, Morrison DA.

Am J Psychother 1973 Oct;27(4):492-505
Anorexia nervosa and psychotherapy.
Szyrynski V.

Am J Psychother 1993 Summer;47(3):353-71
Issues unique to psychotherapy with adolescent girls.
Ponton LE.
University of California, Medical School, San Francisco.
New research on development and risk factors has increased our knowledge of adolescent girls and given those of us working with them more available information to aid our understanding of psychotherapy. Advancing social theory has also promoted an understanding of the problems that adolescent girls begin to face including gender discrimination and conflict around social roles.Educated therapists can utilize this information with their adolescent female patients, providing knowledge about choices available to girls and promoting understanding and problem-solving.

Arch Gen Psychiatry 1975 Jan;32(1):93-6
Treatment of anorexia nervosa with behavior modification. Effectiveness of formula feeding and isolation.
Halmi KA, Powers P, Cunningham S.
Anorexia nervosa has been treated with a variety of therapies. One seemingly successful modality, behavioral modification, has in most cases been used concurrently with

various drugs, making the contributions of each impossible to separate. Eight patients meeting rigorous criteria for anorexia nervosa were treated in this study exclusively with behavioral therapy (reward contingent on weight gain). All had a substantial weight gain while hospitalized, and on short-term follow-up are maintaining or continuing to gain toward their normal weight range on individualized positive-reinforcement programs.

Ariz Med 1982 Mar;39(3):182-5
Treatment of anorexia nervosa.
Sinaikin P.

ASDC J Dent Child 1986 Sep-Oct;53(5):378-81
Eating disorders: anorexia and bulimia nervosas.
Gross KB, Brough KM, Randolph PM.
From both ethical and legal standpoints, knowledge of the symptoms of eating disorders is imperative, since early diagnosis and treatment are directly related to successful therapy. This article provides the dentists with information to aid in the recognition, diagnosis, treatment, referral, and dental support of patients with eating disorders.

Assessment 1999 Mar;6(1):7-20
Development and validation of a multifactorial treatment outcome measure for eating disorders.
Anderson DA, Williamson DA, Duchmann EG, Gleaves DH, Barbin JM.
Louisiana State University, Baton Rouge, 70803-5501, USA.
The purpose of this investigation was to develop a brief self-report inventory which could be used to evaluate treatment outcome for anorexia and bulimia nervosa. The Multifactorial Assessment of Eating Disorders Symptoms (MAEDS) was constructed to measure six symptom clusters which have been found to be central to the eating disorders: depression, binge eating, purgative behavior, fear of fatness, restrictive eating, and avoidance of forbidden foods. While still in the experimental stages, the MAEDS shows promise as a valid and economical measure of treatment interventions for anorexia and bulimia nervosa.

Aust N Z J Psychiatry 1987 Dec;21(4):568-74
The place of family therapy in the treatment of anorexia nervosa.
Hall A.
Department of Psychological Medicine, Wellington Clinical School, Wellington Hospital, New Zealand.
There has been widespread, uncritical support for family therapy as the treatment of choice for all anorexia nervosa patients since Minuchin's report in 1976, but recent research has not been able to validate Minuchin's theories about the functioning of anorexia nervosa families. In the only controlled trial to date, the efficacy of family therapy was found to be superior to that of individual therapy, but only in younger patients.

Aust N Z J Psychiatry 1987 Mar;21(1):5-15
The treatment of bulimia nervosa.
Griffiths RA, Touyz SW, Mitchell PB,

Bacon W.
We review treatment approaches to bulimia nervosa, with particular emphasis on methodology and research design. The following treatments are considered: behaviour therapy, cognitive behaviour therapy, pharmacological treatment, group therapy, psychoanalytic psychotherapy, self-help and support groups, hypnosis and miscellaneous (family therapy and nutritional approaches). Several directions for future research and methodological recommendations are suggested.

Behav Modif 1987 Jul;11(3):373-88
Innovative treatment approaches to bulimia nervosa.
Johnson WG, Corrigan SA, Mayo LL.
Publication Types: Review; Review, tutorial

Behav Modif 1987 Oct;11(4):395-543
Behavioral and cognitive-behavioral treatment of anorexia nervosa and bulimia nervosa.

Behav Modif 1987 Oct;11(4):398-431
Cognitive-behavioral treatment of bulimia nervosa. A critical appraisal.
Garner DM, Fairburn CG, Davis R.
Publication Types: Review; Review, tutorial

Behav Modif 1987 Oct;11(4):432-63
The present status of operant conditioning for the treatment of anorexia nervosa.
Bemis KM.
Publication Types: Review; Review, tutorial

Behav Modif 1987 Oct;11(4):464-86
A review of behavioral treatments for bulimia nervosa.
Rosen JC.
Publication Types: Review; Review, tutorial

Behav Res Ther 1965 Sep;3(2):87-91
Adolescent anorexia nervosa treated by desensitization.
Hallsten EA Jr.

Behav Res Ther 1992 Mar;30(2):193-9
Predictors of short-term treatment outcome in bulimia nervosa inpatients.
Bossert S, Schmolz U, Wiegand M, Junker M, Krieg JC.
Max Planck Institute of Psychiatry, Munich, Fed. Rep. Germany.
Recent studies, mostly performed on bulimic outpatients, did not find consistent predictors of treatment outcome in bulimia nervosa. This is the first study to investigate anamnestic and clinical factors predictive of the short-term outcome of hospital treatment in 31 female bulimia nervosa patients with a mean age of 22.9 yr. Treatment outcome was assessed by several self-rating instruments measuring different features of the specific and unspecific psychopathology ofbulimia nervosa. The majority of predictors tested did not show a strong relationship to treatment outcome. The findings are discussed in relation to results of other studies as well as to possible implications for treatment and research.

Behav Res Ther 2000 Mar;38(3):259-72
Guided and unguided self-help for binge eating.

Loeb KL, Wilson GT, Gilbert JS, Labouvie E.
Department of Psychology, Rutgers University, Piscataway, NJ 08854, USA.
This study compared the relative short- and longer-term efficacy of therapist-guided and unguided use of a cognitive behavioral self-help manual forbinge eating The guided self-help condition was notably superior in reducing the occurrence of binge eating and its associated symptomatology, as well as lowering interpersonal sensitivity.
Publication Types: Clinical trial; Randomized controlled trial

BMJ 1995 Sep 2;311(7005):584
Comment in: BMJ. 1996 Jan 20;312(7024):182
Treating anorexia nervosa.
Russell J.
Publication Types: Editorial

BMJ 1996 Jan 20;312(7024):182
Comment on: BMJ. 1995 Sep 2;311(7005):584
Treating anorexia nervosa. Patients' beliefs hinder treatment.
Sharkey J.
Publication Types: Comment Letter

Br J Clin Psychol 1992 Sep;31 (Pt 3):330-2
Predictors of outcome in the treatment of bulimia nervosa.
Baell WK, Wertheim EH.
Department of Psychology, La Trobe University, Melbourne, Vic., Australia.
Outcome predictors of a cognitive behavioural group treatment for bulimia nervosa were examined here. Pre-treatment self-esteem, binge frequency and ineffectiveness, but not duration of disorder, significantly predicted outcome on at least one measure (binge frequency or overall eating pathology) at post-treatment and/or three-month follow-up. The results are related to previous studies and to theories of maintenance of the disorder.

Br J Hosp Med 1981 Aug;26(2):186
Treatment of anorexia nervosa.
Bruggen P, Lask B, Black D, Schlicht J.
Publication Types: Letter

Br J Hosp Med 1981 May;25(5):434, 437-8, 440
Treatment of anorexia nervosa.
Dally P.

Br J Hosp Med 1989 May;41(5):470-5
The psychological treatment of eating disorders.
Mynors-Wallis LM.
Maudsley Hospital, London.
There has been a considerable increase in the incidence of eating disorders.
This has stimulated research into a variety of therapeutic options. This article examines the psychological treatments currently available, the theories underpinning them and the evidence supporting their use. Where possible the treatments are evaluated separately for anorexia nervosa and bulimia nervosa.
Publication Types: Review; Review, tutorial

Br J Psychiatry 1966 Jul;112(488):671-81
Educative treatment of patients and

parentsin anorexia nervosa.
Groen JJ, Feldman-Toledano Z.

Br J Psychiatry 1979 Jan;134:55-9
Behaviour therapy in anorexia nervosa.
Eckert ED, Goldberg SC, Halmi KA, Casper RC, Davis JM.
In three collaborating hospitals, 81 anorexia nervosa patients were randomly assigned to behaviour modification or its absence and followed over 35 days. There was no overall significant difference in weight gain in the two groups except in a subset of patients: those with no prior out-patient treatments.
Publication Types: Clinical trial; Randomized controlled trial

Br J Psychiatry 1981 Feb;138:164-6
The current treatment of anorexia nervosa.
Russell G.

Br J Psychiatry 1987 Aug;151:185-91
Brief psychotherapy in the treatment of anorexia nervosa. Outcome at one year.
Hall A, Crisp AH.
St. George's Hospital Medical School, London.
Thirty out-patients with severe anorexia nervosa were randomly allocated to either 12 sessions of dietary advice or 12 sessions of combined individual and family psychotherapy. At one-year follow-up both groups showed significant overall improvement, and the dietary advice group showed significant weight gain. A similar mean weight gain for the psychotherapy patients did not reach statistical significance, but this group made significant improvements in sexual and social adjustment.
Publication Types: Clinical trial; Randomized controlled trial

Br J Psychiatry 1987 Aug;151:192-4
Anorexia nervosa: an object relations approach to primary treatment.
Horne M, Gallen M.
Department of Psychiatry and Behavioral Sciences, Stanford University Medical School, California.
Concurrent behaviour therapy and psychotherapy in the treatment of anorexia nervosa creates significant problems in the development of a therapeutic alliance and in the multiple roles staff are required to assume. Our protocol was developed to keep treatment personnel in their usual roles so that their various treatment skills could be fully utilised. A physician treated the anorexia with naso-gastric feeding, freeing the psychotherapist to act in the usual manner. This avoided role confusion, and the split of 'bad' and 'good' treatment personnel was appropriate and therapeutic, rather than pathological.
Four successful cases are described.

Br J Psychiatry 1999 Aug;175:147-53
Compulsory treatment in anorexia nervosa. Short-term benefits and long-term mortality.
Ramsay R, Ward A, Treasure J, Russell GF.
Eating Disorders Unit, Maudsley Hospital, London.
BACKGROUND: Anorexia nervosa is a mental disorder with a high long-

term mortality. Eighty-one compulsory patients were compared with 81 voluntary patients. RESULTS: Predisposing factors to a compulsory admission were a history of childhood sexual or physical abuse or previous self-harm. Detained patients had more previous admissions. Detained patients gained as much weight during admission as voluntary patients, but took longer. More deaths among compulsory than voluntary patients (10/79 v. 2/78) were found 5.7 years (mean) after admission. CONCLUSIONS: Compulsory treatment is effective in the short term. The higher long-term mortality in the detained patients is due to selection factors associated with an intractable illness.

Br Med J 1966 Oct 1;2(517):793-5
Treatment and outcome of anorexia nervosa.
Dally P, Sargant W.

Br Med J 1978 Feb 4;1(6108):303
Anorexia nervosa and family therapy.
Warner J.
Publication Types: Letter

Bull Menninger Clin 1977 Sep;41(5):437-52
On the psychotherapy of patients with anorexia nervosa.
Thoma H.

Bull Menninger Clin 1985 May;49(3):203-26
The outpatient treatment of bulimia.
Yager J.

Can Fam Physician 1994 Feb;40:299-304
Comment in: Can Fam Physician. 1994 Jul;40:1257-8
Practical approaches to eating disorders in adolescence. Primer for family physicians.
Tonkin RS.
Department of Paediatrics, University of British Columbia.
Primary care physicians have an important role in assessing and managing adolescents who present with low weight. Initial diagnosis should be based on current understanding of adolescents' eating behaviours and be followed by obtaining supportive evidence. A practical developmental approach to management should be emphasized. Criteria for hospitalization, a three-step approach to management, and indications for expanding from a primary care to a team approach are discussed.
Publication Types: Review; Review, tutorial

Can Fam Physician 1994 Jul;40:1257-8
Comment on: Can Fam Physician. 1994 Feb;40:299-304
Treating adolescent eating disorders.
Marchessault G.
Publication Types: Comment Letter

Can J Psychiatry 1998 May;43(4):359-6
Coming alive: the psychotherapeutic treatment of patients with eating disorders.
de Groot J, Rodin G.
Toronto Hospital, University of Toronto, Ontario.
This paper describes a dynamic psychotherapeutic approach specifically developed for women with eating disorders. The developmental origins and

psychological disturbances associated with eating disorders are outlined based on a review of the literature and the authors' observations. In the psychotherapeutic treatment of women with eating disorders, a therapeutic posture of sustained empathic enquiry contributes to the patient's curiosity about her own subjective world was understood. Feeling understood in a therapeutic relationship and feeling assisted in organizing and understanding one's subjective experience contributes to the gradual unfolding of the psychological sense of self.
Publication Types: Review; Review, tutorial

Can J Psychiatry 1999 Sep;44(7):665-70
Difficulties in treating patients with eating disorders: a review of patient and clinician variables.
Kaplan AS, Garfinkel PE.
Program for Eating Disorders, Toronto Hospital, ON.
akaplan@torhosp.toronto.on.ca
Patients with eating disorders (EDs) are often difficult to treat. Despite recent advances in treatment, a significant percentage of patients remain treatment refractory. This paper reviews variables that contribute to these difficulties and recent strategies that focus on increasing patient motivation for treatment. Improving understanding of the reasons for treatment refractoriness in patients with EDs is critical to improving their care. New interventions aimed at enhancing motivation may facilitate this process.
Publication Types: Review; Review literature

Can J Psychiatry 2000 Mar;45(2):173-8
Comparison of family therapy and family group psychoeducation in adolescents with anorexia nervosa.
Geist R, Heinmaa M, Stephens D, Davis R, Katzman DK.
Department of Psychiatry, Hospital for Sick Children, University of Toronto, Ontario.
rose.geist@sickkids.on.ca
OBJECTIVE: To compare the effects of 4 months of 2 family-oriented treatments, family therapy and family psychoeducation, on female adolescents with newly diagnosed restrictive eating disorders. Weight restoration was achieved following the 4-month period of treatment in both the family therapy and family psychoeducation groups, but no significant change was reported in psychological functioning by either adolescents or parents. Family group psychoeducation, the less expensive form of treatment, is an equally effective method of providing family-oriented treatment to newly diagnosed, medically compromised anorexia nervosa patients and their families.
Publication Types: Clinical trial; Randomized controlled trial

Can Psychiatr Assoc J 1974 Apr;19(2):169-75
Problems of treatment of anorexia nervosa.
Moldofsky H, Garfinkel PE.

Can Psychiatr Assoc J 1977 Apr;22(3):102-8
Psychotherapy in eating disorders.

Bruch H.

Child Psychiatry Hum Dev 1991 Spring;21(3):163-7
The early care and feeding of anorexics.
Steiner H, Smith C, Rosenkranz RT, Litt I.
Division of Child Psychiatry, Stanford University School of Medicine, CA.
Comparing mothers' reports of early feeding practices in 18 mothers of anorexics and 25 mothers of normal children by means of a questionnaire, it was found that the mothers of anorexics introduced solids earlier and used Schedule rather than Demand feedings more frequently. The mothers of anorexics did not treat patients and control siblings differentially. This study suggests that differences in early feeding and in infant temperament may be operative in the pathogenesis of anorexia nervosa.

Clin Psychol Rev 1997 Nov;17(7):703-18
Meta-analysis of cognitive-behavioral treatment studies for bulimia.
Lewandowski LM, Gebing TA, Anthony JL, O'Brien WH.
Department of Psychology, Bowling Green State University, OH 43403, USA.
A meta-analysis was performed to systematically assess the effect of cognitive-behavioral treatments for bulimia. To protect against past criticisms of meta-analyses, this study focused on well-defined hypotheses with clearly articulated conceptual foundations. These results suggest that the use of a cognitive-behavioral therapy will result in favorable treatment outcomes and implications for future research are discussed.
Publication Types: Meta-analysis

Clin Psychol Rev 1998 Jun;18(4):391-420
Enhancing motivation for change in treatment-resistant eating disorders.
Vitousek K, Watson S, Wilson GT.
Department of Psychology, University of Hawaii, Honolulu 96822, USA.
Denial and resistance to change are prominent features in most patients with anorexia nervosa. Clinicians are encouraged to acquire a frame of reference that can help them understand the private experience of individuals with eating disorders, empathize with their distress at the prospect of weight gain, and acknowledge the difficulty of change. The Socratic method seems particularly well-suited to work with this population because of its emphasis on collaboration, openness, curiosity, patience, focused and systematic inquiry, and individual discovery. Four themes are crucial in engaging reluctant eating-disordered clients in therapy: the provision of psychoeducational material, an examination of the advantages and disadvantages of symptoms, the explicit use of experimental strategies, and an exploration of personal values.
Publication Types: Review; Review literature

Clin Psychol Rev 1999 Nov;19(7):773-88
Evaluating recovery from anorexia nervosa and bulimia nervosa: integrating lessons learned from research and clinical practice.
Jarman M, Walsh S.
Department of Psychology, University of Sheffield, UK.

The aims of this article are to critically examine the conceptualization and measurement of recovery, within the eating disorder outcome literature, and suggest possible ways of developing the clinical utility of outcome research.
Publication Types: Review; Review, tutorial

Compr Psychiatry 1980 May-Jun;21(3):177-89
Anorexia nervosa: controversial aspects of therapy.
Piazza E, Piazza N, Rollins N.

Compr Psychiatry 2001 Mar-Apr;42(2):132-8
Psychoeducation for the families of patients with eating disorders and changes in expressed emotion: A preliminary study.
Uehara T, Kawashima Y, Goto M, Tasaki Si, Someya T.
Department of Neuropsychiatry, University of Gunma Faculty of Medicine, Maebashi, Japan.
Psychosocial variables such as expressed emotion (EE) have prognostic significance, and family psychoeducation has been developed to aid in the treatment of various psychiatric disorders. This study reports relationships among EE, family factors, and symptoms observed while conducting multifamily psychoeducation for eating disorders. EE is an important measure in evaluations of psychoeducation. However, a randomized, controlled trial is needed to clarify the efficacy of this treatment. Copyright 2001 by W.B. Saunders Company

Curr Probl Pediatr 1995 Feb;25(2):67-89
A review of anorexia nervosa and bulimia nervosa.
Woodside DB.
Inpatient Eating Disorders Unit, Toronto Hospital, Canada.
Eating disorders remain an important health care problem for clinicians working with children and adolescents. Although the cause of these illnesses remains obscure, information about the effectiveness of different forms of treatment isavailable to guide the clinician. Individuals involved in the treatment of such patients should be aware of the means of diagnosing the conditions, the common complications of both anorexia and bulimia, the management of these, and the indications for specific treatment modalities. Although the outcome is variable, effective treatment delivered early in the course of illness provides the most likely route to recovery.
Publication Types: Review; Review, multicase

Curr Psychiatr Ther 1975;15:51-7
The treatment of anorexia nervosa.
Liebman R, Minuchin S, Baker L, Rosman BL

Curr Psychiatr Ther 1975;15:59-64
Operant conditioning in anorexia nervosa.
Bhanji S.

Curr Ther Endocrinol Metab 1994;5:15-21
Anorexia and bulimia nervosa: psychiatric approach.
Weltzin TE, McCabe E, Flynn D,

Kaye W.
University of Pittsburgh School of Medicine, Pennsylvania.

Curr Ther Endocrinol Metab 1997;6:18-21
Anorexia nervosa and bulimia: psychiatric approach.
Walsh BT.
Columbia University College of Physicians and Surgeons, New York, New York, USA.
Publication Types: Review; Review, tutorial

Drug Ther Bull 1975 Jun 6;13(12):45-6
The management of anorexia nervosa.

Drugs 1994 Sep;48(3):372-9
Rational therapy of eating disorders.
Crow SJ, Mitchell JE.
Department of Psychiatry, University of Minnesota, Minneapolis.
Pharmacological treatments are one of several strategies used in the treatment of anorexia nervosa and bulimia nervosa. Many studies have found that antidepressants are effective in the treatment of bulimia nervosa and these drugs represent a mainstay of treatment for these patients. Over the past several years, selective serotonin reuptake inhibitors have become perhaps the most commonly used class of drugs.
Publication Types: Review; Review, tutorial

Eur Child Adolesc Psychiatry 1997 Sep;6(3):121-8
Clinical guidelines for anorexia nervosa and bulimia nervosa.
Steinhausen HC.
Department of Child and Adolescent Psychiatry, University of Zurich, Switzerland.

Eur J Oral Sci 1999 Jun;107(3):157-63
Oral status of 81 subjects with eating disorders.
Ohrn R, Enzell K, Angmar-Mansson B.
Public Dental Service, Stockholm, Sweden.
Exploring possible correlations between the oral status of patients undergoing treatment at a special outpatient psychiatric clinic for eating disorders and such variables as psychiatric diagnosis and duration of illness, oral hygiene habits, salivary function, and dietary habits.

Eur Psychiatry 1999 Oct;14(6):333-40
Body experience in eating disorders before and after treatment: a follow-up study.
Probst M, Vandereycken W, Van Coppenolle H, Pieters G.
University Centre Sint Jozef, Kortenberg, Belgium.
Body experience was studied in 290 eating disorder patients, admitted to a specialised unit, after six months and again after one year using the Body Attitude Test (BAT), the Eating Disorder Inventory (EDI), and the Eating Disorder Evaluation Scale (EDES). The clearly negative body experience of eating disorder patients evolved in a positive way after therapy and this improvement lasted for up to one year after admission.

Harv Rev Psychiatry 1994 Nov-Dec;2(4):193-203
Inpatient treatment of anorexia nervosa: review and recommendations.

Bowers WA, Andersen AE.
Department of Psychiatry, University of Iowa, Iowa City, USA.
Inpatient treatment of anorexia nervosa, difficult and at times complex, has been shown to promote enduring change. An integrated treatment approach that includes medical, psychological, nursing, and social interventions can restore patients to a healthy weight, improve abnormal eating behaviors, and ameliorate many of the central psychopathological attitudes and illness-driven behaviors characteristic of the disorder. This article reviews inpatient treatment of anorexia nervosa, evaluating empirical studies and providing a critique of their methodology and potential applicability, combining available published studies with clinical experience to suggest a comprehensive pragmatic treatment approach, and noting research needs for the future.
Publication Types: Review; Review, tutorial

Hillside J Clin Psychiatry 1984;6(2):156-70
Group therapy for bulimia.
Dixon KN, Kiecolt-Glaser J.
Thirty women meeting DSM-III criteria for bulimia were seen weekly in a group setting using behavioral techniques and insight-oriented discussion. Pre- and post-measures using the EAT, Marlowe Crowne Social Desirability Scale, Rotter Locus of Control, and SCL-90-R self-rating scales were performed on 11 group completers. Two comparison groups consisted of bulimic women who received either no treatment or individual psychotherapy. The differences on the parameters measured in comparing group therapy, individual therapy, and no treatment subject groups would suggest that a group therapy approach holds promise for an otherwise poor prognosis disorder and that the changes are measureable.

Int J Eat Disord 1993 Sep;14(2):135-45
Outcome and prognostic variables in bulimia nervosa.
Fahy TA, Russell GF.
King's College Hospital, Institute of Psychiatry, De Crespigny Park, London, England.
The purpose of this paper is to examine the factors that influence treatment response and outcome in 39 patients with bulimia nervosa who were assessed during the course of 8 weeks of cognitive-behavioral therapy, and after an 8-week and 1-year follow-up period. Poor response after 1 year was associated with personality disorder, pretreatment symptom severity, and longer duration of illness. Patients without these poor prognostic indicators are more likely to respond to brief psychoeducational interventions. Patients with poor prognostic indicators are more suited to intensive psychological, pharmacologic, and experimental treatment approaches.
Publication Types: Clinical trial; Randomized controlled trial

Int J Eat Disord 1998 Dec;24(4):339-49
Evaluation of a computer-mediated eating disorder intervention program.
Winzelberg AJ, Taylor CB, Sharpe T,

Eldredge KL, Dev P, Constantinou PS.
Department of Psychiatry and Behavioral Sciences, Stanford University School of Medicine, California 94305-5722, USA.
OBJECTIVE: This study evaluated an eating disorder intervention multimedia program modeled after self-help eating disorder treatment programs. It was hypothesized that women who completed the program would increase their body satisfaction and decrease their preoccupation with weight and frequency of disordered eating behaviors. This study has demonstrated that minimally effective eating disorder intervention programs can be delivered. A revised program that eliminates interface problems and increases the structure of the intervention is likely to be even better received and more effective.
Publication Types: Clinical trial; Randomized controlled trial

Int J Eat Disord 1998 Sep;24(2):157-66
Stress, coping, and crisis support in eating disorders.
Troop NA, Holbrey A, Treasure JL.
Psychiatry Department, Institute of Psychiatry, London, United Kingdom.
OBJECTIVE: Recent research has supported the role of stress in the development and maintenance of eating disorders. However, coping and crisis support, important aspects of this stress process, have received little systematic attention. The present study used semistructured interviews to measure coping and crisis support in response to severe events and/or marked difficulties in 12 women with anorexia nervosa (AN), 21 women with bulimia nervosa (BN), and 21 women without an eating disorder (non-ED). It is concluded that women with eating disorders are less effective in their coping than women without eating disorders.

Int J Eat Disord 1999 Jan;25(1):39-44
Prior treatment received by patients with bulimia nervosa.
Crow S, Mussell MP, Peterson C, Knopke A, Mitchell J.
Department of Psychiatry, University of Minnesota, Minneapolis 55455, USA.
This study examined the frequency with which subjects with bulimia nervosa (BN) presenting for treatment or follow-up studies had previously received either adequate pharmacologic treatment or cognitive-behavioral therapy (CBT). Shown was that although efficacious treatments for BN have been established, they have not been received by most individuals presenting for further treatment.

Int J Eat Disord 1999 May;25(4):361-74
Sequencing of cognitive-behavioral treatments for bulimia nervosa.
Davis R, McVey G, Heinmaa M, Rockert W, Kennedy S.
Department of Psychology, Lakehead University, Thunder Bay, Canada.
OBJECTIVE: This study investigated the efficacy of a stepped-care trial of brief group psychoeducation (PE) followed by individual cognitive-behavioral therapy (CBT) in the treatment of bulimia nervosa. The results of the study provide limited support for offering individual CBT to subjects once they have completed an

initial trial of group PE.

Int J Group Psychother 1990 Apr;40(2):169-87
Why group therapy for bulimia?
Laube JJ.
Mid-Eastern Iowa Community Mental Health Center, Iowa City.
Many treatment approaches for bulimia rely on the use of a group format.
However, descriptions of the treatments do not reveal that the powers of group process are curative in themselves. Case material is offered to illustrate symptomatic expressions and therapeutic responses.

Int J Group Psychother 1993 Apr;43(2):237-42
The use of a group meal in the brief group therapy of bulimia nervosa.
Franko DL.
Harvard Medical School, Boston, MA.
The group meal is a technique that can be easily incorporated into traditional forms of short-term group therapy for bulimia nervosa. It is a modification of the exposure and response-prevention model that has been used in the treatment of this population. A case example is described to illustrate several of the important themes that emerge, including reactions to feeling full, family meals, and the relationship between overeating and feelings about the self.

Int J Group Psychother 1998 Oct;48(4):477-98
A relational approach to group therapy for women with bulimia nervosa: moving from understanding to action.
Tantillo M.
Department of Psychiatry, University of Rochester Medical Center, USA.
This article explains how the psychology of women can inform group treatment by translating relational theory (RT) into practice within a short-term outpatient bulimia group. The goal of treatment is to help members move toward mutually empathic and empowering relationships inside and outside the group.
Publication Types: Review; Review, tutorial

Int J Obes Relat Metab Disord 2001 Jan;25(1):146
Counselling for eating disorders.
Hanswijck De Jonge P.

Int J Psychiatry Med 1981;11(3):291-302
Family therapy in the treatment of anorexia nervosa: theory and technique.
Lagos JM.
This paper describes the dysfunctional characteristics of anorexic families as well as the relevance of these characteristics to the anorexic symptoms. Two approaches to the treatment of these families, one developed by Minuchin and the other by Selvini Palazzoli, are described and the compatability of family therapy with individual therapy isbriefly discussed.

Int J Psychoanal 1984;65 (Pt 4):435-42
On the treatment of anorexia nervosa.
Boris HN.
The omnipotent triumph over the selfpossessed object: this is the anorectic's raison d'etre. The successful evasion of being by love

possessed, this is the methodology. Never to be found wanting, that is her interface. To be totally self-possessed, that is the self she wishes to provide herself. Analysis to such a person is not a welcome procedure. In this report I have set out some approaches I have found helpful and pitfalls to be avoided.

Int J Psychoanal Psychother 1982-83;9:303-12
Treatment in anorexia nervosa.
Bruch H.
A discussion of "Anorexia Nervosa and the Psychotherapeutic Hospital," by Ian Story Ph.D. "Anorexia Nervosa" is a misnomer. "Anorexic" patients do not suffer from loss of appetite but actively pursue self-starvation and are frantically preoccupied with food, and even more with their size and shape. Traditional treatment has emphasized the restitution of weight, which, however, is insufficient for cure. For effective treatment, reparation of the underlying personality deficits is essential. Story's paper on the therapeutic hospital describes the desperate plight of chronic anorexic patients in whose early treatment this important factor had been neglected.

Int J Psychosom 1987;34(3):7-10
The use of group therapy in the treatment of bulimia.
Sykes DK Jr, Currie KO, Gross M.

J Adolesc 1978 Sep;1(3):197-228
An approach to the therapy of anorexia nervosa.Kalucy RS.

J Adv Nurs 1977 Mar;2(2):127-35
Anorexia nervosa: aspects of care and treatment.
Armstrong-Esther CA.

J Am Acad Child Adolesc Psychiatry 1999 Dec;38(12):1482-9
A controlled comparison of family versus individual therapy for adolescents with anorexia nervosa.
Robin AL, Siegel PT, Moye AW, Gilroy M, Dennis AB, Sikand A.
Wayne State University, Detroit, USA. arobin@med.wayne.edu
To compare the effectiveness of behavioral family systems therapy (BFST) with that of ego-oriented individual therapy (EOIT) as treatments for adolescents with anorexia nervosa. BFST and EOIT proved to be effective treatments for adolescents with anorexia nervosa, but BFST produced a faster return to health.
Publication Types: Clinical trial; Randomized controlled trial

J Am Acad Child Psychiatry 1975 Autumn;14(4):646-51
Anorexia nervosa. A case study using behavior therapy.
Werry JS, Bull D.

J Am Coll Health 1984 Apr;32(5):208-15
The group treatment of bulimia.
Weinstein HM, Richman A.

J Am Diet Assoc 1988 Jan;88(1):49-51
Anorexia nervosa: psychological considerations for nutrition counseling.
Omizo SA, Oda EA.
Department of Special Education, University of Hawaii at Manoa,

Honolulu.
This article presents the underlying psychological beliefs and self-perceptions held by individuals with anorexia nervosa. The intent of this article is to help dietitians and other nutrition counselors become more aware of the psychological characteristics of individuals with anorexia nervosa and become familiar with various counseling skills that can assist counselors when they are working toward reaching the goal of re-establishing normal eating patterns and attitudes about food.

J Am Diet Assoc 1993 Dec;93(12):1381
Comment on: J Am Diet Assoc. 1993 Apr;93(4):434-8
Pros and cons of treating anorexia with parenteral nutrition.
Mehler PS.
Publication Types: Comment Letter

J Am Psychoanal Assoc 1988;36(1):153-61
Anorexia nervosa: theory and therapy--a new look at an old problem. Panel reports.

J Behav Ther Exp Psychiatry 1988 Mar;19(1):63-8
Successful self-management of severe bulimia: a case study.
Posobiec K, Renfrew JW.
Department of Psychology, Northern Michigan University, Marquette 49855.
A young woman with a nine-year history of bingeing and purging was given instruction in behavioral principles. She then designed and carried out a program that included paced eating of pre-planned meals, following by differential reinforcement of non-purging behaviors, which featured high frequency of reinforcement early in training. Episodes decreased to a low level after one month and were completely absent nine months later. The amelioration of this problem resulted in progress being made for the first time with her emotional problems that were being treated elsewhere by psychodynamic psychotherapy.

J Child Psychol Psychiatry 1975 Jan;16(1):75-8
The treatment of anorexia nervosa in childhood and adolescence.
Tolstrup K.

J Clin Psychiatry 1988 Sep;49 Suppl:18-25
The treatment of eating disorders.
Yager J.
Department of Psychiatry and Biobehavioral Sciences, UCLA School of Medicine.
Anorexia nervosa and bulimia nervosa are common disorders among adolescent and young adult females, estimated to occur in up to 1% to 3% of these populations.
Important treatment issues include the nature of the disorder, age, degree of malnutrition, motivation, capacity to engage in treatment, personality disturbance, affective state, family situation, and available treatment resources. Based on research data and clinical lore, prudent suggestions for treatment planning are presented.
Publication Types: Clinical trial; Review; Review, tutorial

J Clin Psychiatry 2001 Mar;62(3):164-8

An open trial of light therapy for women with seasonal affective disorder and comorbid bulimia nervosa.

Lam RW, Lee SK, Tam EM, Grewal A, Yatham LN.

Department of Psychiatry, University of British Columbia, Vancouver, Canada.

rlam@interchange.ubc.ca

OBJECTIVE: Many patients with seasonal affective disorder (SAD) have dysfunctional eating behaviors. Light therapy resulted in significant improvement in mood, with a mean 56% reduction in 29-item Hamilton Rating Scale for Depression scores following treatment. These results suggest that therapeutic effects of light therapy on mood and bulimic symptoms in patients with SAD and comorbid bulimia nervosa are sustained over at least 4 weeks. However, the low abstinence rate in bulimic symptoms indicates that light therapy may be most effectively used as an adjunctive treatment to medications and/or psychotherapy for bulimia nervosa.

Publication Types: Clinical trial

J Clin Psychol 1998 Feb;54(2):163-7

The addiction of overeating: self-help groups as treatment models.

Weiner S.

California State University, Dominguez Hills, USA.

This article defines eating disorders and compares it to other addictions, gives a brief etiology, and presents two treatment models: Overeaters Anonymous and Weight Watchers International. The same personality factors that place individuals at risk for substance abuse are often found in individuals with eating disorders. These predispositions are explored from both a developmental and sociological perspective.

J Clin Psychol 1999 Jun;55(6):685-97

Psychosocial and pharmacological treatment of eating disorders: a review of research findings.

Peterson CB, Mitchell JE.

Eating Disorders Research Program, University of Minnesota, Minneapolis 55414, USA.

Research on the treatment of eating disorders has focused primarily on cognitive-behavioral therapy (CBT) and, more recently, interpersonal psychotherapy (IPT). Limited research has been conducted on the treatment of anorexia nervosa, although preliminary studies suggest that psychotherapy and fluoxetine may be helpful in preventing relapse after weight restoration.

Publication Types: Review; Review, tutorial

J Clin Psychol 1999 Jun;55(6):699-713

Cognitive-behavioral therapy for bulimia nervosa: an illustration.

Spangler DL.

Department of Psychology, Brigham Young University, Provo, UT 84602, USA.

Cognitive-behavioral therapy for bulimia nervosa (BN) is a well developed, theoretically grounded treatment for BN with the strongest empirical support for its efficacy of any form of treatment for BN. The treatment package comprises three distinct phases typically delivered

over 20 weeks.
Publication Types: Review; Review, tutorial

J Clin Psychol 1999 Jun;55(6):715-25
Interpersonal therapy for bulimia nervosa.
Apple RF.
Stanford Medical Center, Department of Psychiatry, CA 94305-5722, USA.
Interpersonal therapy (IPT) has been identified as an effective treatment for bulimia nervosa that does not focus on bulimic symptoms. Rather, a detailed assessment culminating in an "interpersonal inventory" identifies core associated interpersonal problem(s) that become the focus of treatment. For that reason, IPT may be particularly helpful for clients who have become "stuck" in their eating disorder for reasons associated with problematic relationships. PMID: 10445862 [PubMed - indexed for MEDLINE]

J Clin Psychol 1999 Jun;55(6):727-39
Family therapy for adolescent anorexia nervosa.
le Grange D.
The University of Chicago, Department of Psychiatry, IL 60637, USA.
Involving the family in the treatment of adolescents with anorexia nervosa has proved to be of benefit for young clients with a short duration of illness. In fact, the benefits of family therapy have been shown to be enduring at five-year follow-up. Engaging in treatment and commitment to therapy are important factors affecting treatment outcome.

J Consult Clin Psychol 1985 Feb;53(1):43-8
Comparison of two group treatments for bulimia.
Kirkley BG, Schneider JA, Agras WS, Bachman JA.
Publication Types: Clinical trial; Randomized controlled trial

J Consult Clin Psychol 1989 Apr;57(2):215-21
Cognitive-behavioral and response-prevention treatments for bulimia nervosa.
Agras WS, Schneider JA, Arnow B, Raeburn SD, Telch CF.
This study was designed to assess the additive effects of major components of cognitive-behavioral treatment for bulimia nervosa. Seventy-seven female patients with bulimia nervosa were allocated at random to one of four conditions: wait-list control, self-monitoring of caloric intake and purging behaviors, cognitive-behavioral treatment, and cognitive-behavioral treatment combined with response prevention of vomiting. All the treatment groups showed significant improvement, whereas the wait-list control group did not. Cognitive-behavioral treatment was, however, the most successful in reducing purging and in promoting positive psychological changes.
Publication Types: Clinical trial; Randomized controlled trial

J Consult Clin Psychol 1993 Apr;61(2):261-9
Cognitive treatments for eating disorders.
Wilson GT, Fairburn CG.
Department of Psychology, Rutgers

University, Piscataway, New Jersey 08854.
Cognitive-behavioral therapy (CBT) is applicable to all eating disorders but has been most intensively studied in the treatment of bulimia nervosa (BN). CBT isdesigned to alter abnormal attitudes about body shape and weight, replace dysfunctional dieting with normal eating habits, and develop coping skills for resisting binge eating and purging. CBT is effective in reducing all core features of BN and shows good maintenance of therapeutic improvement. Although superior to therapy with antidepressant drugs, CBT has not been shown to be consistently superior to alternative psychological treatments. Different hypotheses about CBT's mechanisms of action are discussed.
Publication Types: Review; Review, tutorial

J Consult Clin Psychol 2000 Aug;68(4):564-72
Stepped care treatment for eating disorders.
Wilson GT, Vitousek KM, Loeb KL.
Eating Disorders Clinic, Rutgers, State University of New Jersey, University College-Piscataway 08854, USA.
A stepped care approach would link different patient needs to therapeutic modalities that range from simple advice to intensive inpatient care. Brief methods, including self-help and psychoeducation, may be effective for a subset of patients with bulimia nervosa and binge eating disorder. A stepped care approach poses methodological challenges for clinical research and raises important clinical issues, such as when to switch from 1 level of treatment to another.
Publication Types: Review; Review, tutorial

J Dev Behav Pediatr 1994 Apr;15(2):146
Isolation treatment of anorexia nervosa.
Millman DH.
Publication Types: Letter

J Fam Pract 1980 Jun;10(6):1007-12
Diagnosis and treatment of anorexia nervosa.
Rohde J, Johannes A, Labeck L, Kelly JT.
Anorexia nervosa is much like other psychogenic or psychosomatic disorders in that it tends to run a chronic, relapsing course, with a proportion of patients never fully recovering. This paper draws on both published accounts and original case material to summarize the primary diagnostic criteria and secondary signs of anorexia nervosa. An illustrative history of a young woman with chronic anorexia nervosa is followed by a discussion of treatment alternatives. Although still in the experimental stage, behavior therapy is presented for its apparent efficacy and adaptability to the outpatient family practice setting.

J Fla Med Assoc 1978 May;65(5):345-9
Anorexia nervosa. Current theory and clinical application.
Schussler I, Lazoritz M.

J Hum Nutr Diet 2001 Apr;14(2):i-ii
How can weight control be promoted

without encouraging eating disorders?

J Nerv Ment Dis 1970 Jan;150(1):51-67
Psychotherapy in primary anorexia nervosa.
Bruch H.

J Nerv Ment Dis 1973 Dec;157(6):428-33
Treatment of anorexia nervosa using operant conditioning techniques.
Garfinkel PE, Kline SA, Stancer HC.

J Pediatr Health Care 1996 Jan-Feb;10(1):17-25
Primary care of adolescents with bulimia nervosa.
Muscari ME.
Adolescents with bulimia nervosa present a challenge to pediatric nurse practitioners. These adolescents have a disorder that is secretive and difficult to diagnose, chronic, multifaceted, and difficult to treat. However, armed with the proper knowledge and skills, pediatric nurse practitioners are the ideal primary health care providers for this population.
Publication Types: Review; Review, tutorial

J Psychiatr Res 1985;19(2-3):435-43
The family therapy of anorexia nervosa.
Dare C.

J Psychiatr Res 1985;19(2-3):465-72
The management of bulimia nervosa.
Fairburn CG.

J Psychiatr Res 1985;19(2-3):479-83
Evaluating a group treatment for bulimia.
Huon GF, Brown LB.
A multifaceted group-based approach to the treatment of bulimia is described, that focuses on recovering a sense of control by examining how control isrelinquished, and can be regained by developing adaptive attitudes and behaviour about food and eating, the body, and interpersonal relationships. Results from an end of programme assessment and then at six month, 12 month and 18 month follow-ups indicate that a successful reduction in bingeing and vomiting and a variety of other changes was achieved and maintained by 36 of the 40 participants.

J Psychosoc Nurs Ment Health Serv 1985 May;23(5):16-22
Bulimia. A conceptual model for group treatment.
Reed G, Sech EP.

J Psychosom Res 1967 Jun;11(1):151-5
Anorexia nervosa--long-term follow up and effects of treatment.
Dally PJ.

J Psychosom Res 1993 May;37(4):389-96
The impact of a 'guided self-help group' on bulimic women: a prospective 15 month study of attenders and non-attenders.
Rathner G, Bonsch C, Maurer G, Walter MH, Sollner W.
University of Innsbruck, Dept of Pediatrics, Austria.
Bulimic women (N = 19) interested in a 'guided self-help group' were assessed by structured interviews and standardized tests. Eleven decided to attend the group, eight did not. Attenders showed significant improvement in specific

psychopathology (drive for thinness, bulimia), general psychopathology (depression) and psychosocial adjustment, whereas non-attenders did not. Despite the small sample size our study indicates self-help as a valuable tool in overcoming an eating disorder.

J Psychother Pract Res 1999 Spring;8(2):115-28
Empirical comparison of two psychological therapies. Self psychology and cognitive orientation in the treatment of anorexia and bulimia.
Bachar E, Latzer Y, Kreitler S, Berry EM.
Department of Psychiatry, Hadassah University Medical Center, Jerusalem, Israel.
The authors investigated the applicability of self psychological treatment (SPT) and cognitive orientation treatment (COT) to the treatment of anorexia and bulimia. Thirty-three patients participated in this study. The bulimic patients (n = 25) were randomly assigned either to SPT, COT, or control/nutritional counseling only (C/NC). After SPT, significant improvement was observed. After COT, slight but nonsignificant improvement was observed. After C/NC, almost no changes could be detected.
Publication Types: Clinical trial; Randomized controlled trial

JAMA 1974 Dec 4;230(10):1419-22
Perils of behavior modification in treatment of anorexia nervosa.
Bruch H.

Lancet 1993 Jun 26;341(8861):1635-40
Treatment of anorexia nervosa.
Beumont PJ, Russell JD, Touyz SW.
Department of Psychiatry, University of Sydney, Australia.
Publication Types: Review; Review, tutorial

Lancet 1996 Aug 31;348(9027):611-2
A new treatment of anorexia nervosa.
Bergh C, Eklund S, Eriksson M, Lindberg G, Sodersten P.
Publication Types: Letter

Med Clin North Am 1990 Sep;74(5):1293-310
Medical complications of anorexia nervosa and bulimia nervosa.
Comerci GD.
Adolescent/Young Adult Medicine Section, University of Arizona College of Medicine, Tucson.
The internist plays a critical role in the care of eating disorder patients, especially in the management of the life-threatening medical complications of these conditions. Immediate management of medical complication and correction of nutritional deficits are necessary before patients can benefit from psychotherapy. The need for continued involvement of the internist in the ongoing care of the eating disorder patient is stressed. The high mortality and the likelihood of chronicity without early intervention underscore the need forearly recognition and skilled management of eating disorders.
Publication Types: Review; Review, tutorial

Med J Aust 1989 Nov 20;151(10):583-8
Treatment of the eating disorders.

Szmukler GI.
Department of Psychiatry, University of Melbourne.
Publication Types: Review; Review, tutorial

Med J Aust 1998 Oct 19;169(8):438-41
Comment in:Med J Aust. 1999 Apr 19;170(8):399
Eating disorders revisited. I: Anorexia nervosa.
Gilchrist PN, Ben-Tovim DI, Hay PJ, Kalucy RS, Walker MK.
Weight Disorder Unit, Flinders Medical Centre, Bedford Park, SA.
Anorexia nervosa is a serious psychiatric illness with a high morbidity and a significant lifetime mortality. Successful outcome should be based not simply on body weight but also on the resolution of anorexic thinking.
Publication Types: Review; Review, tutorial

N C Med J 1998 Jan-Feb;59(1):31-4
Eating disorders: effective treatment through understanding. What patients want physicians to know.
Deters SH.
Individual, Child and Family Therapeutic Services, Greenville, USA.

N Engl J Med 2001 Apr 5;344(14):1079-82
Clinical problem-solving. Less is more.

N Z Med J 1975 Jul 9;82(543):10-3
Treatment of anorexia nervosa.
Hall A.
Anorexia nervosa is a well-known syndrome occurring predominantly in adolescent girls, and characterised by amenorrhoea and gross weight loss due to self-induced restriction of food intake. A definite treatment programme isrecommended as likely to improve the prognosis. This consists of hospital admission for restoration of normal weight, combined with family intervention and continuing long-term individual psychotherapy. The hospital regime for weight restoration involves bed rest, refeeding by experienced nursing staff, and a situation where the patient has no opportuinty for avoiding weight gain but receives constant reassurance.

Nurs Stand 1999 Jan 27-Feb 2;13(19):43-7
Anorexia nervosa: a cognitive-behavioural approach.
Sloan G.
Consulting and Clinical Psychology Services, Ayrshire and Arran Community Health Care Trust.
People with anorexia nervosa can be resistant to treatment because they do not feel the therapist is on their side. This article focuses on the need to establish a therapeutic relationship before interventions can begin. The author also outlines important factors in the onset and maintenance of anorexia nervosa.
Publication Types: Review; Review, tutorial

Nurse Pract 1990 Apr;15(4):22, 25, 28 passim
Anorexia nervosa and bulimia: incidence and diagnosis.
Plehn KW.
University of Pennsylvania,

Philadelphia.
The incidence of eating disorders is increasing at an alarming rate. The clinician who sees many female teenagers and young women in the course of practice is a prime candidate for identifying and providing early diagnosis and communication with the anorexic or bulimic client. Vigilance when assessing the client's physical, psychological, personal and family-history status will increase case-finding for eating disorders at an earlier point in the disease.

Nutr Clin Pract 1993 Oct;8(5):220-5
Team treatment of eating disorders.
Landau-West D, Kohl D, Pasulka P.
The treatment of eating disorders requires the expertise of a multidisciplinary team. This case presents the psychologic and physiologic challenges observed in managing these patients. Attention must be directed toward the use of techniques to obtain a commitment from patients to meet a therapeutic goal. Care must be taken to avoid overaggressive feeding of patients with eating disorders to avoid the refeeding syndrome.

Patient Educ Couns 1998 Mar;33(3):217-24
Girls in the 90s: a gender-based model for eating disorder prevention.
Friedman SS.
Salal Communications Ltd., Vancouver, BC, Canada.
Girls in the 90s is an eating disorder prevention program for pre-adolescent/adolescent girls which operationalizes contemporary theories of female development that they face. The flexibility of the program enables it to be used by women with different professional orientations, with different age groups and to address different health and social risks that girls face.

Pediatr Ann 1984 Dec;13(12):892-3, 896-7
Parental and childhood resistance to therapy for eating disorders.
Pauker N.

Pediatrician 1983-85;12(2-3):126-33
Inpatient treatment of anorexia nervosa.
Powers PS.
In this paper the indications for inpatient treatment of anorexia nervosa are reviewed. Although all programs aim at weight gain and normalization of eating habits, the means for achieving these goals vary widely from nursing encouragement, operant conditioning or, rarely, hyperalimentation. Most programs now utilize an integrated treatment program that includes a weight restoration program, individual psychotherapy and family involvement. Nutritional considerations during inpatient treatment are also reviewed.

Postgrad Med 1972 May;51(5):159-62
Diagnosis and treatment of anorexic states.
Rowland CV Jr.

Postgrad Med 1987 Nov 15;82(7):102-4, 109
Eating disorders.
Levine MP.
Department of Psychology, Kenyon

College, Gambler, OH 43022-9623.
Anorexia nervosa and bulimia nervosa present special challenges for physicians. Considerable skill and flexibility, as well as a collaborative spirit, are required to address the important physical, psychological, and social dimensions of these eating disorders. The ideal treatment is an individualized program designed to (1) eliminate the multifaceted effects of a body weight driven well below the biologic set point, (2) develop self-esteem, including a healthy attitude toward the body, and (3) strengthen those aspects of the individual and the family that orient the patient to health instead of illness.

Postgrad Med 1996 Jan;99(1):161-4, 167-9
Anorexia nervosa and bulimia nervosa. When the pursuit of bodily 'perfection' becomes a killer.
Zerbe KJ.
Menninger Clinic, Topeka, Kansas, USA.
Eating disorders probably result from a combination of emotional, physical, and sociologic factors and are encouraged by a society that values appearance as a measure of worth. Primary care physicians may be the first to suspect potential problems, including a patient's fixation on food, weight, dieting, physique, and exercise. Sometimes, patients who have struggled in silence for years turn to their trusted physician for support and understanding. The first step in treatment is to address the medical complications caused by the unhealthy eating habits. Once nutritional health has been restored, patients need to reverse their entrenched and distorted body-image ideas through psychotherapy.
Publication Types: Review; Review, tutorial

Prog Behav Modif 1988;23:11-35
Cognitive-behavioral treatment of bulimia nervosa.
Leitenberg H, Rosen JC.
University of Vermont.
Publication Types: Review; Review, tutorial

Psychiatr Clin North Am 1984 Jun;7(2):235-45
Outpatient treatment of anorexia nervosa.
Sargent J, Liebman R.
The authors discuss outpatient treatment of the anorectic in terms of a process catalyzed in therapy sessions that takes place throughout the patient's daily life. The goal to reverse the physical and psychological symptoms of the disorder within the natural context of family, school or work, and community while enhancing development and adaptation is clearly defined. Treatment isdescribed as holistic; the patient's mind and body are treated in concert.

Psychiatr Clin North Am 1993 Dec;16(4):767-78
Psychopharmacology in the treatment of anorexia nervosa and bulimia nervosa.
Hoffman L, Halmi K.
New York Hospital-Westchester Division, Cornell University Medical Center, White Plains.
Anorexia nervosa and bulimia nervosa

remain enigmatic disorders with poorly understood etiologies. Clinicians continue to find these disorders very challenging to treat. As their underlying pathophysiology is clarified, it ishoped that specific pharmacologic treatments will be developed to alleviate the pain and disability these disorders produce.
Publication Types: Review; Review, tutorial

Psychiatry 1978 Aug;41(3):296-301
Anorexia nervosa: reflections on theory and practice.
Rampling D.
Psychodynamic theory provides a critical element in the conceptual framework necessary for a therapist's understanding of the abnormal behavior exhibited by patients with anorexia nervosa. A model of the syndrome is presented here which the author has found useful in the ongoing treatment of patients. The paper has arisen out of a desire to clarify thinking and practice in the course of treating patients manifesting the classic syndrome identified in those whose symptoms are not secondary to physical disease or psychosis.

Psychoanal Study Child 1988;43:199-211
The terminability of adolescence and psychoanalysis.
Erlich HS.

Psychol Med 1981 Nov;11(4):707-11
A cognitive behavioural approach to the treatment of bulimia.
Fairburn C.

Psychol Med 1986 Feb;16(1):65-70
Bulimia nervosa: treatment and short-term outcome.
Hsu LK, Holder D.
Fifty-six bulimia nervosa patients were treated by means of a behavioural approach and followed for at least one year after completion or dropping out of treatment. Outcome was encouraging in about half of the patients and several psychiatric indicators, such as duration of illness and response to treatment, were identified. The significance of the findings and unresolved methodological issues are discussed.

Psychopharmacol Bull 1993;29(1):121-5
Bulimia nervosa: comparison of treatment responders vs. nonresponders.
Herzog DB, Sacks NR.
Eating Disorders Unit, Massachusetts General Hospital, Boston 02114.
Though psychosocial and psychopharmacological treatments are effective in reducing bulimic symptomatology, bulimic patients often have unremitting behaviors and frequently relapse. The authors sought to identify factors that differentiate bulimic patients who improve while receiving treatment from those who do not. This study suggests that drug therapy may have a differential effect on the outcome of bulimia nervosa; further study isnecessary, however, to ascertain the presence of selection bias.

Psychosomatics 1990 Winter;31(1):1-3
The treatment of eating disorders.
Mitchell JE.
Publication Types: Editorial

Psychother Psychosom 1978;30(3-4):161-9
Anorexia nervosa. Commitment to a multifaceted treatment program.
Whipple SB, Manning DE.
Anorexia nervosa, a complicated and serious illness, warrants the comprehensive use of several treatment modalities: behavior therapy, individual psychotherapy and family therapy. Singular use of and of these three have resulted in high mortality rates. The importance of legal commitment in dealing with this illness is also discussed.

Semin Adolesc Med 1986 Mar;2(1):27-36
Inpatient management of anorexia nervosa and bulimia.
Kreipe RE.
The principles guiding the inpatient treatment of adolescents with anorexia nervosa or bulimia are no different than those guiding the treatment of adolescents with cystic fibrosis, leukemia, or depression. Hospitalization may be required for a number of reasons. Regardless of the indications for admission to the hospital, a consistent, individualized, positively reinforcing plan for evaluation and treatment needs to be developed and executed. By so doing, the hospital team is in a unique position to help the patient and the family develop more healthy patterns of acting and interacting.

Semin Adolesc Med 1986 Mar;2(1):57-64
Individual and family therapy with eating disorder patients.
Carroll AE.

Semin Adolesc Med 1986 Mar;2(1):75-9
Hypnosis in the treatment of anorexic and bulimic patients.
Pettinati HM, Wade JH.

South Med J 1977 Apr;70(4):448-52
Anorexia nervosa: a combined therapeutic approach.
Parker JB, Blazer D, wyrick L.
Ten female patients with a diagnosis of anorexia nervosa were treated with a combination of behavior modification and psychotherapy and, when appropriate, psychotropic medication. Three case histories illustrate the method used. The interrelationship between weight gain and the process in psychotherapy is illustrated and the psychopathologic features typical of this patient population are discussed. It was concluded that the combined therapeutic method described is an effective and appropriate approach to the treatment of patients with anorexia nervosa.

West J Med 1990 Aug;153(2):133-9
Compliance and outcome in anorexia nervosa.
Steiner H, Mazer C, Litt IF.
Department of Psychiatry and Behavioral Sciences, Stanford University School of Medicine, California.
Anorexia nervosa is notoriously difficult to treat, but little is known regarding the relationship of compliance to treatment outcome. Investigated here were 41 adolescents who fulfilled DSM-III-R criteria for anorexia nervosa, the relationship between the completion of a standard psychosocial treatment program,

subtypes of anorexia nervosa, and outcome as determined by standardized measurements. These adolescents were observed for an average of 32.4 months. Overall, 29 patients (70%) improved considerably, but 10 (24%) were symptomatic, and 2 (5%) remained in poor condition. There were no deaths. Of the 41 patients, 14 (34%) completed our entire treatment program, 15 (37%) received major treatment and failed in the outpatient follow-up phase only, 7 (17%) dropped outof inpatient treatment before its completion, and 5 (12%) refused treatment inour system altogether. Treatment completion significantly affected the measures of global clinical functioning and specific psychopathologic features, but only for those patients who completed the initial program.

Wien Klin Wochenschr 2000 Oct 27;112(20):865-75
[Diagnosis and therapy of eating disorders].
[Article in German]
Bailer U, de Zwaan M, Schussler P, el-Giamal N, Strnad A, Lennkh C, Kasper S.
Klinische Abteilung fur Allgemeine Psychiatrie, Universitatsklinik fur Psychiatrie, Wien, Osterreich. ursula.bailer@akh-wien.ac.at Even though there is no convincing evidence that eating disorders in general are on the rise, there has been an enormous increase in "treated" cases of patients with eating disorders. This review will cover important aspects of diagnosis and treatment of eating disorders. Psychotherapeutical and pharmacological treatment strategies in anorexia and bulimia nervosa will be discussed. For both eating disorders, psychotherapy is the treatment of choice. Drugs with a serotonergic function, e.g. serotonin-reuptake-inhibitors (SSRI), have demonstrated significant results in the treatment of bulimia nervosa and eating disorders with comorbid depression. In clinical practice "treatment packages" are offered because of the complexity of the disorders. The paper also deals with medical complications of eating disorders, motivational interviewing in anorexia nervosa and treatment with self-help manuals in bulimia nervosa.
Publication Types: Review; Review, tutorial

AUTHOR INDEX

A

B

C

D

E

F

G

H

I

J

K

L

M

N

O

P

Q

R

S

Y

Z

SUBJECT INDEX

T

U

V

W

TITLE INDEX

B

C

D

E

F

G

H

I

J

L

M

N

N

O

P

Q

R

S

T

U

V

W